Always Been
a Rambler

Contributions to Southern Appalachian Studies

1. *Memoirs of Grassy Creek: Growing Up in the Mountains on the Virginia–North Carolina Line.* Zetta Barker Hamby. 1998

2. *The Pond Mountain Chronicle: Self-Portrait of a Southern Appalachian Community.* Edited by Leland R. Cooper and Mary Lee Cooper. 1998

3. *Traditional Musicians of the Central Blue Ridge: Old Time, Early Country, Folk and Bluegrass Label Recording Artists, with Discographies.* Marty McGee. 2000

4. *W.R. Trivett, Appalachian Pictureman: Photographs of a Bygone Time.* Ralph E. Lentz II. 2001

5. *The People of the New River: Oral Histories from the Ashe, Alleghany and Watauga Counties of North Carolina.* Edited by Leland R. Cooper and Mary Lee Cooper. 2001

6. *John Fox, Jr., Appalachian Author.* Bill York. 2003

7. *The Thistle and the Brier: Historical Links and Cultural Parallels Between Scotland and Appalachia.* Richard Blaustein. 2003

8. *Tales from Sacred Wind: Coming of Age in Appalachia. The Cratis Williams Chronicles.* Cratis D. Williams. Edited by David Cratis Williams and Patricia D. Beaver. 2003

9. *Willard Gayheart, Appalachian Artist.* Willard Gayheart and Donia S. Eley. 2003

10. *The Forest City Lynching of 1900: Populism, Racism, and White Supremacy in Rutherford County, North Carolina.* J. Timothy Cole. 2003

11. *The Brevard Rosenwald School: Black Education and Community Building in a Southern Appalachian Town, 1920–1966.* Betty J. Reed. 2004

12. *The Bristol Sessions: Writings About the Big Bang of Country Music.* Edited by Charles K. Wolfe and Ted Olson. 2005

13. *Community and Change in the North Carolina Mountains: Oral Histories and Profiles of People from Western Watauga County.* Compiled by Nannie Greene and Catherine Stokes Sheppard. 2006

14. *Ashe County: A History; A New Edition.* Arthur Lloyd Fletcher. 2009 [2006]

15. *The New River Controversy; A New Edition.* Thomas J. Schoenbaum. Epilogue by R. Seth Woodard. 2007

16. *The Blue Ridge Parkway by Foot: A Park Ranger's Memoir.* Tim Pegram. 2007

17. *James Still: Critical Essays on the Dean of Appalachian Literature.* Edited by Ted Olson and Kathy H. Olson. 2008

18. *Owsley County, Kentucky, and the Perpetuation of Poverty.* John R. Burch, Jr. 2008

19. *Asheville: A History.* Nan K. Chase. 2007

20. *Southern Appalachian Poetry: An Anthology of Works by 37 Poets.* Edited by Marita Garin. 2008

21. *Ball, Bat and Bitumen: A History of Coalfield Baseball in the Appalachian South.* L.M. Sutter. 2009

22. *The Frontier Nursing Service: America's First Rural Nurse-Midwife Service and School.* Marie Bartlett. 2009

23. *James Still in Interviews, Oral Histories and Memoirs.* Edited by Ted Olson. 2009

24. *The Millstone Quarries of Powell County, Kentucky.* Charles D. Hockensmith. 2009

25. *The Bibliography of Appalachia: More Than 4,700 Books, Articles, Monographs and Dissertations, Topically Arranged and Indexed.* Compiled by John R. Burch, Jr. 2009

26. *Appalachian Children's Literature: An Annotated Bibliography.* Compiled by Roberta Teague Herrin and Sheila Quinn Oliver. 2010

27. *Southern Appalachian Storytellers: Interviews with Sixteen Keepers of the Oral Tradition.* Edited by Saundra Gerrell Kelley. 2010

28. *Southern West Virginia and the Struggle for Modernity.* Christopher Dorsey. 2011

29. *George Scarbrough, Appalachian Poet: A Biographical and Literary Study with Unpublished Writings.* Randy Mackin. 2011

30. *The Water-Powered Mills of Floyd County, Virginia: Illustrated Histories, 1770–2010.* Franklin F. Webb and Ricky L. Cox. 2012

31. *School Segregation in Western North Carolina: A History, 1860s–1970s.* Betty Jamerson Reed. 2011

32. *The Ravenscroft School in Asheville: A History of the Institution and Its People and Buildings.* Dale Wayne Slusser. 2014

33. *The Ore Knob Mine Murders: The Crimes, the Investigation and the Trials.* Rose M. Haynes. 2013

34. *New Art of Willard Gayheart.* Willard Gayheart and Donia S. Eley. 2014

35. *Public Health in Appalachia: Essays from the Clinic and the Field.* Edited by Wendy Welch. 2014

36. *The Rhetoric of Appalachian Identity.* Todd Snyder. 2014

37. *African American and Cherokee Nurses in Appalachia: A History, 1900–1965.* Phoebe Ann Pollitt. 2016

38. *A Hospital for Ashe County: Four Generations of Appalachian Community Health Care.* Janet C. Pittard. 2016

39. *Dwight Diller: West Virginia Mountain Musician.* Lewis M. Stern. 2016

40. *The Brown Mountain Lights: History, Science and Human Nature Explain an Appalachian Mystery.* Wade Edward Speer. 2017

41. *Richard L. Davis and the Color Line in Ohio Coal: A Hocking Valley Mine Labor Organizer, 1862–1900.* Frans H. Doppen. 2016

42. *The Silent Appalachian: Wordless Mountaineers in Fiction, Film and Television.* Vicki Sigmon Collins. 2017

43. *The Trees of Ashe County, North Carolina.* Doug Munroe. 2017

44. *Melungeon Portraits: Exploring Kinship and Identity.* Tamara L. Stachowicz. 2018

45. *Always Been a Rambler: G.B. Grayson and Henry Whitter, Country Music Pioneers of Southern Appalachia.* Josh Beckworth. 2018

Always Been a Rambler

G.B. Grayson and Henry Whitter, Country Music Pioneers of Southern Appalachia

Josh Beckworth

Contributions to Southern Appalachian Studies, 45

McFarland & Company, Inc., Publishers
Jefferson, North Carolina

Library of Congress Cataloguing-in-Publication Data

Names: Beckworth, Josh, 1983– author.
Title: Always been a rambler : G.B. Grayson and Henry Whitter, country music pioneers of southern Appalachia / Josh Beckworth.
Other titles: Contributions to southern Appalachian studies ; 45.
Description: Jefferson, North Carolina : McFarland & Company, 2018. | Series: Contributions to southern Appalachian studies ; 45 | Includes bibliographical references and index.
Identifiers: LCCN 2018007788 | ISBN 9781476667294 (softcover : acid free paper) ♾
Subjects: LCSH: Grayson and Whitter. | Grayson, G. B. (Gilliam Banmon), 1887–1930. | Whitter, Henry, 1892–1941. | Country musicians—Appalachian Region, Southern—Biography. | Old-time music—Appalachian Region, Southern—History and criticism.
Classification: LCC ML421.G735 B43 2018 | DDC 781.642092/2 [B] —dc23
LC record available at https://lccn.loc.gov/2018007788

British Library cataloguing data are available

ISBN (print) 978-1-4766-6729-4
ISBN (ebook) 978-1-4766-3186-8

Front cover record label images are from the author's collection

Printed in the United States of America

McFarland & Company, Inc., Publishers
Box 611, Jefferson, North Carolina 28640
www.mcfarlandpub.com

To my mother, Kathie,
and my wife, Sarah.

I couldn't have done it without you.

Acknowledgments

I cannot take sole credit for this book. I owe a huge debt to two researchers who came before me: Archie Green and Jim Meadows. These men studied Henry Whitter and G.B. Grayson, respectively, and through interviews conducted during the 1960s and 1970s with people who had personally known the duo, they amassed a wealth of knowledge that would otherwise have been lost to history. The details about Grayson's and Whitter's lives I was able to acquire could not have been known without their foresight and diligence.

I would also like to thank all of the people who generously contributed photos and their time for interviews: Brian Forehand, Ann Baker Forehand, Kada McNeil, Lee Eller, Benson Jones, Haynes Baker, Thornton Spencer, Kilby Spencer, Marshall Wyatt, Tony Russell, Charles Meadows, June Hubbert, Ted Trivette, Bessie Brown, J.C. Kemp, and Frank Grayson. The information they provided was invaluable in creating a detailed portrait of Grayson and Whitter.

On a more personal note, this book could not have been completed without the assistance of my father, Lee Beckworth. He is an avid music historian himself, and his ability to track down information and make connections with musicians, historians, and relatives of Grayson and Whitter was instrumental in putting this book together. His help and encouragement kept me motivated, and I feel he is largely responsible for the final product.

Table of Contents

Preface

I first became interested in traditional music as a teenager. At that time, I was trying to learn to play the three-finger banjo and had begun listening to bluegrass recordings for guidance. Since I was largely unfamiliar with the genre, I confined myself to the most obvious selections. I didn't know that traditional music had roots any deeper than Bill Monroe.

One day, I was at my grandmother's house in Crumpler, North Carolina. In her basement, I ran across an old cardboard box full of brittle 78 rpm records. I had never even seen a 78 record, and I was certainly unfamiliar with the artists listed on the labels. Vernon Dalhart, the Skillet Lickers, and Fiddlin' John Carson were total strangers. But as I went through the stack of records, I began recognizing the titles of songs I had heard before: "Tom Dooley," which I had heard Doc Watson sing, "Nine Pound Hammer," a song featured on the Nitty Gritty Dirt Band's *Will the Circle Be Unbroken* album, "Train 45," which I had heard at local jam sessions, and "Handsome Molly," one of my favorite Country Gentlemen tracks. I started to notice that almost all the songs I recognized in this stack of early country records were from the same group: Grayson and Whitter. I didn't know who they were, but seeing their records made me realize there was more to traditional music than I had previously thought.

Less than ten years later, I was taking folklore classes at Appalachian State University. I had grown more knowledgeable about traditional music and was enjoying learning about varied forms of Southern folk music. I was introduced to ballad singers from Kentucky, fiddlers from Mt. Airy, blues guitarists from the North Carolina Piedmont, and Cajun bands from Louisiana. During this time, I received a copy of a CD, *Music from the Lost Provinces*, which had recently been released on the Old Hat label. This album showcased early string bands from my home county of Ashe. I was shocked to discover that one of the groups featured was Grayson and Whitter. Not only were they influential, we were also from the same place. I suddenly felt connected with traditional music in a way I never had before.

Since that time, I have tried to find out everything I could about G.B. Grayson and Henry Whitter. I began by reading the few articles and liner notes that had been published about them, but, after talking to people who had personal connections to the pair, I knew there was more to be said about them than had previously been published. This book is my attempt to finally provide a full portrait of the duo that had such a profound impact on me in hopes that they may do the same for others. I am presenting the information about the duo in two parts: the first deals with aspects of their personal lives and careers, and the second focuses on their recorded output, exploring both the performance and history of their recorded songs. I feel by approaching them in this way, the artists, as well as their art, are given a full appreciation.

However, the book is not meant to focus exclusively on the recording careers of Grayson and Whitter. I hope additionally to use Grayson's and Whitter's experiences to discuss life in the southern Appalachian Mountains around the beginning of the 20th century. To this end, I have included details about their hometowns, their marriages, the Civil War in Johnson County, Tennessee, and the events of the Hillsville Courthouse shooting. I have done this in an attempt to contextualize Grayson and Whitter, to show how their music was shaped by the world that created them. I have also chosen to spend time exploring Henry Whitter's solo career, which was itself very influential and which, up until now, has been largely ignored. I feel that Whitter's experiences as a solo artist are vital to understanding the career of the Grayson and Whitter duo and should be fully examined.

I have chosen to present the information as a series of loosely connected essays. I hope this will give readers the ability to focus on topics of most interest to them, without necessarily having to read the book from beginning to end in a set order. I begin with a broad overview of Grayson's and Whitter's biographies, and each subsequent essay elaborates on a more specific topic. Sometimes these subsequent essays will include information already mentioned in the biographical overview; I included these occasional repetitions in order to allow each essay to function independently.

The second part deals with the songs of the duo; I have tried to categorize their songs into manageable groups, so as to allow readers to focus on types of songs of interest to them. Like with many folksong collections, this section attempts to describe the history of each song while including references to other versions and variations, but unlike other folksong collections, which put sole emphasis on the song, I have tried to confine my focus to Grayson and Whitter's recordings, describing arrangements as well as how each song fits into the duo's overall repertoire.

I have not included a discography of Grayson and Whitter's record releases. Numerous other works featuring this information currently exist, and I felt it would be redundant to include it here. For anyone interested in seeing a discography of the duo's recorded output, I would recommend Tony Russell and Bob Pinson's *Country Music Records: A Discography, 1921–1942* or Marty McGee's *Traditional Musicians of the Central Blue Ridge.*

Most of the information about G.B. Grayson and Henry Whitter I have gathered has been acquired from interviews and archives, and much of it has never before been published. Many of the photos were acquired directly from members of the Whitter and Grayson families and have never before been seen by the public. I hope that as a result of this new information, readers of this book will be able to feel the same excitement I felt when I ran across my first Grayson and Whitter records all those years ago.

Biography and History

A Dark Road Is a Hard Road to Travel

Brief Biographies of Grayson and Whitter

Scholars of Appalachian musical and cultural history generally focus on large scale movements for study. The rise of commercial folk music, twentieth-century industrialization, impacts of the Civil War, and other topics are analyzed as sweeping phenomena that affected huge populations. Although this approach is necessary to see how wide-ranging change was manifested in different areas and among different groups, it sometimes seems sterile, turning distinct individuals into statistics and census data. In order to really see how all these clashing cultural, industrial, and social shifts manifested themselves on a day-to-day level, it is sometimes useful to take a close look at a few single individuals caught up in the midst of these sweeping changes, and it is especially interesting if those individuals left behind a legacy that still resonates. It is in this capacity that the duo of Grayson and Whitter serves not only the small community of hillbilly music fans but anyone interested in exploring life in the southern Appalachian region as it existed in the early twentieth century. Their records are a testament to their music, but their biographies are no less important for appreciating their art.

Because of their recording successes on the Victor and Gennett labels, these two individuals, G.B. Grayson and Henry Whitter, will forever be remembered as a duo, but their shared musical career was a short one, lasting only from 1927 until 1930. Before these joint recording sessions as Grayson and Whitter, sessions that would make them celebrities among aficionados of early country music, these two men had already crafted independent careers.

Speaking generally, their backgrounds were quite similar—both were products of the southern Appalachian region, both had learned to play music through oral traditions, relying on regional folk songs and melodies to populate the majority of their repertories, and both were relatively successful local musicians—but if not for the commercial impetus provided by the early country record industry, these two would have never played together. Additionally, a careful analysis of the duo reveals two folk musicians whose influences, impulses, and impacts were wildly different. For this reason, a true study of Grayson and Whitter is a study of the two men themselves, Gilliam Banmon Grayson and William Henry Whitter, men whose individual lives give an incisive glimpse into their vibrant and changing worlds.

G.B. Grayson was the artistic heart of the pair. He provided vocals, instrumental breaks, and, consequently, was responsible for most of the song selections. As a result, when discussing the duo, most attention is naturally directed toward him, but untangling the realities of his background has proven challenging. G.B. Grayson was born. That much is certain. The details surrounding his early years cannot be as readily assured. Grayson himself, along with his wife, and many friends and playing partners, died before his musical impact was apparent, leaving few clear sources available to testify about his life. Accordingly, much of Grayson's life story is so dependent on unreliable sources and faded memories that any accounting of his early life must be viewed as theory rather than fact. This lack of information has resulted in scholarship about him being focused on his recording years, often ignoring the realities of his earlier life. For example, his name wasn't G.B. Those were his initials, but his true first name, Gilliam, was never used by those who knew him. It is only on record labels, in discographies, and, ironically, on his headstone (purchased by a folk music aficionado decades after his death[1]), that his name is ever recorded as "G.B." Legal documents from the era usually recorded his name as Gillum B. Grayson, but friends, relatives and some census takers all remember his name as Banmon, the only name he ever used, which was frequently spelled "Bandman."

Grayson's place of birth is also a contentious question. Most liner notes and biographies place his birth in Ashe County, North Carolina, in the northwest corner of the state. Specifically, his birthplace is often cited as being in the community Walnut Hill, near the modern-day community of Crumpler. These claims are not without merit. Ashe County borders Johnson County, Tennessee, where Grayson would spend almost all of his life; his mother was a native of Ashe County, and his parents were living together in Ashe in 1880, seven years before Grayson was born. Also, on a document establishing a guardianship for him after the death of his mother, a sixteen-year-old Grayson had to have his identity authenticated. On a sworn affidavit, his uncle W.M. Roark noted his birthplace as Walnut Hill. In 1917, Grayson had to fill out a draft registration card for the First World War, and, although he couldn't write, he did sign his mark to a card that listed his birthplace as Crumpler, Ashe County, North Carolina.

Despite all this, there are a few reasons this birthplace claim could be disputed. For one, the Walnut Hill birthplace is very unusual given the family's living arrangements. Grayson's father was a native of Johnson County, Tennessee. Although he did reside in Ashe County briefly, being recorded in the 1880 census as a resident, his listed address was in the Horse Creek Township, in the western part of the county, near the Tennessee border. Walnut Hill, by contrast, would have been much further east. The idea that perhaps Grayson's parents moved around between census recordings is also difficult to sustain. There are no easily identified relatives living around the Walnut Hill community in these census records, and there is no record of property being owned in the area by Grayson's parents. One would have to wonder what would drive the Grayson family to briefly live in Walnut Hill in the absence of these obvious connections. In fact, official documents suggest the family was much more likely to move west, toward Tennessee, than toward eastern Ashe County. Official records show that in 1885, two years before his birth, G.B. Grayson's parents were married in Johnson County, and in 1888, a year after G.B. Grayson's birth, his father appears on official documents with his address listed as Laurel Bloomery, Tennessee, where Grayson would spend his entire life, from infancy onward. The idea that the family would move from Horse Creek, back to Tennessee, back to Walnut Hill, and then back to Laurel Bloomery, all within the course of eight years, seems unlikely, although it is possible.

Another reason to wonder about his place of birth comes from Grayson's mother, Martha Roark Grayson, who was recorded in the 1900 census living as a widow in Tennessee. During this census, she was asked to account for the states in which she, her spouse, and her children were born. She notes Tennessee as the birthplace for all her children, G.B. Grayson included.

Despite the argument over his birthplace, it is clear that Grayson's life was spent in Laurel Bloomery, in northern Johnson County, Tennessee, an area his father's side of the family had inhabited for years.

The Grayson family's residence in the area began during a wave of migration that came into western North Carolina and eastern Tennessee during the early nineteenth century. Johnson County, where the Graysons would ultimately settle, was formally established in 1836, carved out of land that had once been part of the short lived state of Franklin—an American geographical anomaly that had existed for about three years between 1786 and 1789. During these two decades after its founding, Johnson County experienced the most rapid rate of growth during anytime in its history, expanding in population by around 3.5 percent between each census.

One of these settlers pouring into the area around the time of the Johnson County's founding was William Grayson, G.B. Grayson's grandfather. William seems to be the first generation of the family to live in America, and he first appears in the 1830 census, living where G.B. Grayson's mother and brother are currently buried, in what would today be considered western Watauga County, North Carolina, very near its current border with Johnson County, Tennessee. Family tradition holds that William, born around 1800, was a shipwright who immigrated from either Scotland or England sometime before 1830. Although he arrived in America with his brother, Charles, they seemed to have quickly gone their separate ways. William moved to the Cove Creek community of Watauga County, North Carolina, where he married Rebecca Reese, the daughter of one of Watauga County's earliest permanent settlers.[2]

William Grayson's direct connection with the Old World would tempt one to argue that surely he brought with him ballads and tunes from the British Isles which he then imparted to his son, G.B.'s father. This would allow a direct line to be established from G.B. Grayson recordings of the late 1920s to the folk tradition of the British Isles, something that would have greatly excited early folk music scholars like Cecil Sharp, who were convinced that the Appalachian Mountains held pockets of residents, untouched by time, holding onto stores of British folksongs. Unfortunately, Grayson's direct line to England was erased very quickly. According to family history, sometime around 1841, when G.B. Grayson's father, Benjamin, would have been three years old, William Grayson picked up his rifle and told his wife he was going hunting. He never returned. Whether that is an accurate accounting of what happened or not, it is clear that after 1840, William Grayson ceases to exist in documents and censuses. His wife and two young sons were left alone.

G.B. Grayson's father, Benjamin, growing up without the presence of his father, also struggled to maintain a steady household. After returning from service in the Civil War, Benjamin married Catherine Johnson Daughtery on October 8, 1867. Catherine Daughtery was herself a widow, bringing three young children with her to this marriage. Catherine and

Benjamin seemed to have had a child together, a child that would have been G.B. Grayson's half-sister, Martha, born around 1869. Sometime between the birth of this daughter and the 1880 census, Benjamin and Catherine Daughtery were divorced. By 1880, Benjamin was living in Ashe County with a new partner, Martha Jane Roark, a girl sixteen years his junior.

Martha, only twenty-six in 1880, was also embarking on her second marriage, having been previously married to a Henry Lewallen, according to Roark family genealogy. In 1880, she was living, unmarried, with Benjamin Grayson, and three children, Amanda, known as Manda, Rebecca, and Caroline. The oldest child, Amanda, had been born in 1873. Given the complexity of the family living arrangements, ascertaining the definite parentage of these children is difficult, although Tom Gentry, a genealogist from Johnson County who did research for the Grayson family, lists all of them as being children of Benjamin and Martha. They were either full or half siblings to G.B., but there is no clear way to tell.

Grayson did have at least one full sibling; his brother, James Benjamin, was born in 1883, after the 1880 census had recorded Benjamin and Martha living together (but before they were married). G.B. was the only child born after the marriage of Benjamin and Martha and would have been the youngest of their children.

From the earliest, G.B. Grayson had a difficult childhood. His father was ill and died when G.B. was seven years old, making him the second consecutive generation to grow up in a single parent household (oddly, G.B.'s own tragic death in 1930 would leave a third generation of Grayson children to grow up without a father). Complicating the situation, G.B. was born with some kind of impairment to his vision. The true nature of Grayson's blindness is another family story that seems to be shrouded in mystery. According to Grayson's son Clarence, Grayson's sister held him up to a window on a sunny day and blinded him. A similar story claims that he was blinded from staring at the snow from his crib.[3] Whether these stories have any truth to them is dubious, but it seems to be a fact that Grayson's blindness wasn't total. It has been reprinted in several sources that Grayson could tell time by holding a watch close to his eyes and could make out figures by their shape. One of Grayson's musical partners, Callie Trivette, always remembered that Grayson had been able to compliment her on a brooch she was wearing when he had seen it reflect the sunlight.[4] His son Clarence noted that he could see well enough to travel by night, which was when he often came home from playing.[5] One of the most interesting stories about Grayson's visual ability comes from Ray Dowell, who played with Grayson as a young man. Dowell recalled that "G.B. was partial blind but he could see better than you might think. One day in the fall, when the chestnuts were getting ripe and were falling, someone suggested we go pick up chestnuts. G.B. wanted to go too. So he did and by the way he picked up as many chestnuts as anybody."[6] Taken together, stories about Grayson's blindness seem to suggest that his vision was severely impaired when he was looking straight ahead but improved when he looked downward.

Grayson's blindness, even if it wasn't total, was sufficient to keep him from most forms of labor. Because of his disability, Grayson was eligible to collect his father's Civil War pension, which provided his family with a reliable, although small, income. Luckily, his interest in music gave him a way to make additional money, but it isn't obvious where this musical ability originated. Grayson's daughter Lillian claimed that he was surrounded by musicians, learning from his older sister, his brother, his father, his mother and his neighbors.[7] By contrast, his son Clarence claimed in an interview that nobody in G.B.'s family before him had played.[8] Wherever he got the idea to play music, he seemed to have a natural gift for mastering it. He was known in his life to play not only the fiddle but also the guitar, the harmonica, the organ, the piano, the mandolin, and the dulcimer.[9]

Despite his varied musical talents, his earliest love was for the banjo, which was probably the first instrument he learned. As a child, he had mastered maintaining rhythm while playing by sitting in a straight-backed chair and tapping his foot on the upper rung to keep time.[10] During his adulthood, when he was most often thought of and referenced as a singer and fiddler, Grayson continued to play the banjo at home. His son Clarence even argued that his father was a better banjo player than a fiddler. Grayson would often be asked to play the banjo rather than the fiddle when at home and playing with friends and neighbors. Unlike some other more traditional clawhammer players, Grayson played in an odd frailing style that involved picking up on the strings. His son Clarence recalled the excitement he felt hearing his father play "Joe Turner," which Clarence claimed was his most impressive banjo piece. At the end of his life, Grayson's widow provided an accounting of his personal possessions. Aside from his house, a fiddle and banjo were his only property.

Just as Grayson developed a somewhat unusual banjo playing style, his fiddle playing was also quite unique, indicating that he was at least partially self-taught. Unlike many fiddlers, he kept his thumb through the bow, between the hair and the stick, using it to control the tension of the hair as he played. He also held the fiddle on his arm, rather than near his

A publicity photograph of Grayson and Whitter. Unusually, Grayson played with the fiddle pressed against his chest rather than under his chin (courtesy Southern Folklife Collection, Louis Round Wilson Special Collections Library, University of North Carolina at Chapel Hill).

chin, rocking it up and down while playing. Friel Alderman, who had seen Grayson play in person, remarked, "It was sort of comical to see him do this."[11]

One observation that can be made about Grayson unequivocally is that, unlike his grandfather, William, he was a loyal and devoted father and husband. In 1908, he married a girl who had grown up in neighboring Washington County, Virginia, Fannie Mahaffey, and by 1909, the couple had their first child, Edgar.

G.B. Grayson's wife, Fannie Mahaffey, and their youngest daughter, Dallas. Dallas was born in 1925, so this photograph probably dates to 1927 or 1928 (courtesy Charles Meadows).

Edgar would be followed by Lessie, who died in 1929; other children soon followed: Clarence, Lily, Rosa, Howard Franklin, and the youngest, Dallas, born five years before Grayson's death in 1930.

These seven children recalled their father fondly, and their descriptions of him capture a devoted parent forced to spend many hours away from home in pursuit of a musical career. In a letter written in 1974, Rosa Grayson recalled how memorable it was when her father would come home after his long trips. Similarly, Clarence Grayson recalled that his father's long absences were interspersed with joyful homecomings, when neighbors would come by Grayson's house and a party atmosphere would emerge. Grayson told jokes and ghost stories to entertain his children and would liven up gatherings by showcasing one of his non-musical talents: throwing his voice while hiding in neighboring rooms.

Clarence Grayson, born June 6, 1912, was G.B. Grayson's third child. He would later become a musician himself and was an important source of information about Grayson's life (courtesy Charles Meadows).

However, his absences were long. His children recalled that he was rarely home during the week, even before his days of recording. Because of his handicap, he had to try to make a living through "busking," playing in public for donations. He traveled constantly to make money this way: performing at parties, social gatherings, coal mines, community dances and on street corners. Because of his limited transportation during these trips, he stayed with friends and other musicians. During these years he also began making appearances at fiddlers' conventions, which were only beginning to emerge in the region during the 1920s. These conventions allowed performers from the area to mingle with performers from other states and regions, something that would prove to be instrumental in propelling G.B. Grayson to national recognition.

The first fiddlers' convention in Mountain City, the closest large town to Grayson's home, was held 1925, organized by N.B. "Nimby" Parsons and partially sponsored by the Ku Klux Klan.[12] Grayson competed in this convention and did well. Many sources claim he won first place playing "Cumberland Gap," but Charlie Bowman, who also participated, claims that Dudley Vance was the actual first place winner, playing "Twinkle Little Star." All accounts support the belief that Grayson was at least a top finisher in the contest. Regardless of how Grayson performed at this convention, he did get to interact with several other professional musicians who were launching careers in the new country music record industry. One of these, Fiddlin' John Carson, had been paid to travel from Atlanta. Organizers of the convention had hoped to attract a larger crowd through his celebrity as a recording artist. According to Ray Dowell, Carson, who had been launched to stardom after becoming one of the first country artists ever recorded, heard Grayson playing "Don't Let Your Deal Go Down" with Tom Ashley on a street corner in Mountain City and remarked that Grayson was the best fiddler he'd ever heard.[13]

The 1926 fiddlers' convention the following year further introduced Grayson to the professional music world. It was during this convention that Elvis "Tony" Alderman, who was already achieving professional success in vaudeville, on records, and on the radio with the Hill Billies, set up a rudimentary radio station in the lobby of a Mountain City hotel. From this homemade station, around a hundred amateur fiddlers were able to be broadcast over the airwaves for the first time, fielding requests that were being phoned in from around the area.[14] Grayson was one of the fiddlers who was able to participate, and the experience of performing for an invisible audience listening from far away only increased his desire to enter the professional world. Frank Grayson, a musician from Johnson County and a great nephew to Grayson who did extensive research about G.B., recalled in an interview that "he was tickled to death to get to play over the transmitter … and he wanted desperate to make a record but never had the chance to."[15]

By the 1927 convention, Grayson's chance to leap from obscurity to national notoriety was about to arrive. For walking through the crowd of this convention was a man who had come to Mountain City seeking an undiscovered talent, a man who had the will and the connections to help launch a professional career: Henry Whitter.

William Henry Whitter was born in Sulphur Springs, a community in Carroll County, Virginia, in 1892. Like Grayson, Whitter was the product of a blended family unit. His father, James Ellis Whitter, had married his mother, Mary Caroline Ring, in 1888. Mary was listed as a Reeves at the time of their marriage, having been previously married (at age fourteen) to J.D. Reeves. She brought a daughter, Martha Reeves, from this previous marriage. In 1900, the Whitter family, with seven-year-old William Henry, were living in the Old Town district of Grayson County. By 1910, the family had moved six miles up the New River to the newly-created mill town of Fries, Virginia, and were working in the Washington Mill, which processed textiles out of raw cotton bales. Most of the Whitter family began work in the mills, and this industrial life would be a defining factor in Whitter's formative years.

Whitter seems to have possessed more musical talent than he is given credit for. Like Grayson, he was a multi-instrumentalist, playing not only the guitar but the harmonica, banjo, fiddle, piano, and organ.[16] Whitter's mother had herself been a fiddle player, and the family was interested in music. His father was an avid singer,[17] although he couldn't play an instrument; after gaining employment in the Washington Mill, the family's love of music led them to spend a portion of their new found disposable income on a cylinder phonograph, allowing them to suddenly hear music from performers around the country and the world.

The young Henry Whitter, born in the Virginia countryside, would spend the majority of his adolescent years laboring, like his family, in the Washington Mill, but between shifts, he spent his time on the streets of Fries. It was within this tight-knit community that he began to develop into a performer. Whitter played harmonica and guitar everywhere he could: at work, at home, and on street corners. Along with his guitar and harmonica performances, Whitter also entertained passersby with performances from his "limberjacks"—wooden figures that rhythmically danced when the performer patted his foot.[18]

Whitter married a young girl, Orene Eunice Jones, in February 1913. Their son, Paul, was born June 24, 1916. Despite Whitter's blossoming interest in musical performance, this period of his life was still dominated by work at the Washington Mill. His parents, father-in-law, brother-in-law, sister-in-law, and, later, his son Paul, would all come to be employed at the Mill. In Whitter's early days he had lived with his parents in company owned housing, but after marrying Orene, Whitter moved to Stevens Creek, into the home of his brother-in-law, Albert Jones.

Stevens Creek was a bustling community at the time, one that predated the nearby town of Fries. Prior to the establishment of the Washington

Left: **Orene Jones, Henry Whitter's first wife and mother of Paul Whitter (courtesy Brian and Ann Baker Forehand).** ***Right:*** **Henry Whitter (left) and his son Paul Whitter. Paul, born June 24, 1916, was the son of Whitter and Orene Jones (courtesy of Brian and Ann Baker Forehand).**

Mill, Stevens Creek had held the original post office, and, as far back as 1877, the community had a grist mill and an academy. One of the older stores in the community was located at the entrance to Stevens Creek Road, and it was here that local residents, many of whom worked in the nearby Washington Mill, would gather in evenings and on weekends. The store owner, John Rector, was a musician himself, playing banjo with customers who would pass through during the day.

One day, sometime around 1923, Henry Whitter was playing with Rector in his store when a traveling salesman stopped by. Although he had meant to stop only briefly on a routine sales call, he stayed long enough to enjoy the music. Feeling obliged to encourage the local talent, he told Whitter and Rector that, through his travels, he had heard of a record company in New York called OKeh and suggested the two take their talents there and attempt to make a recording. Rector, tied to his business and suspicious of such a bold undertaking, shrugged off the suggestion, but Henry Whitter saw an opportunity to change careers.

Shortly thereafter, Whitter apparently wrote to the OKeh company inquiring about making a record but received no response. Undeterred, Whitter carried his guitar case aboard a train leaving the Fries station heading north. Whitter wound his way through numerous stops along the Norfolk and Western line, chugging through Pulaski, Roanoke, Washington, D.C., and Philadelphia before finally arriving in New York.[19]

The definite date of Whitter's first recording session is one that is difficult to firmly establish. When asked about it years later, Ralph Peer, the head talent scout for OKeh, asserted that Whitter's first appearance in his office did not come until December of 1923, but other evidence points to Whitter's first recordings being made in March of 1923.[20] During this initial session, Whitter used his claims of talent and his unflinching determination to convince Fred Hager, the studio manager, to agree to a few test recordings. These recordings were shelved and were no doubt quickly forgotten as Henry headed back to life in the mill with his family in Fries.

Whitter's original test recordings would have no doubt faded into obscurity if it hadn't been for the chance meeting that same summer of Ralph Peer and Fiddlin' John Carson. Peer had been traveling through the South in search of songs that could be used by blues performers who were becoming popular on the OKeh label. In Atlanta, a local talent scout and furniture store owner, Polk Brockman, encouraged Peer to record Fiddlin' John Carson, a local celebrity known for composing and playing songs on the streets of Atlanta. Peer, who was not accustomed to the unpolished sound of John Carson's authentic folk music, felt that the recordings produced by Carson were terrible, but after Brockman ordered some copies of the Carson recordings for sale in his store, and after those recordings began flying off the shelf, Peer realized that an untapped market for Southern folk music existed in the rural areas of the country. Luckily for Peer, he had already made contact with another country artist who could quickly be called upon to help OKeh capitalize on this newly discovered market: Henry Whitter.

In December, Whitter again found himself in New York City, recording for the OKeh label. During this first official session, Whitter would record numerous songs, the most notable of which was his rendition of "The Wreck on the Southern Old 97." Whitter was called back to record several times over the course of the next year. The years 1924 and 1925 would be the high point of Whitter's solo recording career. He recorded songs at a feverish pace, stepping into the New York studio nine different times. In a period of seventeen months, running from February 25, 1924, to July 1, 1925, Whitter would record thirty-eight songs, more than he and Grayson would record together in their entire three-year partnership.

As soon as Whitter began succeeding as a recording artist, he left the textile mill in Fries and began a new life as a full-time musician. He traveled to schoolhouses and other community gatherings, performing both alone and with other early recording celebrities. Around 1926, Whitter relocated to Mooresville, North Carolina. His failed first marriage to Orene had been left behind in Virginia, and on May 6, 1927, he married a new wife, a native of Mooresville, whom he had met in the summer of 1926.

Henry Whitter (left) and James Sutphin on the road to New York. Sutphin and Whitter would make several records, along with John Rector, as Whitter's Virginia Breakdowners (courtesy Brian and Ann Baker Forehand).

Unlike his time in Fries, Whitter's life in Mooresville was one defined by long absences and distant travels. Whitter traveled from one show to the next, stopping by radio stations in between and occasionally working in recording sessions for OKeh.

Eventually the musical tastes of country music consumers were becoming more discerning, and with new musical options appearing every day, Whitter's appeal began to decline. He knew that his own songs and talents were no longer capable of sustaining a successful livelihood, and so he began searching for someone new to step in and help save his fading career.

In 1927, Henry Whitter's and G.B. Grayson's lives were about to be permanently entwined. Whitter hadn't been successful in his previous attempts to find an undiscovered talent to assist the rebooting of his career, so he made the long journey to Mountain City, hoping that he might finally get lucky, finding a talented musician who had somehow been passed over by the booming recording industry. Sometime during the course of this Mountain City fiddlers' convention, the same convention that had given Grayson his first taste of radio broadcasting the year before, Grayson and Whitter met. The two men saw in each other something their respective musical careers had been lacking. For Whitter, Grayson was the talent that would push him back in the spotlight; for Grayson, Whitter was a pathway out of Laurel Bloomery and into the alluring world of professional musicians. The two committed to starting a partnership, one built on Grayson's untapped talents and Whitter's music industry connections.[21]

Their first stop was the Starr Piano company, which had begun a small record label, Gennett, named for the company's owners. In 1922, Gennett, along with Brunswick and OKeh, had won a lawsuit against Victor, arguing that they should be allowed to create discs using the lateral recording method on which Victor and Columbia records claimed patents. This victory allowed the small labels to stake out a viable place in the recording world, as their discs could now be played on the commonly-owned Victor and Columbia record machines. These small labels began by attempting to find niches of music that were unrepresented on the larger labels, and for several years in the early 1920s, Gennett released large numbers of jazz records. Beginning in the mid–1920s, though, the label had begun to focus on pressing records for the Sears mail-order catalog labels, like Challenge and Silvertone. Gennett also developed its own economy label, Champion. Because the Sears mail-order catalog largely catered to rural customers, to find material for these new discs, the label had begun relying heavily on hillbilly performers.[22]

For an aspiring musician, Gennett was not the best label to work with. The sound quality of their recordings was notably inferior to other companies. They paid little in royalties, and they were able to avoid paying even more by releasing songs on alternative labels under pseudonyms, but they were very unrestricted in their management of performers. They did not use studio musicians and maintained little oversight over the recording process. They also did not place a great emphasis on royalties and copyrights, allowing artists to record songs they chose rather than songs believed to produce lucrative royalty payments.[23] In October of 1927, Grayson and Whitter recorded eight songs for Gennett in their first session as a duo. They would come back in February of 1928 to record nine more, but in the meantime, they also began recording on the Victor label. Victor was much more prestigious than Gennett and paid artists more for their recordings, but they were much stricter about the material that could be recorded. Victor put a greater emphasis on copyrights and steered artists away from songs that could not generate royalties. Grayson and Whitter were obviously willing to make the trade-off; from July of 1928 until their final session in October of 1929, they did all of their recordings for Victor, ultimately releasing twenty-two songs on the label.

With G.B. Grayson, Whitter had restored much of the success he had experienced in his early recording heyday. Similarly, Whitter had finally given Grayson the chance to showcase his talents for a larger audience and achieve the fame and recognition he had so desired. For a brief period, G.B. Grayson, who had spent his entire life struggling to make a living with music, was a true celebrity, able to bill himself as a recording and radio star.

During the peak of Grayson and Whitter's popularity, the country music industry was in a state of rapid transformation. The Carter Family and Jimmie Rodgers, both of whom made their recording debuts in 1927, were permanently reinventing the genre, bringing it into mainstream popularity and attracting artists and audiences outside of the rural South.[24] Although Grayson and Whitter's success meant that they were able to continue recording into the late 1920s, when other artists had seen their recording output rapidly dwindle, tragedy would abruptly end their brief partnership.

G.B. Grayson's partnership with Whitter had resulted in an influx of money from royalties and performances, and suddenly the Grayson family was looking forward to a future they assumed would be financially stable. During this period, G.B. Grayson had been attempting to buy his family's home place outright from his brother, and, with his newly-acquired finances, he finally had enough money to pay the debt he still owed.

On August 15, 1930, Grayson prepared to leave his house in Laurel Bloomery and travel to Damascus, Virginia, about seven miles north, to arrange for the final purchase of the house from his brother. Grayson's daughter, Rosa, who was nine years old at the time, hadn't seen much of her father during the years he was recording with Whitter and could remember the excitement she felt whenever her father was home. Rosa particularly recalled the morning of August 15: her father took her in his lap and sang her favorite song, "Don't Go Out Tonight, My Darling," a mournful temperance song about a man leaving his home never to return alive.[25] It would be the last time she ever saw her father.

Grayson's trip to Damascus that day was uneventful. He carried his fiddle, which was typical, presumably to entertain himself and others, spent the night, and was ready to return home on August 16. Steve Rupert, a friend of Grayson's who often sold milk to the family, was also in Damascus, preparing to haul a load of chestnut logs back to Tennessee. To save Grayson the seven-mile walk back to his home in Laurel Bloomery, Rupert arranged to meet him that morning so Grayson would be able to ride home on Rupert's wagon.

Unbeknownst to Grayson, Rupert had been delayed and didn't make it to the prearranged meeting spot in time. Grayson was no doubt eager to get back to his family after spending the night away from home and probably thought it was quite a lucky break when Curtis Milhorn, driving his wire-wheeled Pontiac coupe, pulled up, offering to give Grayson a lift. Unfortunately for Grayson, Milhorn's car was already full of family members and couldn't accommodate another passenger. Grayson's fiddle case could ride in the back seat, but Grayson himself would have to stand on the car's running board in order to get home. Having spent his entire adult life as a legally blind musician travelling the mountain back roads, Grayson probably thought nothing of this unusual arrangement. He threw his fiddle case in the back seat, situated his feet on the narrow running board, clinging to the side of the car for his final ride.

Immediately outside the southern town limits of Damascus, the road, Highway 91, crossed a bridge over Laurel Creek. This road has since been straightened and moved slightly downstream; a modern bridge has been built, but the abutments that mark the placement of the old bridge still stand. These buried concrete supports are all that remain today to mark the location of Grayson's tragic death. Sometime around 10:30 a.m., Milhorn, driving erratically, sped across the bridge, crossed the center of the road and entered into the northbound lane of the highway. At the same time, a logging truck loaded with extract timber heading to Damascus approached the bridge with no way to stop.

The details of the actual wreck have no doubt been embellished over the years of retelling; supposedly Ferd Gentry, the driver of the log truck, saw Grayson crash through the windshield of his vehicle and careen through the open passenger side (the logging truck had no doors), dropping a pack of cigarettes from his shirt pocket on the way. After colliding with the truck, the Milhorns' car skidded off the road and barreled through the wall of a nearby barn, leaving a hole that would stand as a memorial to the fatal accident for many years afterward.

Grayson, severely injured and unconscious, was rushed to the nearest hospital in Abingdon, which was nearly fourteen miles away. He had suffered a fractured right arm, right leg, and serious head trauma. He never regained consciousness and was pronounced dead at 5:15 p.m., August 16, 1930. He was forty-two years old.

Shortly after the accident, Steve Rupert, plodding along the road with his wagon team, came upon the site of the wreck. In shock over what he saw, he picked up one of Grayson's shoes lying on the highway and carried it back to Laurel Bloomery to present to Grayson's wife. He would forever blame himself for causing Grayson's death by failing to meet him on time in Damascus.[26]

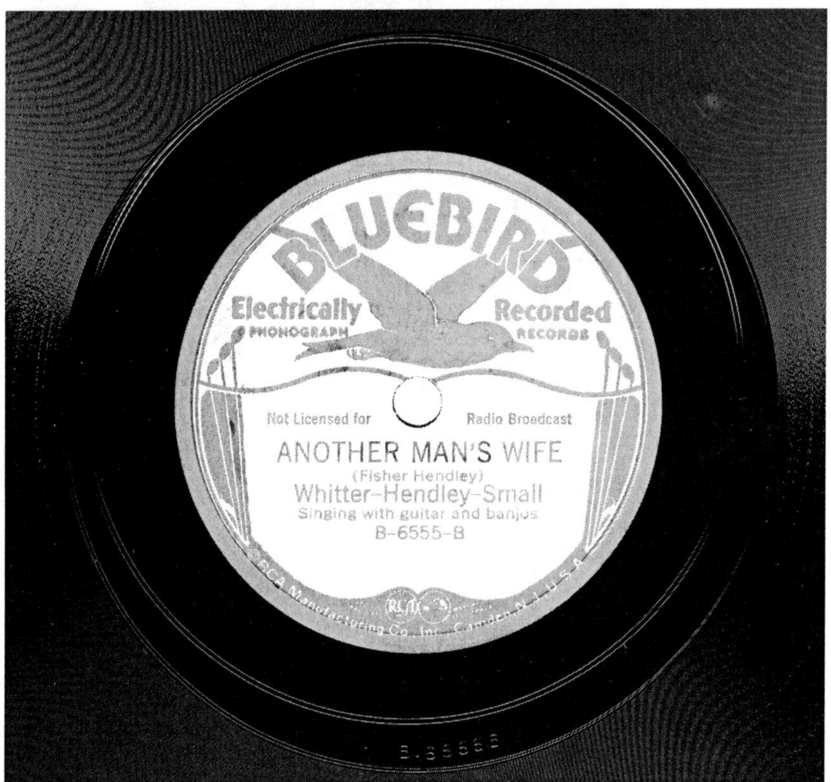

One of Henry Whitter's last records. Whitter partnered for a final time with Marshall Small and Fisher Hendley for this session. This recording was made on November 28, 1930, just over three months after G.B. Grayson's death (courtesy Marshall Wyatt).

Without his financial support, Grayson's family was soon forced to separate. The oldest sons, Edgar and Clarence, musicians themselves who had hoped to someday join their father on records and on tour, instead began work in sawmills and coal mines. Much of the family eventually settled in Pennsylvania, returning only periodically to visit friends and relatives in Laurel Bloomery.

After Grayson's death, Whitter's recording career effectively ended. He would travel to the recording studio only once more, performing with Marshall Small and Fisher Hendley on two records that were recorded in November of 1930. By 1933, he had left Mooresville and moved to Crumpler, North Carolina, the supposed birthplace of his former partner. Here he married another young bride, Hattie Baker, whom he had met while performing a show at the nearby Healing Springs High School.

Henry Whitter with the Ford Model A he purchased in 1928. This is the car Whitter drove to show dates and recording sessions later in his career (courtesy Brian and Ann Baker Forehand).

Whitter's health during this period was in a state of decline. He suffered from diabetes, which he left untreated. This in turn caused ever more frequent bouts of erratic behavior and dementia. He continued to tour locally and made a living as a performer, but the Depression years left little avenue open for success as a travelling musician. Whitter tried to find a replacement for Grayson, but his unpredictable behavior made performing with him difficult. One of his performing partners during this period, Albert Hash, recalled his worsening health:

> I played with him for about a year until his nerves went to the bad, you know, and I got afraid of his driving. I was reluctant to go with him because he wouldn't see a car until it was right at you and it would scare him almost to death and he'd run his car plumb off the road to dodge that. Something was eating on him in some way or other so his vision didn't work, or he wouldn't concentrate on what was coming up in front of him, and it was pitiful.[27]

By the 1940s, Whitter's health had become so poor that he could no longer live at home, and on October 1, he was admitted to the Broughton Psychiatric Hospital in Morganton, North Carolina. He survived for just over a month and died in Morganton on November 17, 1941, from complications related to his diabetes. He was forty-nine years old.

Ironically, G.B. Grayson and Henry Whitter, men of such success during their heydays, were both laid to rest in unmarked graves, their respective families unable to provide them with headstones. Only decades later, when scholars and musicians began to rediscover the music of this duo and to come to North Carolina and Tennessee seeking out any person or relic that might connect them to these mythical performers were the families able to find parties interested in financing the erection of markers for their graves. As lone individuals Grayson and Whitter would almost certainly have passed into obscurity, their lives, like their graves, neglected and forgotten, but as a recording duo, they have been able to achieve something greater than records sales or royalty checks: a permanent place in the history of traditional music.

Straddling the Appalachian Divide

Fries and Laurel Bloomery

It is quite common when attempting to understand an artist to look first at where he comes from. It is often believed by scholars that artists do not function independent of the world around them but are rather reflections of their society. In the world of country music, this belief has led scholars to see traditional ballads, instrumentation, playing styles, and song selection as products of Southern society. This society has been itself subdivided. Piedmont musicians are seen as significantly different from Appalachian musicians. Musicians of the upland South are viewed through a different lens than musicians of the lowland South.

That said, it is interesting to note the extent to which even these subdivisions fail to capture the societal variations that can exist even in locations that would seem very similar. As the crow flies, Henry Whitter's hometown of Fries, Virginia, is a mere forty-five miles from G.B. Grayson's hometown of Laurel Bloomery, Tennessee, and both towns would be considered part of the southern Appalachian region for all intents and purposes. These two seemingly similar locations are in fact vastly different, showcasing wide discrepancies in terms of economics, residential patterns, and industry. To fully understand G.B. Grayson, the obscure but driven fiddler, and Henry Whitter, the entrepreneurial and revolutionary self-promoter, one need look no further than their respective hometowns.

Like Henry Whitter, Fries was a place that was in a constant state of self-invention. In fact, when Whitter was born in 1892, Fries as a town didn't even exist. Whitter was born in Sulphur Springs, near Hillsville, Virginia. When Whitter was born, his family was scratching out a living as subsistence farmers, very much like the classic image of stereotypical Appalachian residents living in the late nineteenth century, but a few miles away, a new town was in the works, one that would permanently change the region.

Fries was named after its founder, Francis Henry Fries, who was originally from Old Salem. There his family had made a small fortune building and operating textile mills along the Mayo River, a tributary of the Dan that flows north of modern-day Winston-Salem, North Carolina. These mills were operated by damming up the river and using the force of flowing water to power the machinery used to create textiles. Because of the need for a river and the difficulty in finding an ideal spot to place a dam, these mills were often built away from established towns, attracting the residents and infrastructure needed for an industrial operation after the mill's construction was already underway.

In the early 1900s, a southwest Virginia land owner, Jim Carico, felt that a piece of property he owned along Bartlett's Falls on the New River would make an ideal spot for a dam. Hoping to sell his tract for the most money possible, he contacted the Fries family of Winston-Salem and asked them to come see his property. Francis Fries himself set out from Mt. Airy, North Carolina, to examine the plot, which was located in the rural countryside of Grayson County, just north of Galax.

Fries approved the site, and soon construction of a dam was underway. By 1901, the impending construction of the Washington Mill caused a railway line to be extended into the area, the same railway line that would later carry Henry Whitter to New York City for his first recording sessions. By 1903, the mill was complete. Attracted by the promise of good wages and stable employment, hundreds of families began migrating into the new town.[1]

As was the case with most mill towns, the homes for these workers were constructed by the mill company and were laid out to maximize efficiency and land usage. Around three hundred homes were quickly built. These houses, which would be used to accommodate the families working at the mill, were nearly identical and were laid out in a tightly-packed grid pattern. This layout resulted in an oddly urban environment, especially when compared to less centralized nearby towns like Galax and Hillsville.

Before the construction of the mill, and the ensuing growth of the new mill town, most local commerce was anchored in nearby Stevens Creek, which had a post office dating from 1877. Stevens Creek had at one time been the site of a grist mill and an early academy, both of which served the outlying farming community, but Stevens Creek's importance was soon overshadowed by the emerging nearby town. The post office would soon be relocated and the community would acquire a new name. The mill town

The Washington Mill in Fries, Virginia. This was the mill where most of the residents of Fries, including Henry Whitter, spent their working days (courtesy Grayson County Historical Society).

was originally going to be called Carico, after Jim Carico, the original landowner, but the decision was made to instead name the town after its creator, and soon Fries would become a bustling hub of migration and commerce for the nearby area.

The Washington Mill, as the new textile plant in Fries would come to be called, required a large labor force to operate, and in 1903, the area around Stevens Creek was not populated sufficiently to meet the industrial needs of the mill. Heeding the call for employees, people began pouring into the area for the opportunity to make a new life, a more industrial life, for themselves in the new town. The first census taken after the construction of the mill was in 1910. At this time, the town of Fries, which had only existed for seven years, already had a population of 1,775. By 1920, the population was more than 2,000. Many of these families were not natives of the area, migrating from neighboring counties and states to find work in the mill. In 1900, the population of Grayson County was 16,853; by 1910, it was 19,856, the largest population jump that Grayson county would experience for the next sixty years.

One of the families swept up in this tide of immigrants was the Whitters, who, some time after 1900, relocated to Fries. Textile mill workers in the southern Piedmont have sometimes been viewed by historians as hard-

The Washington Mill and Fries, Virginia. The mill and town were designed for industrial operation. The highly-organized layout of the identical mill worker houses was unusual for a town in the Southern Appalachian region (courtesy Grayson County Historical Society).

pressed, making the move from agriculture to industry out of desperation or lack of alternatives.[2] This belief is no doubt a generally correct one. However, in the case of the Whitter family, this decision to move does not seem to be one that came out of dire necessity. In 1900, three years prior to the mill's opening, the family was living near Galax, Virginia. Henry Whitter's father worked on a farm, which he owned debt-free, and Henry and two of his siblings, Rose and Callie, were attending school. To abandon this relatively stable life and move up the road to Fries indicates the same desire for self-improvement on the part of the Whitters that motivated much of the immigration to mill towns across the South. No doubt the commerce, the promise of steady pay, the vibrant community life, and the urban luxuries offered in Fries were a compelling lure. Sometime after the opening of the mill, the Whitter family arrived, initially renting one of the company houses near the mill at 109 Main Street. Although dating the exact year of the Whitter's migration is difficult, by 1910, the family seemed well settled into mill life. Henry, then eighteen, along with his father and his two sisters, the youngest only sixteen at the time, were punching the clock every morning at the Washington Mill.

Fries was a mill town, and, as a result, life for local residents like the Whitter family was much more controlled, mechanized, and regimented than for their agrarian neighbors. In Fries, like most mill towns, private property was practically non-existent and the company exerted incredible control over the everyday lives of citizens. A report commissioned by the United States Senate in 1910 sought to explore the lives of Southern textile mill workers, and its findings give a keen insight into life in Fries and other towns like it.

> All the houses in which the operatives live are owned by the mill company. None of the land is privately owned. The company has donated land for churches and a school, and has built or helped to build the church and school buildings. Usually it selects the teachers and controls the school. It assists in supporting the pastor of a church or perhaps the pastors of several churches. It provides a water supply and regulates the use of the water. It provides for lighting: the streets, for cleaning the streets, and for cleaning outhouses. There is a company store, where a great variety of merchandise is sold, and in which the village post-office is located. Often the company sells fuel, and occasionally electricity for lighting the houses of operatives. The company decides whether cows and swine shall be allowed in the village; sometimes builds stables and pens for them, and sometimes provides a pasture. The company plants trees in the streets and sometimes provides a park. Occasionally the company conducts welfare work, and provides athletic grounds, a skating rink, a dancing pavilion, a library and a club house, or a Y.M.C.A. building, and contributes liberally to their support. If the mill village is large enough to have a hotel and a livery stable they are owned by the company and managed by employees or lessees of the company. In some mill villages the company chooses the doctor to attend the operatives and their families, making regular deductions from their wages to pay him. In fact, all the affairs of the village and the conditions of living of all of the people are regulated entirely by the mill company. Practically speaking, the company owns everything and controls everything, and to a large extent controls everybody in the mill village. Indeed, in some mill villages every man but one, the railroad agent, is under the direct or indirect supervision of the mill.[3]

Fries mirrored many of these assertions. Along with the workers' houses, the mill owned the larger homes near the dam that were inhabited by the mill's managers. The two boarding houses in the town were owned by the mill. The only hotel in town, The Washington Hotel, was built by the company operating the mill and named after it. The same company built the first gym found in either Grayson or Carroll counties, the Lyceum, which would be converted into a Y.M.C.A. in 1923. By 1924, a two-story concrete school had been built by the mill company on land owned by the company. Francis Fries had himself donated the land used to build the first church in the town.[4] Overall these construction projects show the tradeoff inherent in mill life: superior infrastructure and increased opportunities at the cost of local control and self-determination.

Perhaps nowhere is the control exerted by the mill more clearly seen than in the bell. This bell, situated on the roof of the Washington Mill, was a constant reminder of the mechanized life found in an industrial town. On weekends and holidays, when the mill was closed, the bell was used to toll time. It was also used to warn of floods and fires. Its primary purpose, though, was to regulate the lives of the town residents. When the mill was first built, it employed a single ten-hour shift, meaning that virtually every resident of the town would report for work and leave work simultaneously. To manage this incredible tide of workers coming and going, and to ensure productivity and efficiency, the bell was sounded as a way of organizing the workers' hectic morning routines. At 5:00 a.m., Mondays through Fridays, the wakeup bell echoed through the town. For anyone who tried to sleep in, another bell was rung at 5:30. The toll at 6:00 was used as an indicator that all employees should be fully awake and dressed. Beginning at six o'clock, the bell began tolling every fifteen minutes, each toll designed to pair with an employee's morning routine. Eat breakfast by 6:15, be out the door by 6:30. To accelerate the process, at 6:30 the bell began tolling every ten minutes, and at 6:40 came the warning bell, only twenty minutes to get to your station. By the 6:50 toll, responsible employees would be at their stations, while the less reliable would be running to catch up. Anyone arriving after the final bell, which tolled precisely at 7:00, would be considered late.[5]

Although this level of automation on the part of both the factory and the populace would seem to be a dehumanizing force, in some ways it helped to cultivate a strong sense of community in Fries. This was because almost every person in the town worked together. For the first years of the mill's operation there was only a single shift; consequently, the mill's workers all came to work at the same time, took breaks together, and left together; in essence, the employees lived essentially identical lives. They faced tragedies together, like the massive 1916 flood that threatened to destroy the mill and the flu epidemic of 1918. They also shared in the rewards. Because of its status as the largest taxpayer in Grayson County, the Washington Mill provided Fries with resources other towns in the area didn't have: high-quality education, indoor plumbing, and, eventually, electricity, provided by generators that were used by the mill to replace the more primitive water wheels.[6] These realities made Fries a world unto itself, a very unified atmosphere in which people, who were often brought together from far-flung regions and backgrounds, could intermingle, exchanging stories, ideas, and music.

Historian Patrick Huber has already noted the importance of Southern mill towns like Fries in bringing together what were traditionally disparate groups. He writes that

> with the rapid construction of textile mills and the gathering of displaced white farm families to tend their whirring spindles and beating looms, a new world of cities and towns, roaring factories and crowded mill villages rapidly emerged. Amid this modern world, with its factory whistles, industrial discipline, clattering machines, and low wage labor, Piedmont textile workers created a vibrant regional working class culture out of which was born a new commercial sound.[7]

These workers were always on the move, migrating from one town to the next looking for work. Henry Whitter's sister, Callie, began working at the Washington Mill but eventually moved to find work at a mill in Mooresville, North Carolina. She ultimately moved to Kannapolis to work in the Cannon Mill.[8] Kelly Harrell, another musician who would eventually record for the OKeh label, was working in the Fries mill in the early twenties but would move to the Fieldcrest Mill in Fieldale, Virginia, before dying of a heart attack.[9]

Henry Whitter and his sister Callie Payne. Whitter lived with Payne briefly after leaving Fries (courtesy Brian and Ann Baker Forehand).

This migration of workers from one town to the next allowed for a steady flow of information, including songs, from one region to another. This flow of people and information is what brought Henry Whitter in contact with the most profitable song of his career. This song found its way to Whitter through two textile mill migrants, Charles Noell and Fred Lewey. Charles Noell was working in a textile mill in Lynchburg, Virginia, when Fred Lewey played him a partially completed song which Lewey had been working on. This song, which Lewey had begun writing in Danville, Virginia, told the story of a train wreck that had occurred on September 27, 1903. The fast mail train Number 97, running behind schedule, had leaped off the tracks and crashed into a ravine. Lewey had been on the scene of the accident and had begun composing a ballad telling the story of the wreck. Noell would take up the song and help Lewey finish it. This song, which is still sung today as "The Wreck of the Old 97," probably would have faded away if it hadn't been for textile mill migration. Noell and Lewey moved to various mill towns: Danville, Lynchburg, and Fries. As they went, they sang the song to their fellow mill workers. No doubt the song, whose message about the dangers of fast living and the killing power of steel and steam, appealed to the textile mill audience. One of the people who heard Noell and Lewey's song was Frank Burnett, who began singing it himself sometime around 1904. Around 1914, Burnett taught the song to his childhood friend and fellow mill worker Henry Whitter, who would propel the song to national prominence when he recorded it for the OKeh label in December 1923.[10]

Huber notes that this convergence of mill workers was vital to the genesis of country music, both in its creation and consumption. Because mill workers suddenly found themselves with disposable income, and because mill towns were well connected to the outside world through radio and rail, the market for early country music recordings was suddenly becoming more easily accessible to Northern companies. Henry Whitter's family was one of those that used their income from the Washington Mill to invest in cylinder players and recordings, recordings which helped fuel Whitter's pursuit to expand the country music genre.

An early publicity photograph of Henry Whitter. The ability to play harmonica and guitar simultaneously made Whitter unusual in the world of early country performers (courtesy Brian and Ann Baker Forehand).

But it was in the creation

of music by individual workers that mill towns like Fries excelled. Huber writes,

> When hard-pressed white farm families moved to find work in the Piedmont's cities and textile towns, they brought with them their fiddles, banjos, mandolins, guitars and musical traditions, and although many of them were already accomplished singers and musicians when they arrived, their exposure to a wide range of musical influences and their access to factory-made instruments, radios, phonographs, sheet music, songbooks and musical instructional booklets led to a flourishing musical culture within Piedmont mill villages.[11]

These influences led mill town performers to alter tradition and develop progressive styles. Henry Whitter's first recordings, using a harmonica rack and guitar simultaneously, did not fit the mold of "traditional" Southern music, composed of a banjo and fiddle. In fact, Whitter was one of the first county musicians to play with a guitar and harmonica at the same time.[12] Charlie Poole, who was also a product of a mill town environment, learned a unique three-finger banjo roll rooted in a classical style.[13] Howard Dixon, another cotton mill native, began playing a new instrument, the Hawaiian-style steel guitar, after seeing Jimmie Tarlton.[14]

These new styles, born out of the commercial awareness and cross-pollination afforded by the mill towns, created concentrated pockets of musicality. Fries may be the best example of a mill town bursting with musical personality. The town seems to have exuded a musical presence. Performers played on the streets; music was played through phonographs in houses; even at their jobs, the mill workers sang to pass the time. The repetitive and stationary nature of mill work made singing a commonplace occurrence.[15] One song, making fun of the mill's superintendent, a Mr. Kinsey, was fondly recalled by Henry Whitter's sister, Callie, who had worked in the mills since she was eight. Henry Whitter, Kelly Harrell, and Ernest Stoneman were all working in the Washington Mill in the 1920s, and later musicians like Glen Neaves would also grow up in and around the mill. That isn't to say that Fries only produced hillbilly music. From its inception, the town sponsored a community coronet band which performed in full uniforms,[16] and many residents, Henry Whitter included, could play instruments like organs and pianos, not usually associated with traditional string bands.

Consequently, Fries' reputation was as a musical town, a reputation commemorated in a historical marker declaring Fries to be the "Center of Early Recorded Country Music." This modern, industrial town is forever tied to the traditional sounds of guitars, fiddles, and banjos.

This was the unique nature of Fries that allowed an artist like Henry

Henry Whitter and friends in Fries, Virginia, around 1922. The woman on the passenger side of the back seat is probably Whitter's first wife, Orene. The industrial economy of Fries would have made the ownership of goods like cars more common than in other areas of the southern Appalachian region (courtesy Southern Folklife Collection, Louis Round Wilson Special Collections Library, University of North Carolina at Chapel Hill).

Whitter to form. His natural desire for attention and fame, coupled with the hierarchical, capitalist world of a mill town, drove him to actively pursue a life outside of demeaning industrial labor. Huber notes that all across the Piedmonts of North Carolina and Virginia "millhands constructed new social identities for themselves in part around their production and consumption of this commercial music."[17] In Fries, this desire to reimagine oneself away from the shadow of the mill, along with the exposure Whitter had to performers from other areas, the recordings, instruments and music books that were widely available and affordable, the railway, connecting Fries to every major city on the eastern seaboard, all converged in a single individual, at a single moment. Whitter, and the role he would play in launching a new musical genre, didn't come from Fries by coincidence. He was a living embodiment of everything, good and ill, a mill town had to offer.

Fries was a town born from nothing whose rapid growth was fueled by an industrial economy. By comparison, G.B. Grayson's hometown of

Laurel Bloomery, Tennessee, was a world of history and tradition. Located in the far northeastern corner of Tennessee, Johnson County, in which Laurel Bloomery is situated, was one of the first areas settled in the state. The area was at one time part of the lost state of Franklin, an autonomous territory lying west of the Blue Ridge in North Carolina. Before its dissolution, Franklin had attempted to enter the Union as the fourteenth state, but the attempt failed.

By the early 1800s, Franklin was gone and its territory absorbed into the new state of Tennessee. Settlers to this region began trickling in from North Carolina and Virginia to establish homes in this wild frontier, G.B. Grayson's paternal grandfather among them. The first community established in the area was named Ward's Forge, after Major John Ward, a veteran of the war of 1812 who came to the area in pursuit of iron ore.

The selection of northeast Tennessee for his iron forge was no coincidence: the area was rich in the ore necessary for raw iron production. Two other early settlers, John Wills and William Gentry, had also started a forge sometime around 1800. Soon, the abundance of ore discovered caused a small industrial boom to come to the area, as several forges popped up along Laurel Creek, which winds north from Tennessee to the Holston River in Virginia.

Writings and liner notes about G.B. Grayson have sometimes referenced the name of Grayson's hometown, Laurel Bloomery. Generally, writers comment on the beauty of the name. It does seem to conjure up images of lush pink and white flowers cascading down forested ridge lines. Ironically though, the name has nothing to do with laurel bushes or blooms; the reality is much more industrial. The bloomery, in fact, referred to a primitive method used to melt iron ore. The ore would be placed in what was called a Catalan forge, essentially a large box surrounded by iron plates that connected to blast pipes. Iron and charcoal were placed inside (about four hundred pounds of ore were used in each run) and immense heat was generated by the burning charcoal. After about two hours, melted iron would run out of the forge through tap holes. This melted iron was collected on rods as it cooled, forming large balls or "blooms" which would be beaten into shape with a giant anvil and hammer.[18]

Because of the location of these "bloomeries" along Laurel Creek, the new community, which first obtained a post office in 1882, was named Laurel Bloomery, a commemoration of the area's industrial roots.

Although iron production was the most predominant industry in Laurel Bloomery during the nineteenth century, the community was not an industrial area. There was a church, which also served as a school, established in 1852. There was a grist mill, and there was a mineral spring. This supposedly medicinal mountain water would eventually be sent north and sold at hotels. But largely, the community G.B. Grayson would grow up in was one comprised of poor subsistence farmers.

When compared to Grayson County, Virginia, the county in which Henry Whitter's hometown of Fries is located, the disparity in wealth and industry is obvious. In 1930, the year G.B. Grayson died, Grayson County was home to twenty-eight manufacturing establishments. G.B. Grayson's home, Johnson County, had eight. Grayson County was averaging $464,392 in wages from manufacturing jobs. Johnson Country was averaging $97,092. In 1920, three years before Henry Whitter would make the trek to New York seeking fame, his hometown of Fries had a population of 2,029 people. That same year, the largest town in all of Johnson County, Mountain City, had a population of 724.

Iron production, the only real industry Laurel Bloomery had ever supported, didn't even last. The bloom forges were too primitive and the ore too limited to support long-term production. One writer notes, "Though in 1859 iron manufacturing accounted for 26 percent of the value of commercial manufacturing in northeast Tennessee and southwestern Virginia ... the majority of iron production in northeastern Tennessee used primitive methods little changed from the industry's frontier origin."[19]

Consequently, iron production was replaced in the early twentieth century by another industry, timber extraction, which was rapidly expanding in the Appalachian region immediately after the Civil War. In his book *Reconstructing Appalachia: The Civil War's Aftermath*, Andrew Slap notes that "earlier logging depended on use of the river to transport timber from the woods to processing centers. The late 1870s and early 1880s saw the expansion of railroad lumbering, in which a network of small-gauge rail lines stripped larger acreages of woods with ruthless efficiency."[20]

Laurel Bloomery and the area surrounding it were not immune to this new encroachment of outside profiteers. The T.W. Thayer Lumber Company, a Northern enterprise, was in need of timber. They had exhausted their supplies in Michigan and were attracted to the large stands of virgin pine and hardwood around southwest Virginia. In 1906, the Thayer Company built a narrow gauge line into Johnson County, Tennessee, looking for timber to supply its planing and dimensioning mill in Damascus, Virginia (this mill in turn supplied planed lumber to a plant in Cazenovia, New York, which used the Tennessee and Virginia timber to make doors and other finished products). In addition, bark from oak, hemlock, and chestnut trees was also being bought and sold in large quantities. This tanbark was processed in order to extract valuable tannic acid, which could be sold for considerable profit. A truck laden with this valuable tanbark would eventually be involved in the accident that would claim G.B. Grayson's life.

Like with most timber extraction operations of that time, the cutting of trees in Johnson County, Tennessee, and southwest Virginia was an exploitative operation. In 1907, a Mr. H.E. Clark of Glen Campbell, Pennsylvania, working in partnership with the Thayer Lumber Company, purchased 15,000 acres of timber in Washington and Grayson counties, Virginia, Johnson County, Tennessee, and Ashe County, North Carolina.[21] This land, which might have accommodated a growing population and been converted into new farms, would instead be purchased by the encroaching timber companies, clear cut, and left useless. Land that was once available for hunting and fishing would be stripped and barren. As the trees were systematically removed, the land lost its ability to contain runoff and erosion from heavy rains, and soon flooding became a major problem, making what farming remained in the area even more difficult.[22]

The environmental destruction wrought by these lumber companies in the Appalachian Mountains would create profound, long-term problems, as limbs and debris from the timber extraction would be left in place of the once-standing timber. The lumber companies, who had no interest in creating a sustainable future for the land they purchased, exploited timber resources until they were totally exhausted. The federal government was often forced to step in and attempt to remedy the situation. In fact, the existence of Cherokee National Forest, which encompasses much of modern-day Johnson County, Tennessee, was made necessary as a way of saving land ruined by unregulated timber production.[23]

The timber industry was fundamentally different than the textile industry in many significant ways, but one of the most prominent was the lack of mobility it afforded. Huber notes that mill towns, as a result of their railroad connections and ample job opportunities, were in a constant state of flux. He notes, "The perpetual movement of dissatisfied workers from one mill to the next meant that the dynamic musical culture of almost every Piedmont mill village was continually being reenergized and transformed through the constant introduction of new singers and musicians, who brought with them new songs and tunes, new instrumental techniques and new musical ideas."[24] By contrast, no energized culture was cultivated by the timber industry. Although the timber extractors did bring rail into areas like Laurel Bloomery, these rails were often narrow gauge, used primarily for the moving of timber, not people. Unlike the mill towns, which were largely residential and centralized, the areas of timber extraction continued to be rural and spread out. As a result, locals did not have close contact with incoming workers, who were often brought by the lumber companies and moved regularly from one timber camp to another.[25] Similarly, the fact that timber extraction took place in areas that were already inhabited, as opposed to mill towns like Fries, which were often rapidly built from nothing, resulted in a sense of division, the local population and the temporary timber workers never fully intermingling. Unlike Henry Whitter, G.B. Grayson would not have the opportunity to move from his native town to a new area, and unlike Whitter, Grayson would not have been surrounded by a flowing tide of neighbors and co-workers, arriving and moving, bringing with them new musical influences. Grayson did indeed learn new material throughout his life, and it is quite possible that some of that new material, specifically the railroad-themed songs, filtered into the region through the timber industry; however, there was no explosion of new musical styles in Laurel Bloomery following the arrival of the timber industry as occurred in the mill towns of the Virginia and North Carolina Piedmont.

Unlike the Washington Mill in Fries, which, although exploitative in its own way, gave back to the community in the form of schools, electricity, and infrastructure, the Thayer Lumber Company, which was owned and managed by capitalists in far-away cities, sought only to take out timber. As a result, the livelihood of the local residents was of no concern to them. Workers were brought in to operate the train, build tracks, and cut timber, leaving few job openings for the native population. In the period between 1900 and 1910, Laurel Bloomery saw its population increase from 1,220 to 1,934. The Appalachian Land Ownership Task Force has written that "corporate acquisitions by lumber and coal interests and the subsequent exploitation of coal and timber at the turn of the century limited the amount of land available to the Appalachian farmer. As a result, farmers were often left to farm land that they had never intended to use as their sole means of support. With this intrusion began the decline of mountain agriculture."[26] The result was that while the textile industry worked to improve the quality of life for many poor farmers, the timber extraction industry only made things worse. Given that G.B. Grayson's father and grandfather had been farmers, this destruction of timber and reduced land ownership options would have been acutely felt.

Essentially, both G.B. Grayson and Henry Whitter were the products of a southern Appalachian region that was being rapidly transformed by early twentieth century industry, and in both cases the industries that were affecting them succeeded through the exploitation of local resources. The mill in which Whitter found himself created a vigorous environment full of new people and new ideas commingling. Whitter grew up in a world brimming with possibilities, where the allure of material luxury and entrepreneurial success lay all around him. Grayson's environment, by contrast, was one of repression. The exploitation by the timber industry cut off avenues for mobility and made it increasingly difficult for local residents to maintain even the meager lifestyles that they had known in a preindustrial era. For Whitter, music was a tool to achieve the life he knew was possible; for Grayson, music was a desperate attempt to keep himself relevant in a world that was leaving him behind.

When Grayson and Whitter first joined as a duo, it wasn't just a partnership of musicians but rather a uniting of influences: the radically modernizing, industrial southern Appalachia, embodied by recording star and talent agent Henry Whitter, meeting with the poor and exploited agrarian Appalachian regions, embodied by obscure and impoverished G.B. Grayson. This blending of a deep musical tradition and savvy business knowledge is what made the duo unique. They weren't a traditional Piedmont mill band, which would have often been characterized by more modern song selections and virtuosic performances, but neither were they rustic, backwoods musicians steeped in folk tradition but unfamiliar with marketable song structures and recording techniques. They were the best of both.

Henry Whitter and the Creation of Country Music

Henry Whitter's role in early country music has often been to serve as an easy punchline. The tale is often retold of Ernest Stoneman hearing Whitter's early recordings for the first time and declaring that his former co-worker was so bad that surely anyone else could do better. Whitter's nasally delivery and rough guitar work are referenced when one wants to point out how far country music has come since its amateurish early years. If it hadn't been for his discovery of G.B. Grayson, virtuosically playing his fiddle in relative obscurity, at that infamous Mountain City fiddlers' convention, some would be quick to argue that Whitter would have faded away as a forgotten relic, a man who happened to be in the right place at the right time to make some early records, but who was ultimately unworthy of prolonged attention.[1]

The real Henry Whitter was something else altogether. To view Whitter solely as a musician is to miss where his real talents lay. Whitter may have been a subpar guitar player and a less than impressive singer, but he had a talent nonetheless: shameless self-promotion. It was this ability to exude confidence, to stand in an office in downtown New York, stare across official-looking desks, and tell skeptical men in suits that he was without a doubt "the world's greatest harmonica player"[2] that allowed Whitter to make a living for himself in an industry that didn't even exist at the time.

This aggressive self-confidence, coupled with an underlying business acumen, was not lost on his contemporaries. One critic, writing in 1929, summarized Whitter in this way:

> Henry Whitter, as the leader of this [hillbilly] movement is entitled, perhaps, to a few lines of description. Though probably the world's worst singer, he is really good upon his chosen instruments. He is also, I hear, a peculiar combination of simplicity and shrewdness and has his own business ideas, one of which is to stand on a street corner,

A promotional photograph of Henry Whitter (courtesy Brian and Ann Baker Forehand).

announcing his identity and distributing photographs of himself. I was informed by a local photographer that Whitter once introduced himself to him somewhat as follows: "Howdy do? I guess you've heerd tell on me. I'm the celebrated Mr. Henry Whitter, of OKeh recording fame. I made 'The Wreck of the 97' what it is today. They's been millions of copies of it sold. OKeh give me a good contract and that record made me barrels o' money. I got money to burn, by God!"[3]

Although the truth of this anecdote is probably questionable, there is no doubt that Henry Whitter was somehow able to use a natural talent for self-promotion and confidence to overcome any musical deficiencies he may have had. Even though it may be difficult to imagine, country music as we know it today owes a huge debt to an untrained youth whose nasally warblings helped launch a commercial genre.

Whitter's musical career can actually be traced to his youth in Fries. As a resident of a mill town, Whitter was a minor cog in a community-based industry. In 1910, his father, sisters and Whitter himself were all working in the mill. In fact, a brief glimpse at the census records from Fries during the early twentieth century clearly advertises the ubiquitous force of the Washington Cotton Mill. Almost every name is listed as an employee of the mill, their trades reflecting the reality of their daily lives: spoolers, spinners, doffers, weavers, oilers, and, in the case of the young Henry Whitter, laborers.

Trapped as a faceless automaton serving the interest of an industrial machine clearly didn't appeal to Whitter, and from his early days he was

The weaving room of the Washington Mill. This room is where laborers like Henry Whitter, Ernest Stoneman, and Kelly Harrell spent their days before launching recording careers (courtesy Grayson County Historical Society).

seeking means to escape. Whitter's sister, Callie Payne, who began working in the Washington Mill when she was only eight, remembered her brother's musical career being driven by a desire to escape the mill life.[4]

Luckily for Whitter, the mill did provide something that a more romantic, agrarian life would not have: money. With the disposable income suddenly available to them, Whitter's family, like many mill families, was able to afford luxuries that would have been unattainable otherwise. Sometime during the mid-teens, Whitter's parents acquired a cylinder machine, and Whitter was for the first time exposed to the world of recorded music. Of course, during this period, cylinder selections were limited, but Whitter was able to listen to a steady stream of unfamiliar music, no doubt many classical and operatic pieces performed by professional musicians. Whitter's favorite recordings, however, were those of Uncle Josh.[5]

Uncle Josh, the character created by vaudevillian Cal Stewart, first appeared on records as early as 1897. For years, Uncle Josh monologues were churned out by fledgling record companies. These comedic monologues followed the rustic Uncle Josh from the fictional town of Punkin Center as he encountered all kinds of confusing situations. "Uncle Josh on a 5th Avenue Bus," "Uncle Josh on a Bicycle," "Uncle Josh in an Automobile," and "Uncle Josh in a Chinese Laundry" are just a few of the humorous situations in which Uncle Josh found himself.

It is easy to see why the career of Cal Stewart, although Stewart was not a musician himself, could excite the imagination of a young boy laboring in the obscurity of a Virginia mill town. Stewart was himself a native of Virginia, born, as he said, "on a little patch of land, so poor we had to fertilize it to make brick."[6] From these humble beginnings, Stewart clawed his way up, working menial agricultural and industrial jobs before finally launching a career on the professional performer circuit. From minstrel shows, circuses, and medicine shows, Stewart, and his developing Uncle Josh character, was able to land a gig performing monologues on records. Although Whitter was probably unaware of Stewart's backstory, he would definitely have been aware of the fact that Uncle Josh didn't sound like the classically-trained musicians also popular on cylinder recordings. Although the character was supposedly a rube from a small town in New England, Cal Stewart's Southern roots allowed him to impart an accent and folksy charm into his Uncle Josh recordings that was unique in a recording industry dominated by Italian opera singers. Because of these recordings, Whitter would have no doubt been aware that even though Southern folk music had yet to appear on record, rural culture had the capacity to attract an audience.

Of course, Whitter had to start somewhere. Coming from a musical background, Whitter seemed to immediately gravitate toward musical performances as a means of escaping the menial mill work that occupied most of his day in the Washington Mill spooling department. He had learned to play the harmonica first, but seemingly aware that a solo harmonica artist would have limited opportunities, Whitter set out to learn the guitar. True to his nature as someone willing to aggressively challenge his own limitations, Whitter ordered a guitar and began playing with no real knowledge of how the instrument was played. He began by wildly flailing the strings, but he practiced regularly, sitting on an empty gas tank that had been rolled off a train car in front of the Fries depot.[7]

It was also during this period that Whitter began working on his trademark mode of performance, utilizing a guitar and harmonica simultaneously. With the help of a fellow worker, John Summer, who worked in the machine shop of the Washington Mill, Whitter fashioned a holder that would allow him to play the harmonica while backing himself up on a guitar. With these tools at his disposal, Whitter began performing all around Fries in the hours he wasn't at work.[8]

His desire to appeal as a showman as well as a musician was also evident from this period prior to his first recording session. Those who witnessed his early local performances recalled that Whitter utilized something similar to a limberjack during his performances: a hand carved wooden puppet that could be made to dance with a string that Whitter tied to his leg.[9]

Practicing and performing were no doubt fun for Whitter, as they were for other musical millworkers around the Virginia and North Carolina Piedmont, but unlike many amateur musicians of the time, Whitter never lost sight of music as a means to escape the mills.[10] Fortunately for Whitter, he was about to be in the right place at the right time.

The place was John Rector's general store. By 1923, Whitter had left the rented company house in the town of Fries where he had grown up and was living instead with the extended family of his wife in the nearby community of Stevens Creek. At the time, Stevens Creek was a well-populated area, inhabited by many mill workers who commuted to work in Fries every morning. The hub of this small community was a general store located on the banks of the creek. The store had been in operation for years, even predating the founding of Fries itself. Once run by a man named Henry Isaac, by 1923, the store was under the operation of John Rector, a banjo player who enjoyed playing with local musicians who came in to shop. Whitter was a regular participant in the impromptu jams and

John Rector's store in Stevens Creek, Virginia. This store, shown on the left, with the large crowd on the porch, was where Henry Whitter first got the idea to make a record in New York after being encouraged by a travelling salesman (courtesy Grayson County Historical Society).

happened to be playing with Rector one afternoon in early 1923 when a salesman stopped by to drum up business. Impressed by the music, he suggested that Whitter and Rector travel to New York. He'd heard on his travels about a record company, OKeh, that was seeking new talent, and he suggested that the two audition.[11]

Whitter was excited by the prospect of traveling to New York to launch a professional musical career, but Rector, a responsible and successful business owner, deferred. Whitter would have to go alone. Undaunted, Whitter told everyone at the Washington Mill of his plan to break into the world of professional musicians, a world dominated at the time by formally-trained performers, not rustic mill workers. Whitter's boss, no doubt reflecting the sentiment of many of Whitter's co-workers, responded, "Henry, you will be seen walking back up the railroad tracks, dragging your guitar behind you."[12]

But again, if there is one word that describes Henry Whitter, it is tenacious. Despite discouragement, Whitter began diligently saving money out of his paycheck to purchase a ticket to New York. His wife remembered,

"He just wanted to go. He always wanted to be famous."[13] Preparing to leave, and brimming with his trademark self-confidence, Whitter reminded those around him, "You know, after I make this record, I'll never have to work in a cotton mill again."[14] With guitar in hand, the thirty-year-old Whitter boarded the train for the long, fateful journey to New York City.

The details of this trip have been a bit controversial ever since researchers began attempting to ascribe a specific date to early country recordings. Ralph Peer, who recorded Fiddlin' John Carson in Atlanta on June 19, 1923, adamantly contended that Whitter's appearance did not predate the Carson recording. His contention was that Whitter had written a letter to OKeh prior to the Carson recording, but it was only after the success of that recording, when Peer formally invited him, that Whitter travelled to New York. Based on Peer's timeline, Whitter would have showed up some time later in the year of 1923.[15]

By contrast, Archie Green contended in his famous essay "Hillbilly Music: Source and Symbol" that Whitter's trip predated Carson's by several months. He cited interviews with Whitter's family members, Whitter's own claims during his lifetime, and Polk Brockman's (the OKeh talent scout who had discovered John Carson) assertion that the Whitter test pressing existed prior to the Carson recordings as evidence. In addition, Whitter maintained possession of a postcard sent back to Fries from New York that was postmarked 1923 as well as a souvenir picture of himself taken in New York during the initial trip, also bearing the date March 1, 1923. Whether the date was added afterward in order to support Whitter's claim is impossible to prove, but given the fact that Whitter died in 1941, years before any controversy about the recording date existed, it seems unlikely that he would have actively attempted to craft a fraudulent story about the date. Peer, whose reputation hinged on his ability to identify unknown talents, would have had a vested interest in arguing that his discovery of Carson was the first time a rural singer was recorded and that Whitter's arrival in New York was only made at Peer's behest.

According to Fred Hager, who operated the recording studio used by OKeh in New York, Whitter showed up in their offices sometime in 1923 and was ushered into the studio to make a few test recordings. These records, which no longer exist but were no doubt unimpressive to the ears of OKeh executives, were shelved. Whitter went back to Fries and returned to work in the spooling department of the Washington Mill.

However, a musical revolution was about to explode in Atlanta. Fiddlin' John Carson's field recordings, issued in a limited run for local sale, began to take off in popularity. Peer and Brockman, suddenly aware of a great

A souvenir photograph taken during Whitter's first trip to New York. The date of this initial recording session is not settled; the back of this photograph is dated March 1, 1923 (courtesy Brian and Ann Baker Forehand).

untapped market of people who favored rural musicians to classically-trained ones, frantically looked around for a way to keep the momentum going. They found their answer in Whitter's test recordings and quickly summoned the obscure mill hand back to New York in December for what would become his first official recording session.

Initially, Whitter favored harmonica solos. The harmonica had been his first instrument, and he apparently felt that it was his best chance at success, but Ralph Peer, who was actively attempting to shape rural musical forms unfamiliar to him into something marketable, felt that these first sessions needed something more. His accounting of this first session gives insight into both his astute sense for marketable music as well as his disinterest in the rural talents providing it:

> I finally found out by talking to [Henry Whitter] that he worked in a cotton mill someplace. Charlotte or someplace like that. And he said he was the world's greatest harmonica player.... So, I finally took him down to the recording studio and we ran off a half a dozen of these things, and he was a great harmonica player. There was no doubt about that. Then we issued one or two records. And, to me, they were something lacking. They needed something more. So I brought him back, because he was successful, I brought him back to New York to do some more recordings. And then I discovered that the dope could sing. So then I began making recordings where he would sing a chorus and play a chorus, you see. All these things are so simple but I had to learn, or somebody had to learn, by experiment. And we, we had Henry Whitter as an artist for a number of years.[16]

These first recordings, with Whitter's pinched delivery interspersed with uncomfortably long harmonica solos, are difficult for modern listeners to appreciate. However, like fellow trailblazer Fiddlin' John Carson, Whitter was standing on the cusp of a momentous transition from true folk music, designed to appeal to amateur performers and regionally defined, untrained listeners, to commercial country music, something that was polished and consciously designed to appeal to wider audiences. In that light, "Wreck on the Old Southern 97," Whitter's most popular early recording, sounds less like harsh dissonance banged out by an untrained musician and more like the trumpet heralding a new age of popular music.

Despite its tedious harmonica solos and pinched vocals, "Wreck on the Old Southern 97," and other songs like it, exploded in popularity during the years of 1924 and 1925. Dock Walsh, who would soon be propelled into stardom himself, recalled that he could "remember the first record I ever heard [Whitter] play was 'Going Down the Road Feeling Bad' or 'Wreck of Old 97.' I knew I was in Winston Salem at the time and they was playing that thing all over, every house you went by."[17]

Back in Fries, Whitter's popularity was disproving the statements of

THE LEADING LINES

WEAVER PIANOS PLAYER PIANOS

PHONOGRAPH RECORDS O. K.

HENRY WHITTER'S LONESOME ROAD BLUES

LARGEST STOCK OF RECORDS AND MUSICAL INSTRUMENTS IN N. C.

L. C. DULA, *Distributor*

604 North Liberty Street 904 Shallowford Street

PHONES 2466—2440 WINSTON-SALEM, N. C.

During the height of Whitter's career, he was a preeminent recording artist. This business card, from a music store in Winston-Salem, North Carolina, mentions Whitter by name to advertise their record inventory (courtesy Brian and Ann Baker Forehand).

a lot of doubters who had questioned the merits of his trip to New York. His sister, Callie Payne, who was living in Mooresville, North Carolina, at the time, remembered Whitter visiting her immediately after the first recordings had been released. Whitter waited for his sister to leave the room, then put his record on the Victrola. Payne recalled her shock when she returned to the room, and, hearing music, expected to see Whitter playing. Instead she found he had hidden, hoping to surprise her with his accomplishment.[18] Friends and family in Fries were also picking up copies of the "Wreck of the Old Southern 97," and Whitter was becoming something of a local celebrity.

Unfortunately for Whitter, this initial recording trip had not thrust him instantly into a career as a professional musician. Although his records were starting to gain popularity early in 1924, Whitter was still laboring at the Washington Mill in Fries. Having separated from his first wife in 1921, Whitter soon left Fries, travelling to Mooresville, the home of his sister, but his professional music career was still insufficient to make a livelihood, and he once more found himself laboring in a cotton mill.

Whitter's career was about to gain traction, though. As 1924 wore on, Whitter would keep getting called back to New York to record: three sessions in February, three more in July and two in November would produce twenty-seven songs. During the July sessions, Whitter attempted to expand his sound, arriving in New York with two of his neighbors, John Rector and James Sutphin. This group would record eight songs as Whitter's Virginia Breakdowners. This move was probably motivated by the OKeh record company, who had just recorded several songs by John Carson's new group, the Virginia Reelers, in April of 1924.

One of the moments that would solidify Whitter's presence in future histories of early country music was the recording of "Wreck on the Southern Old 97" by Vernon Dalhart in 1924. Dalhart, a trained singer who had an established career in the recording industry, heard Whitter's early recording and felt the song (as well as the less than stellar singing on the original record) offered him an opportunity to break into the suddenly emerging hillbilly music world.[19] Having recorded for several years on the Edison label, and feeling that they possessed superior sound reproduction technology, Dalhart first recorded the song for Edison. Dalhart, originally from Texas, was not an active practitioner of folk music styles and so adhered to Whitter's version as closely as possible in order to retain the authentic sound of the original. He learned the lyrics from Whitter's record, garbling several words in the process, and even included harmonica accompaniment similar to that found in Whitter's version. This Edison record was successful enough for Dalhart to attempt to record the song again, this time for the more prestigious Victor label, a label that had yet to aggressively enter the emerging hillbilly market.

Dalhart's second

Whitter's Virginia Breakdowners on the road to New York for their 1924 recording session. From left to right: John Rector, Henry Whitter, and James Sutphin (courtesy Brian and Ann Baker Forehand).

A publicity photograph of Henry Whitter. The incorporation of fox hounds makes reference to Whitter's most popular instrumental, "The Fox Chase" (courtesy Brian and Ann Baker Forehand).

recording of the song, which would forever rename the it as the more concise "Wreck of the Old 97," probably would have meandered, unheralded, into the Victor back catalog if it hadn't been for the inclusion of a strong B-side, something the original Edison recording lacked. The B-side to the Victor release, "The Prisoner's Song," would help launch Dalhart's record to the top of the hillbilly market, ultimately becoming the first million-selling country record and ensuring Dalhart a place in the hillbilly genre for several years to come.

Apparently, Henry Whitter was not as fond of Dalhart's recording as everyone else seemed to be. He complained that the success of Dalhart's record took sales away from his own version. Dalhart himself felt guilt over the slight to Whitter. He wrote in a letter, "I am sorry to learn that my efforts have in any way damaged any other artist, and this goes especially for Henry Whitter as I liked him very much personally, as well as his recordings. I have always claimed that the popularity of one singer or song helped others, as no one man could do them all."[20]

Whitter's life was made increasingly difficult when the success of Dalhart's record resulted in a lawsuit. As a result of the song's popularity, and the lucrative copyright that went with it, a controversy over the original authorship of the song erupted. David Graves George, responding to a request for information about the song's origin printed in a local newspaper, stepped forward, claiming that he was the song's composer and was entitled to royalty payments. Unfortunately for Whitter, his ambition and desire to make a name for himself put him in the middle of this sudden controversy. Whitter had learned the song from Frank Burnett, who had in turn learned the song from Charles Noell, one of the musicians who were eventually given credit as the song's co-authors; however, in his first recording of the song for OKeh, Whitter failed to make this point public, instead allowing himself to be listed as songwriter on the published sheet music for the song.[21] When the controversy over the authorship arose, thrusting Whitter into the middle of a high-profile lawsuit, he began to panic. Ernest Stoneman remembered Whitter's distressed mindset during this period, as he feared what retribution might befall him as a result of the court's ruling. Stoneman was also quick to point out that the blame for Whitter's involvement lay in his unceasing desire for self-promotion. He recalled that "if [Whitter] said I don't know who is the author of it, but I own the copyright, he'd of had 'em, but the trouble of it is he said 'I wrote it' trying to get credit for writing it."[22]

The case of *George v. Victor Talking Machine* took years to settle. After numerous delays, it finally arrived in court in 1931. For almost a decade the case wound its way through the court system, eventually arriving before the United States Supreme Court in 1940. Ultimately, it was decided that the songwriting copyright belonged jointly to Henry Whitter, Charles Noell, and Fred Lewey, but by the time it was finally decided, Whitter was no longer involved. In a panic, he had sold his interest in the song to Fred Hagar, the man who had first arranged to record Whitter. Hagar, in turn, sold it to the Shapiro-Bernstein company, the company that still maintains rights to the song today.[23]

By 1925, hillbilly music was becoming all the rage in the recording world. Gennett, a label started by the Starr Piano Company, which would later be the label of the first Grayson and Whitter records, was gravitating toward "old-time" tunes as the biggest-selling market available to them. Although OKeh had started the country boom with their recordings of Whitter and John Carson, Columbia, a rival record company, was vying for dominance. In 1924, they recorded their first country artists, Ernest

Thompson, Samantha Bumgarner, Eva Davis, Gid Tanner, and Riley Puckett. By 1925, Columbia would begin issuing the 15000-D series of records exclusively for country recordings.[24]

Fiddlin' John Carson

ASSISTED BY

Henry Whitter

Will Play a Full Program of Jazz Music and Ballads at

The Tabernacle

Friday, Sept. 18th, at 8 P. M.

Under Auspices Galax High School

During the mid–1920s, Henry Whitter and Fiddlin' John Carson were two of the biggest hillbilly stars on the OKeh label. This newspaper clipping, from 1925, advertises an upcoming show in Galax, near Whitter's home town of Fries (courtesy Brian and Ann Baker Forehand).

One thing all of these companies lacked was any knowledge of what they were doing. Labels like OKeh, Gennett, and Columbia were based in urban areas and had developed methods to market music produced by professional artists who were often members of organized musician and songwriter unions. The executives running these companies couldn't distinguish between good and bad when it came to rural musicians and certainly were incapable of finding artists living in the rural South to record. During the period before 1925, many artists, like Whitter, began seeking out record companies themselves, often because they realized the material being released was of subpar quality. The story of Ernest Stoneman deciding to make a record after hearing the pinched, nasally delivery of Whitter has often been used to besmirch Whitter's qualifications as a musician, but it was hardly the only example. Fiddlin' Powers was inspired to record after hearing a John Carson record. Powers had beaten John Carson in a fiddler's contest, and, as a result, felt he was also entitled to make a record. Other artists, like Dock Walsh and Elder Golden Harris, were also seeking out New York recording companies, suddenly realizing they could make it as recording artists.[25]

This dependence on artists' initiative was not a very sound method of insuring a steady recording output, however, so recording companies began turning to field scouts to provide connections to rural artists, a method

Riley Pucket Is Here

(Columbia Phonograph Artist.)

ASSISTED BY

HENRY WHITTER

WILL GIVE A 90 MINUTE GROGRAM AT

STEVENS CREEK SCHOOL HOUSE

Saturday, June 19th, At 8 O'clock P. M. 1926

Their program consists of all kinds of singing, old time melodies and up-to date selections. Be on hand and hear a real honest to goodness musical entertainment. Mr. Puckett and Henry are two good musicians and will give a program that will please everybody.

You all know "Henry" and will know "Riley."

"Riley is from Atlanta, Ga., and "Henry" is one of our home boys. Bring a friend with you and enjoy 90 minutes of good music and entertainment. at the Stevens Creek School House, Saturday night, June 19th., at 8 o'clock P. M. 1926

PROCEEDS FOR BENEFIT OF SCHOOL

Admission 20c & 35c.

Grayson-Carroll Gazette, Galax, Va.

One of the performers Whitter often partnered with was Riley Puckett from Georgia. Puckett's virtuosic guitar playing and singing was very popular with live audiences. This flyer advertises an upcoming show in Whitter's former home of Stevens Creek, Virginia, in 1926. By the end of the 1920s, Whitter's own guitar playing had improved dramatically, no doubt aided by his frequent appearances with Puckett (courtesy Brian and Ann Baker Forehand).

that tended to be more reliable than advertising and open auditions.[26] Naturally these scouts were generally rural artists themselves who had a preexisting connection to the record labels.

Henry Whitter was used heavily as a scout, initially for OKeh records, and it is through his position as a conduit to New York–based recording companies that his influence on early country music was truly exerted, a point often ignored by people commenting on Whitter's career.

In fact, almost all the early musicians from southwest Virginia can trace their careers to Whitter at some point. Whitter had traveled to New York in 1924 with his neighbor John Rector and James Sutphin to record as the Virginia Breakdowners. This session in turn gave Rector the connection to OKeh that he would use a year later to land a recording deal for his second band, the Hill Billies. Elvis Alderman, who played fiddle for the Hill Billies, even said that the band insisted on using OKeh because they had been willing to record Whitter.[27] Rector wasn't the only musician in Fries to directly benefit from Whitter's original trip to New York. Whitter's fellow mill worker, Kelly Harrell, a singer who didn't even play an

A rarely-seen publicity photograph of Whitter's Virginia Breakdowners. From left to right: John Rector, Henry Whitter, and James Sutphin (courtesy Brian and Ann Baker Forehand).

instrument,[28] would be personally introduced to OKeh field recorders by Whitter.[29] Ernest Stoneman, another employee of the Washington Mill, would also follow the path to New York carved by Whitter. Stoneman would later serve as a talent scout himself, encouraging his own friends to record, further perpetuating the dominance southwest Virginians held over early hillbilly records. In fact, thanks to Henry Whitter, in 1924, one would be tempted to say that Fries was one of the world's most prolific producers of hillbilly music.

During this period, record companies were not interested in representing a variety of folk traditions or regions and were no doubt unaware of any difference between a Virginia fiddler and one from Arkansas. Their only interest was in steadily producing new records that would sell to rural audiences. Consequently, a few efficient talent scouts, like Whitter, Stoneman, and Polk Brockman in Atlanta, could cause small areas to be systematically strip-mined for all musical talent while the musicians of adjacent areas were totally ignored. Unfortunately, because these early records are oftentimes our only windows to the folk traditions that predated them, certain areas, like Atlanta, Georgia, and Grayson County, Virginia, have gained accidental dominance over these studies. In essence, Whitter's placement in Fries during the time of his first recording session forever shaped the way country music itself is understood.[30]

During the folk music renaissance of the 1960s, many of these early recording artists were sought out for interviews and emulation, and researchers quickly noted that a disproportionate number of them lived around Galax and Fries, leading many to assume that this area was just especially fertile ground for traditional music. However, in his book *Virginia's Blues, Country and Gospel Records 1902–1943: An Annotated Discography*, Kip Lornell astutely theorizes that the Galax area, which still holds a claim to being the center of the old-time music world, owes its entire identity to Henry Whitter. He asks, "If Henry Whitter had come from Franklin County rather than Fries, would today's string bands be playing the tunes of Ferrum artists like Dr. Lloyd and Howard Maxey with equal vigor and reverence?"[31]

Aside from establishing a gateway to commercial country music for the southwest Virginia area, Whitter's scouting was also blazing trails off the mountains. The sheer number of records Whitter was recording for OKeh between 1923 and 1926 was causing him to gain a reputation as a person of importance in the recording world, and he was attracting the attention of other musicians, lured not by his masterful singing but rather by his connections. In an article published in the national trade magazine

Talking Machine World describing a hillbilly field recording session in Asheville, North Carolina, Whitter is the only artist mentioned by name:

> Three hundred applications for a test recording were received and from these twenty-five were selected. Some of the most famous fiddlers and singers of the South were heard and many old-time tunes were recorded. Henry Whitter was the only professional who attended and he recorded some records which bear all the marks of being wonderful sellers.[32]

Ads like these telegraphed Whitter's importance, whether earned or not, to other artists struggling to make it. In 1925, while recording in Asheville, another musician, Fisher Hendley, was also trying to break into the music world. Hendley, unlike Whitter, was not trying to escape a laborious and underpaid existence; in fact, he was quite successful as a businessman, owning and operating a service station in Albemarle, North Carolina. Hendley did, however, have a strong interest in musical performance and wished to try his hand in the recording world. After performing on WBT in Charlotte in April of 1925, he was asked to make a test recording during the Asheville session, the same session that Whitter was attending. However, Hendley's recordings did not launch him into immediate recording stardom, and he returned to Albemarle to continue working on his musical career. When he was finally ready to make another attempt at breaking into the world of country records several years later, he turned to any connection he could find to give him an edge. He originally sought out the sponsorship of Gibson, the instrument manufacturing company that had crafted Hendley's banjo,[33] but they were unable to provide assistance. It took a letter to Henry Whitter, who Hendley probably remembered as being an artist of importance from his first recording session, to give Hendley the avenue to recording stardom that he needed. Whitter, who by that time had made several well-received records along with G.B. Grayson, on the Victor label, was able to secure Hendley a recording session, something Hendley would have probably been unable to do on his own.[34]

As Whitter's recording career became more prolific during the years of 1924 and 1925, so too did his career as a live performer. Whitter secured the assistance of George Bridges, a booking agent from West Virginia, a state with a voracious appetite for hillbilly music. Like professional musicians today, Whitter was aware that to escape the cotton mill life and make a sufficient living, he would have to rely predominantly on live performances. During this time, Whitter was between marriages and was relying heavily on his mother for support. She kept track of his correspondences with New York and sent him supplies on the road[35]; Ernest Stoneman remembered Whitter's mother also frequently traveling to live shows with him.[36]

Fisher Hendley, the last musician to record with Henry Whitter. Hendley owned a garage in Albemarle but was able to break into the musical world with Henry Whitter's help (courtesy Marshall Wyatt).

Fred Hager, the studio director for OKeh records, credited Whitter's unusual use of a harmonica and guitar as a primary reason for his early successes as a live act. Unlike many artists who had to travel in groups, arranging all transportation and boarding to accommodate several people, Whitter was able to serve as a one-man band, providing vocals, rhythm

HEAR

FISHER HENDLEY

AND

HENRY WHITTER

Victor and Radio Artists

AND FORGET YOUR BLUES

These superb artists are no strangers to Phonograph and Radio fans. Hendley, recognized champion banjo player of North Carolina, presents his famous banjo duet with Marshall Small of Badin, which is in a class by itself. Whitter, who has become world famous with his "Wreck of Old Ninety-Seven", and "The Fox Chase", will be present with his guitar and his voice that has charmed millions.

These artists have a date with the Victor Record Company to make a number of new records this month. While they are practicing upon their new material, you are offered an opportunity to hear them in some of their new interpretations.

It's a rare opportunity and if you have the price you can't afford to miss it.

TROY HIGH SCHOOL

Thursday Night, October 9th

8:00 o'Clock

ADMISSION . . . . 15c and 25c

Before recording together, Fisher Hendley and Henry Whitter performed a series of shows around Hendley's hometown of Albemarle. This show, at the Troy High School, was advertised for October 9, 1930, less than two months after the death of G.B. Grayson (courtesy Brian and Ann Baker Forehand).

and lead instrument from a single performer. This ability to play with no assistance from other musicians allowed efficient and rapid movement from one performance location to another and made him more attractive to venues than a solo singer or a lone instrumentalist would have been.[37]

Whitter began touring vigorously, and soon he had quit cotton mill work altogether, making his living solely through his musical career, primarily through live appearances. These performances were held anywhere Whitter could attract an audience. Like many touring performers of the time, he primarily used schools and theaters for his evening shows, but he also performed at the homes of individuals. Friel Alderman, cousin of fiddle player Tony Alderman, remembered how Whitter would work a community during his touring: "Henry would make the rounds for two weeks and visit different places. Then he'd put a show on at the schoolhouse and charge to go in and see him. 'Course everybody went in to make a donation to him, give him some spending money."[38]

As with his recording career, Whitter's touring was built on connections to other artists. Whitter generally traveled alone, but he was able on many occasions to pair up with other well-known acts in order to increase ticket sales. Along with artists like G.B. Grayson and Fisher Hendley, with

One of Henry Whitter's business cards. Beckley, West Virginia, probably refers to the location of Whitter's booking agent, George Bridges (courtesy Southern Folklife Collection, Louis Round Wilson Special Collections Library, University of North Carolina at Chapel Hill).

whom he made records, Whitter also performed with Fiddlin' John Carson and Riley Puckett. Whitter, ever a conscientious businessman, seems to have been quite aware of the limits of his own abilities, and from early in his career was more than willing to share top billing with more talented performers as a way of prolonging his own success. Ernest Stoneman, a fellow Fries millworker who had launched his own recording career, remembered how effective the use of these other musicians was to attracting audiences for Whitter, especially around 1926, when their popularity was on the rise and Whitter's was on the decline. Stoneman recalled that he would accompany Whitter on stage without compensation when Whitter performed with Riley Puckett, just to be in the presence of Puckett's outsized talent.[39]

It was undoubtedly this self-awareness of the need for support to prop up his career that led Whitter to the Mountain City fiddlers' convention in 1927, but Whitter was looking for more than raw musical talent when he encountered G.B. Grayson: he also needed songs.

By the time Grayson and Whitter teamed up in 1927, Ralph Peer, who had first recorded Whitter for OKeh, had moved to the more prestigious Victor label. Victor, seeing the money being made in hillbilly music by competitors like Columbia and Gennett, wanted to hire Peer to establish Victor's presence in the hillbilly market. Peer felt he wasn't being offered a sufficient salary for his expertise and made Victor a counteroffer: he would work for nothing if he could retain ownership of copyrights. Victor accepted the offer and Peer set out to establish himself at this new label. He mimicked practices that had worked at OKeh. He utilized a portable recording studio, something that would work to great effect at the famous Bristol sessions. He also tried to keep costs down by paying hillbilly artists at the same rate they had been paid through OKeh: twenty-five dollars per side recorded. However, Victor, seeing itself a more prestigious label than OKeh or Gennett, felt it would reflect poorly on them to pay so little. They insisted he give artists fifty dollars per side for their recordings.[40]

The amount paid to the artists was of no concern to Peer; he was after copyrights. The first artist he recorded for Victor was Ernest Stoneman, who had recorded earlier for Peer on the OKeh label. These Victor recordings quickly sold 60,000 copies. Other successful recordings followed, and Peer claimed he earned a quarter of a million dollars in a few months solely through copyright royalties.[41]

It is interesting to note that Peer's massive success was largely due to his desire to treat recording artists as valuable rather than disposable. Although he had little respect for the rural music he recorded, Peer did understand that artists sought out people who seemed to treat them as professionals. Consequently, Peer never bought an artist's copyright outright; he just collected royalties on their recordings. He then paid the artists 25 percent of their mechanical royalties (royalties earned for each record pressed). This system encouraged artists to not only stick with Peer but also to consistently come up with songs which had yet to be copyrighted, thereby benefiting both Peer and the artist. Peer seemed well aware of how important the use of financial incentive was for encouraging his growing stable of artists. He said, "One trouble about dealing with any of these people is you don't want to figure out how much money they might earn and then give it to them, cause then they have no incentive. You see, they've got everything. No incentive to work."[42]

Peer demanded that any artist who recorded for him be able to provide new material. This is no doubt one of the factors that made a partnership with G.B. Grayson so desirable to Henry Whitter. Whitter had been recording for four years and had probably exhausted his knowledge of non-copyrighted songs. Grayson, however, was able to provide dozens of new songs which had never been recorded before. This seems to be what Peer thought, when Henry Whitter, who Peer hadn't seen for several years, walked into his new Victor office in New York with a blind fiddler in tow. Peer recalled what he thought when he first met Whitter's new partner:

> He was a fiddle player. I just don't know where he fit in ... my policy was always to try to expand each artist by adding accompaniment or adding a vocalist, what have you, and that's the way this fellow came in. He was either a better singer than Whitter or he had the selections which would be another reason to bring him in. Finding the new stuff continuously month after month was not easy.[43]

Almost immediately, Grayson and Whitter's recordings were met with success. Walter Jones, who ran a furniture store in Galax, Virginia, near Whitter's hometown, recalled that along with Riley Puckett, Grayson and Whitter were some of the biggest sellers. According to Jones, he once submitted an order for two hundred copies of the duo's new records sometime around 1927. The distribution company, which was located in Baltimore, wrote back to tell Jones that he must have made a mistake, they would send twenty instead. Knowing the record market around Galax was eager for new Grayson and Whitter discs, Jones replied, "Hell, send me 300."[44]

With Grayson as a partner, Whitter suddenly was able to breathe new life into his flagging career. In the entire year of 1928, Henry Whitter was able to record two songs as a solo artist; as half of the Grayson and Whitter partnership, he recorded nineteen. These recordings by the new duo had started on Gennett, where Grayson and Whitter had earned a fairly paltry sum. On their October 10 recording session they had each earned ½ cent per record sold, less 10 percent in royalties, and had been paid $150 in traveling expenses for the recording of eight songs.[45] With Peer's move to Victor, Whitter saw an opportunity to use his connections to switch labels, and soon the duo were recording, along with artists like Jimmie Rodgers and the Carter Family, on the prestigious Victor label, earning more money both in expenses and from the royalties generated by copyrighting their songs. After recording for Victor in October of 1927, they would return once more to Gennett, recording nine songs in February of 1928. From that point onward, all of their recordings would be done for Victor.

Whitter, through perseverance, business acumen, and luck, had finally achieved the high point of his professional career. With Grayson's clear and soulful singing and clean, precise fiddle playing, Whitter was able to stay in the background, providing solid guitar backup (which showed dramatic improvement from his first recording sessions, apparently influenced by Whitter's occasional live performance partner, Riley Puckett). Whitter also chimed in with off-handed remarks and asides which give these records much of the vibrancy that contribute to their continued popularity. Although Grayson and Whitter never achieved the levels of success experienced by other Victor artists, like Jimmie Rodgers and the Carter Family, they were able to make a notable impact on the record market. "Train 45," paired with "Handsome Molly," was their top seller, staying in print until 1934, well into the dismal Depression years. It ultimately sold around 50,000 copies. "Nine Pound Hammer," coupled with "Short Life of Trouble," sold around 10,000 copies. Other popular selections that sold more than 1,000 copies were "Barnyard Serenade," "Red and Green Signal Lights," "Little Maggie," "Tom Dooley," and "Going Down the Lee Highway." During a time when many artists languished in obscurity and cut only one or two sides, which often sold just a few hundred copies, Grayson and Whitter's popularity was worthy of note.[46]

Even though he was experiencing the highest level of success he would ever obtain, Whitter was ever the forward-looking businessman, searching out the next step for his career. Having seen the power of forming a partnership, Whitter began looking for new artists who could benefit from his connections to the music industry. One of Whitter's ideas was to expand the Grayson and Whitter duo into a trio by incorporating a banjo player. Ralph Peer encouraged artists to expand their sound to be more appealing, and it seems that Whitter felt he and Grayson would benefit from an additional member. Grayson had already been playing occasionally with a young banjo player, Fred Miller, who lived in nearby Ashe County. According to Miller, both Grayson and Whitter were interested in adding him to their lineup:

> Banmon Grayson, he was a blind man, a blind fiddler. Oh boy, he was good. He could sing, my Lord he had a real voice. I played with Grayson, and he wanted me to go out with Henry and make some records with them. He lived in Laurel Bloomery, Grayson did. He went back over there and he got in touch with Henry, and Henry came down here to Calhoun's place, and I went down to that brick house. I went down there and we played and sung. He sung, I didn't. He said, "Boy, I think you'll fit right in there," said "we'll get an arrangement, and appointment." 'Bout a week before we had to go to New York, Grayson got killed in a car wreck. That stopped it. If he ever made any more records, I don't remember. He might have found someone else to play with. I wanted to go so bad. But they had to cancel when Grayson got killed.[47]

Luckily for Miller, he was not deprived of his chance to record; he performed with Frank Blevins and His Tar Heel Rattlers on several sides for Columbia. These rollicking recordings capture the exuberant playing that would have no doubt fit right in on a Grayson and Whitter record.

Fred Miller, the banjo player for Frank Blevins and His Tar Heel Rattlers. Miller briefly played with Grayson and Whitter and was offered a position in the group before Grayson's death. This photograph was taken the year of Grayson's death, 1930 (courtesy Marshall Wyatt).

One of the often repeated bits of folklore associated with Grayson and Whitter is that after Grayson's death in August of 1930, Whitter was so upset, he gave up recording and retreated to a life of isolation. This seems to overlook the fact that throughout his partnership with Grayson, Whitter continued to make solo live appearances. In fact, Whitter was already planning his next recording session when Grayson was killed. He had already made contact with Fisher Hendley, a banjo player from Albemarle, North Carolina, who was hoping to break into the music business, and by October 1930, not even two months after Grayson's death, the two had worked up a routine and were putting on shows around Albemarle in preparation for an upcoming recording date.

Unfortunately for Whitter, lightning would not strike twice, and his recording partnership with Hendley would be short-lived, resulting in eight songs, but only two issued records. Although Fisher Hendley's recording career would quickly take off, resulting in more than thirty songs being recorded through the Depression years, Whitter had been replaced. The man who had been one of the original pioneers of country music would never record again.

It is tempting to see this as a testament to Grayson's influence: without him, one could argue, Whitter was nothing. The truth of the matter is much more practical. Because of the economic crash of the Great Depression, the period between 1930 and 1931 saw a complete shift in the country music industry, as recorded discs, and artists like Whitter who had popularized them, were eclipsed by radio, which provided free entertainment. Almost immediately, the 1920s model of

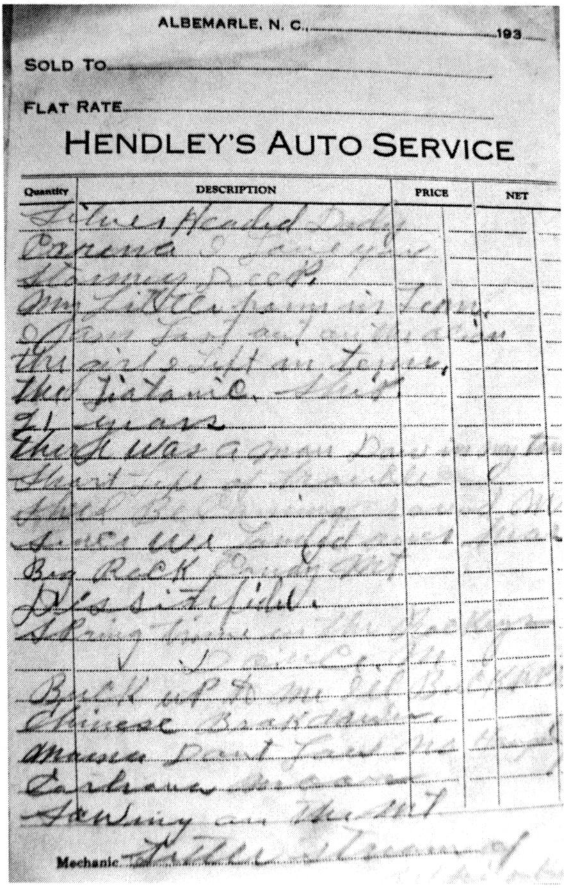

ALBEMARLE, N. C., 193

SOLD TO

FLAT RATE

HENDLEY'S AUTO SERVICE

Quantity	DESCRIPTION	PRICE	NET

Mechanic

A setlist of songs performed in live shows by Henry Whitter and Fisher Hendley. The list was handwritten on a blank receipt from Hendley's garage in Albemarle. The list includes the Grayson and Whitter song "Short Life of Trouble" (courtesy Brian and Ann Baker Forehand).

the country industry was dismantled, and the performers who had achieved success following it found their careers evaporating.[48]

Through his career, Whitter had wisely stepped from one role to another: mill worker, solo artist, talent scout, and member of a duo. By 1930, he had nowhere left to go. But, ever determined, Whitter never let certain defeat discourage him, and even during the Depression, when almost every artist from the heyday of the 1920s gave up a full-time music career to pursue other work and other commitments, Whitter continued to do what he could to prolong his career as a professional musician. In the 1930 census, when asked his profession, Henry listed "musician"; lacking record or radio work, he was forced to list his employer as "stage." Radio was becoming the preferred media for country music, and Whitter had at various times performed on some of the largest broadcasting hubs in the South, even appearing on WSM in Nashville with Fisher Hendley as late as 1930. The radio shows of the 1930s were dominated by younger talent with fresher sounds, acts like Mainer's Mountaineers and the Monroe Brothers; there wasn't much demand for a relic from the early 1920s.[49] Consequently, Whitter had nowhere to turn but to live performances as a means of maintaining an income. He continued to use schools but also found himself frequently performing in movie theaters between film showings. He appeared at the Lyric Theater, the Sears Palace Theater, and the Jeffersonian Theater in West Jefferson, North Carolina, through the 1930s.

Whitter also continued to market himself, using his notoriety as one of the first artists to record, and his association with the wildly popular "Wreck of the Old '97" to book appearances. At these live shows, Whitter would bring a portable record player, play one of his early OKeh discs, and explain all the intricacies of the recording process to the crowd. He would then demonstrate to the curious audience the methods he used in the studio to ensure his voice would be picked up by the primitive recording machines.[50]

After Grayson's death, Whitter was on the lookout for a new partner. In his songbook he wrote, "I met G.B. in Mountain City Tenn. in 1927, and we booked together on records.... I will be glad to do for others as I have done for Mr. Grayson." This desire to use live shows to attract the interest of local untapped talent can be seen in the following section from a performance poster:

> If there are any musicians in this territory that would like [Henry Whitter] to recommend them to phonograph companies in the future, you are invited to come to this entertainment, as the admission is reasonable and after the program each musician or band can play about two tunes so he can see and hear your type of playing and singing,

> and remember he is willing to recommend each musician or band absolutely free.... There are so many musicians that have played on stages and broadcast that have never had the opportunity of recording a phonograph record, so bring your music and come, no matter what type of music you play, or what kind of instrument you use.[51]

In these post-recording years, Whitter was able to attract a few aspiring local musicians around the Ashe County area, where Whitter now lived. He frequently played with his stepson, Earl Baker, who had learned to play the harmonica from Whitter. He also appeared with Worth Taylor, a local fiddler. These two were advertised as featured artists at the 1934 Dogwood Festival in Chapel Hill, where Whitter was billed as a "famous musician from the mountains of Ashe County and composer of the ballad 'The Wreck of the Old 97.' [He] will sing and play a number of songs that are nowadays seldom heard."[52]

Whitter was also accompanied for a year by Alonzo Black, a young fiddler from Ashe County who would later play semi-professionally on a small radio station in Mooresville, North Carolina, Whitter's former home town. However, their partnership was short lived. Believing Whitter was exploiting the young musicians hired to accompany him, Black and Whitter eventually had a falling out. Black recalls "We went to Chapel Hill, to what they call

TAYLORSVILLE, N. C.

In Person February 4-5

HENRY WHITTIER

Saturday February 6

Monday & Tuesday Feb. 8-9

A Tale of Two Cities

with

RONALD COLEMAN

ELIZABETH ALLAN

During the 1930s, Henry Whitter found it harder to attract live audiences. He began playing at movie theaters between film screenings. This clipping, from 1935, advertises his upcoming performance at the Palace Theater in Taylorsville, North Carolina (courtesy Brian and Ann Baker Forehand).

Jeffersonian Theatre

West Jefferson, North Carolina

HEAR

HENRY WHITTER

Nationally Known Phonograph Record Artist and Radio Entertainer

Fri. & Sat. Feb. 28-29

Show Starts at 10:15 A. M. on Saturday

Bring the Whole Family to Hear This Great Artist

Regular Prices—No Advance in Admissions

Also on the Screen

Gene Autry

Radio's Singing Cowboy, in

"Tumbling Tumbleweeds"

Hear Henry harmonize on the harp and guitar. He will furnish a world of entertainment for young and old, the same HENRY WHITTER who made the "Southern Old 97," "Fox Chase," "Lonesome Road Blues," "Many a Time With You I Have Wandered," and many others.

PRESS OF THE SKYLAND POST

During the 1930s, Whitter's career was nearing an end, but he continued to play locally. This flyer advertises a show in West Jefferson, near Whitter's home. Whitter played sets between film showings at the local movie theater (courtesy Brian and Ann Baker Forehand).

the Dogwood Festival, me and him and, I can't think of that boy's name who played the five string banjo ... They give [Whitter], I believe it was forty dollars, but he didn't give me and that boy a dime of it, and he quit and I quit."[53]

The most widely recognized artist who would get his start playing with Whitter during this period was Albert Hash, who, years later, would become quite well known as a fiddler. Albert had been a fan of Grayson and Whitter's records and had sought Whitter out after Grayson's death. Whitter was impressed by Hash's fiddling prowess and took him on as a partner; the two steadily toured the schools and towns of northwest North Carolina and southwest Virginia until the late 1930s. During this period, the young Albert Hash, who would later be famed for his abilities as a luthier, didn't own a fiddle nice enough to play at live shows, so Whitter loaned him one that he had built from a kit. Whitter also tried to support Hash's growth as a musician. Ironically, Hash learned many of G.B. Grayson's fiddle songs not from Grayson, but from Whitter, who was himself an adept fiddler and wanted the young Hash to be able to mimic the sounds of Grayson's playing at live shows.[54]

Henry Whitter (left) and Albert Hash on the porch of Whitter's home in Healing Springs, North Carolina. The record player has been moved on the porch to provide a backdrop for this amateur publicity shot. Whitter and Hash regularly played together during the 1930s (courtesy Brian and Ann Baker Forehand).

Whitter continued to do live performances until the late 1930s, prolonging his career far beyond most rural musicians of his generation. Unfortunately, Whitter's health was rapidly deteriorating. He was suffering from diabetes, which was left untreated, and his mental state soon began to suffer. In 1941,

The box containing Henry Whitter's personal record collection at the time of his death was decorated with this homemade collage under the lid. It includes photographs of other artists Whitter admired, indicating that Whitter was staying abreast of contemporary country records. These artists include Riley Puckett, the Delmore Brothers, Jimmy Rodgers, Mainer's Mountaineers, and the Monroe Brothers (courtesy Brian and Ann Baker Forehand).

as country music recording finally began to fight its way back to life following the Great Depression, Henry Whitter passed away from complications stemming from his diabetes.

Whitter's legacy is not only one of records and live performances. Throughout his career, he seems to have genuinely cared about the welfare of the other musicians with whom he came in contact. Ernest Stoneman remembered, "As far as I can find out, Whitter was very fair with everybody he worked with.... I never did find out anything else, he was very fair with all of them." Albert Hash recalled that he "liked him, he treated me good like I was his own boy and we had a good time together."[55] Whitter was a self-promoter to the very end, so perhaps the best eulogy to his career and his influences comes from Whitter himself. In the introduction to his songbooks he wrote, "He is the same honest, jovial, good natured Henry Whitter yesterday, today and tomorrow. He is always kind and courteous to everyone and is anxious to help aspiring musicians over the rough road he has travelled."

The Long Shadow of G.B. Grayson

In the early 1960s, the Country Gentlemen were quickly becoming one of the pre-eminent bluegrass bands to emerge during the folk music boom. They would eventually help the bluegrass genre to progress beyond the traditional sounds of Bill Monroe and the Stanley Brothers and into new realms, featuring contemporary songs and innovative playing styles. Although they would come to stand for a new style of bluegrass band, their early repertoire, released in a series of albums recorded for the Folkways label, was indebted to songs and groups from the earliest days of country recording. When their album *The Country Gentlemen Sing and Play Folk Songs and Bluegrass* was released in 1961, an astute observer may have noticed something interesting about the track arrangement. The lead song of side A was "Train 45," and the lead song of side B was "Handsome Molly": the two sides of Grayson and Whitter's single most successful record. Although they had not performed in more than thirty years, the duo was still making its impact felt in the folk music world.

One of the reasons Grayson and Whitter maintain a position of importance among those interested in the history of country music is the wide impact they have had on generations of musicians who have come after them. While other, sometimes more successful, acts are often forgotten, or given cursory treatment by music historians, Grayson and Whitter continue to cultivate interest. This long-reaching impact can primarily be traced to Grayson's musicianship rather than Whitter's. It was Grayson who was largely, if not solely, responsible for the duo's song selection; it was Grayson's clear, strong voice that made the lyrical content of the songs he sang easy to understand, a quality not universally found in singers from his era; it was Grayson who chose which verses to sing and which to leave out, thereby establishing canonical versions of folksongs that traditionally existed in varied forms; and it was Grayson whose unembellished fiddle style helped craft clear, direct melodies that could easily be imitated by others. Compare his style, for example, to that of Fiddlin' John Carson, an artist no doubt as influential, and probably more well known, but whose songs were often characterized by radical melody shifts and uneven bar lengths. It is clear that if one had the choice of a version of a song to learn, Grayson's would often take priority over many others, not only because of his technical abilities but also because of his clarity.

Clearly this influence was felt almost immediately. Unlike many other musicians of the era, whose rough styles or forgettable song selection drove them inevitably into obscurity, Grayson's songs quickly began to gain traction with other performers, who continued to perpetuate his song selections, lyrics, and phrasing. This perpetuation, like ripples on the surface of a pond, quickly began to magnify Grayson's musical importance after his death as his influence spread to successively more well-known performers, eventually resulting in G.B. Grayson songs being peppered into the discographies of performers as varied as Bob Dylan, Doc Watson, and Mick Jagger.

One of the clearest connections between Grayson himself and the popularization of his song versions in commercial country recordings can be directly traced to Steve Ledford, the famous North Carolina fiddler. Ledford had learned to play from a very large, very musical family. He was born in Mitchell County, North Carolina, in 1906. He was one of twelve children and began learning to play the fiddle at age seven. With the advent of country recording in 1923, Ledford began to gravitate toward the sounds of fiddlers who were being captured on record. Two of his favorites were Fiddlin' John Carson and G.B. Grayson. In an article assessing the role Ledford played in the history of bluegrass music, Clarence Green notes that "although Steve learned some songs directly from Carson, most of his commercially recorded examples during the late 1930s owe a substantial debt, both in style and repertoire, to the late fiddler from Laurel Bloomery, Tennessee, G.B. Grayson."[1] Ledford personally knew Fiddlin' John Carson, who he'd met at a fiddlers' convention, Charlie Bowman, one of the fiddlers for the Hill Billies, and G.B. Grayson. It was from Grayson, and his recordings, that Ledford would learn many of the songs he would play throughout his life.

It is worth noting that Ledford's younger brother Taft claimed that Grayson had actually learned the songs he recorded from Ledford rather than the other way around,[2] but several factors make this seem unlikely. For one, Ledford was only twenty-one at the time Grayson, who was almost forty, began recording. Additionally, Ledford never recorded a song during Grayson's lifetime, and, as result, would have had little standing to give Grayson instruction. Also, Ledford seems to have had little personal contact with Grayson. Although the two probably crossed paths, when asked in interviews about Grayson, Ledford discussed him with a sense of detachment, seeming to know him more from his records than from any firsthand experience.

Although he never made a record during Grayson's lifetime, Ledford would soon be a recorded artist himself. In 1932, he made a record with the Carolina Ramblers String Band. Because of the dismal market conditions created by the Great Depression, this record never launched Ledford to stardom. However, it did establish him as a viable professional fiddler. When Buddy and Bucky Banks, nephews of Wade Mainer, performed in nearby Spruce Pine, Ledford showed up for an audition and soon found himself in contact with Wade Mainer, who was establishing himself as a top act on the flourishing medium of radio.[3]

Wade Mainer had just recently parted ways with his brother, J.E., and was looking for a new fiddler. According to Mainer, "[Steve Ledford and his father] came to see our show, just him and his dad. Steve brought a fiddle with him; after he saw the show he said, 'I play the fiddle a little bit.' I said, 'How would you like to play a tune or two with us?' So that's when we struck off.... That's where we come up with that 'Train 45' and made such a big hit."[4] This version of "Train 45," recorded in 1937, is clearly indebted the version G.B. Grayson recorded ten years earlier. Although Ledford's version is a bit more upbeat, featuring extra train effects and including four verses not found in Grayson's version, the similarities to the Grayson and Whitter recording are obvious. The melody is identical; the first three verses sung are identical to Grayson's version; and the recording also features side remarks, hollers, and the repeating of the song's title between verses, all of which were aspects of the original record.

Ledford himself claimed that his version was the original and that he had taught Grayson "Train 45," a song that Ledford claims he first heard being played by a musician named Fred Winters. Ledford said he added verses to the song, which Grayson then copied on record.[5] Although this is possible, by the time Ledford recorded his version, Grayson's version had been in print for ten years, and although Ledford's version does contain verses not found in the Grayson and Whitter original, Ledford was not shy about improvisation and adding verses to established songs. In home recordings he made in the 1970s, Ledford recorded "Train 45" several times with verses added to celebrate Tweetsie Railroad, a local line that had run from Johnson City, Tennessee, to Boone, North Carolina. Whether or not Ledford's 1937 version was in fact the original and the Grayson and Whitter recording was the copy will never be known for sure; what is certain is that in many other ways Ledford was definitely indebted to Grayson's recorded repertoire.

In later years, Ledford, as a member of the Ledford String Band, would record a song entitled "He's Coming from Vietnam." This song, with slightly altered lyrics, is clearly a re-recording of G.B. Grayson's "He's Coming to Us Dead." In his home recordings, which showcase the wide array of songs that Ledford played regularly, numerous Grayson songs are found: "Rose Conley," "Handsome Molly," "I Saw a Man at the Close of the Day," "Going Down the Lee Highway," and "A Dark Road's a Hard Road to Travel."

With the help of Steve Ledford, Wade Mainer served as a bridge between Grayson and other musicians who would come after. In addition to "Train 45," Mainer would record at least six other songs from Grayson's repertoire during the Depression years. One group that was heavily influenced by Mainer, and would go on to international notoriety, was the Stanley Brothers, Carter and Ralph. In the book *Lonesome Melodies: The Lives and Music of the Stanley Brothers*, David W. Johnson notes that the Stanleys were using Mainer as inspiration before they themselves even began playing. During these formative years, the Stanleys were also being exposed to the original recordings of Grayson and Whitter. Johnson notes that Carter was especially enthralled with these original recordings. He cites an interview with music historian Joe Wilson, who remembered that "[Carter] used a lot of Grayson's melodies and songs. Obviously he had been exposed—not only to all the Victor but all the Gennett records."[6] Ralph Stanley himself emphasized this connection saying, "We never got to see Grayson play, but we had his records and we couldn't get enough of 'em. The way some boys studied schoolbooks, we studied these old 78-rpm records, and we learned 'em good."[7]

These influences can clearly be heard on several early recordings by the Stanley Brothers. "Little Maggie" was a song originally recorded by Grayson and Whitter and later re-recorded by Wade Mainer, Zeke Morris, and Steve Ledford. This song was also recorded early in the Stanley Brothers' career. In his autobiography, Ralph Stanley noted, "One of our biggest mail pullers was 'Little Maggie.' I heard Steve Ledford do that on an old 78 record, I believe it may have been with the Carolina Ramblers. He was later the fiddle player with Wade Mainer and Zeke Morris in the thirties and he featured 'Little Maggie' a lot then too."

Although "Little Maggie" was probably the best known G.B. Grayson song in the Stanley Brothers repertoire, it was hardly the only one. Clearly, Grayson and Whitter's catalog had profoundly influenced them. This may be because Carter and Ralph Stanley felt a strong connection to G.B. Grayson, a man they had never met. Ralph recalled, "Our favorite records were by the Carter Family, and Grayson and Whitter, and Fiddlin' Powers and Family; they came from places that weren't so far away, less than a hundred miles. They sounded familiar to us, like people we knew back in our mountains." Additionally, he said, "[Grayson] played the prettiest lonesome fiddle and he was a good singer too, which was rare for a fiddle player. Grayson sang a lot of the lonesome ballads my dad sung: 'Omie Wise' and 'Rose Conley.'" Over the course of their recording career, the Stanleys would continue to revisit the catalog of Grayson's recordings. They would eventually record versions of "Short Life of Trouble," "Handsome Molly," "The Lee Highway Blues," "Train 45," "The Banks of the Ohio," and even G.B. Grayson's obscure temperance song, "Don't Go Out Tonight, My Darling."

Aside from the songs themselves, Grayson and Whitter's influence can be felt in other ways when listening to some of these recordings from the early days of bluegrass. Specifically, their vocal asides and exclamations, which gave such vitality to the original recordings, were repurposed by these later artists. As earlier noted, Ledford's version of "Train 45" featured a series of comments between verses similar to those that were interjected by Grayson and Whitter in 1927. The Stanley Brothers' original version of "Little Glass of Wine" features Carter calling out the title of the song during the mandolin's instrumental break—a stylistic choice directly traceable to Grayson and Whitter's recordings, specifically when Henry Whitter shouts out, "Handsome Molly" during that song's first fiddle break.

"Little Maggie" and "Train 45," G.B. Grayson standards that had gained early traction with other artists, quickly found new lives outside of Steve Ledford and the Stanley Brothers. Bill Monroe was playing "Little Maggie" by 1946. Earl Scruggs made several personal recordings of the Opry Shows he played when he first joined with Monroe (establishing what many would argue was the first true bluegrass band). Among the songs collected by Scruggs during this period was "Train 45."[8] In 1962, Monroe released *Bluegrass Ramble*, his attempt to capitalize on the folk revival of the early 1960s with traditional folk songs from his early repertoire. Two of the songs selected were originally recorded by G.B. Grayson, "Little Maggie" and "Nine Pound Hammer," which Monroe had arranged by combining the version recorded by Grayson with the version recorded by the Hill Billies,[9] showing how far the influence of the fiddler from Laurel Bloomery was spreading.

Through Steve Ledford and the Stanley Brothers, Grayson's songs and style were broadcast to an audience larger than he had been able to reach in his own lifetime, most of whom would have been unaware of G.B. Grayson and his original recordings, but his influence, was more directly felt by some players who were acquainted not only with his music but with the man himself.

One fiddler who was heavily indebted to Grayson was Glen Neaves, who would be recorded numerous times, most notably as the leader of the Virginia Mountain Boys. This group recorded several albums for Smithsonian Folkways beginning in 1974. The first three volumes of this recording series predominately feature Neaves as lead fiddler and vocalist on many songs. On the third volume, a brief track is included in which Neaves explains his influences. He says, "Well, old G.B. Grayson, I listened to him a whole lot. He was raised up in my country, around close by. That was over in Ashe County, close to West Jefferson. Yeah, I learned, tried to follow him, play his kind of tunes, all that stuff. He was a fine man, a fine man."

Neaves' connection to Grayson is even more direct than it sounds on the recording. In an interview conducted by Frank Weston, and published in the *Old Time Herald*, Neaves recalled meeting Grayson personally: "[Grayson] was born right next to home down in Ashe County. He come by, to my grandfather's and he played the fiddle of a night just by himself, nobody playing with him, down at the house. I was just a little old barefoot boy.... I play a lot of his tunes, I like his music."[10]

Neaves went on to recall seeing a show featuring Grayson that would have occurred prior to his partnership with Whitter.

> I was pretty small but I remember a contest, him and Smokey Davis and a bunch, that was before [Grayson] run up with Henry [Whitter]. Smokey, he had a group of musicians (I don't remember too much—it's been so long ago) but I went to fiddle at this schoolhouse and he had a little girl that danced—about five or six years old. [There was] a wailing good crowd and when they went to divide up their share of the money taken at the door they gave it all to Grayson. This was around Jefferson around where he was born. He'd been gone a long time and come back with Smokey. Smokey played guitar and there were several more but I don't know who they were, they just come in and put on a show.[11]

Clearly, Grayson's music impacted Neaves profoundly and, by extension, all who listened to the recordings of the Virginia Mountain Boys. In the first three volumes of the series, six songs were almost identical versions to the Grayson originals. These included some of Grayson and Whitter's more obscure material like "Where Are You Going Alice?," "Don't Go Out

Tonight, My Darling," and "The Red and Green Signal Lights." By including these songs, which Neaves had learned directly from the original recordings, a wider audience was able to discover the songs of Grayson, further ingraining his canon of songs into the bluegrass tradition.

Neaves was one of the bluegrass artists who was helping to repurpose and reinvigorate Grayson's material for a newer generation of players. Another artist helping to expand the music to new audiences was Ola Belle Reed. Like Neaves, Reed was an Ashe County native, growing up near Grayson's home of Laurel Bloomery. Reed did not stay in Ashe County but at an early age traveled north to Pennsylvania with her family. As a migrant from Ashe County to Pennsylvania, Reed is an example of a large-scale migration from the Appalachian region to the mid–Atlantic and Midwestern states that took place in the Depression era. This migration would bring Appalachian musical forms into new regions, where it was able to flourish among these transplanted populations. Ola Belle Reed is a perfect example of this pattern. Reed's songwriting and her appearance at two traditional music parks—the New River Ranch and later Sunset Park—made her one of the key figures working to spread Appalachian folk music to new audiences in the post-war years.

Like Neaves, Reed was herself personally inspired by G.B. Grayson. She noted in an interview that her father, whose musicality had helped inspire Reed, played with Grayson. She remembered, "They used to play. My father didn't play with his group, but they used to play together at times in our community because that's the way people used to do—they'd get together and play."[12] In the same interview, she recalled meeting Grayson personally at a performance in West Jefferson. Ola Belle Reed retained a knowledge of Grayson's songs when she moved north, and she actually ended up living near and knowing Grayson's oldest son, Edgar, who had also migrated to Pennsylvania. She remembered that around the Pennsylvania area versions of "I've Always Been a Rambler" based on Grayson's versions were being played. Cleverly, these versions changed the lyrics "I left old North Carolina, to Marion I did go," found in the original recording, to "I left old North Carolina, to Maryland I did go."

Back home in east Tennessee and northwest North Carolina, Grayson's influence never really faded: after the record-buying public had moved on to newer artists, his name still carried weight in these areas because his influence locally had been so immense. His list of performing partners was extensive and made up a healthy portion of the recording artists performing in the area during Grayson's lifetime.

One of the most frequently cited of these partners is Clarence "Tom"

Ashley, a fellow resident of Johnson County, Tennessee, who often worked with Grayson at local performances. In fact, in a famous photo of the performers taken at the 1925 fiddlers' convention, Ashley is standing next to Grayson.

Ashley was about seven years younger than Grayson when the two began playing together. Although he would go on to mentor Roy Acuff, contribute to the discovery of Doc Watson, create a recording career of his own, and re-establish his fame during the folk revival of the 1960s, Ashley owes much of his career to Grayson, with whom he had first honed his playing skills. Ashley was not as well practiced as Grayson when they began playing together. G.B. Grayson's son Clarence recalled that when they first started performing together Ashley "wasn't much of a musician."[13] However, they did play together extensively, traveling as far north as West Virginia to perform for miners on Friday nights, a trek that Grayson would also make with Henry Whitter after the two formed their famous partnership. During their travels, Grayson and Tom Ashley joined with other musicians in the region. They were traveling with Ted Bare around Saltville, Virginia, when they met Hobart Smith who would later be an icon of the folk revival. Ted Bare was himself a regionally well-known musician, a notorious rambling mandolin player who would later assist in recording a single side, "Governor Al Smith for President," with the Carolina Night Hawks.

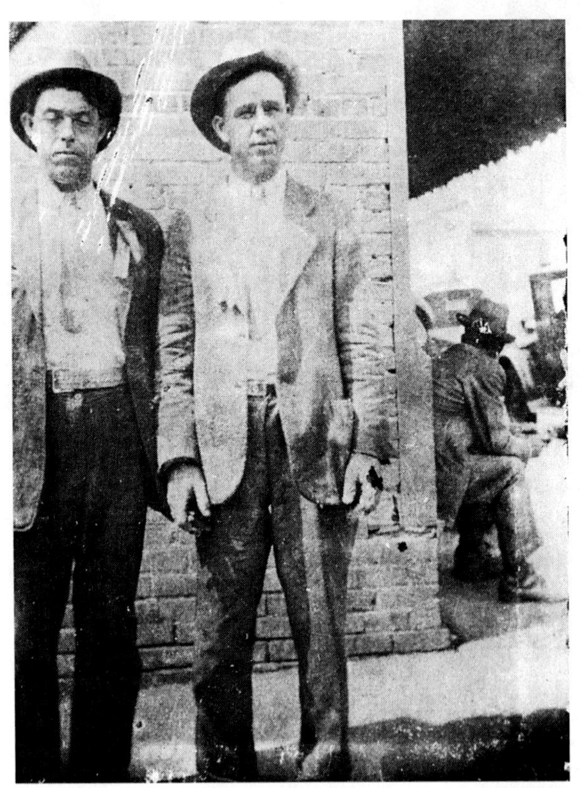

G.B. Grayson (left) with his frequent playing partner Clarence "Tom" Ashley. This photograph was probably taken on the streets of Mountain City, Tennessee (courtesy Tony Russell/Old Time Music collection).

Eventually, Grayson

and Ashley parted ways, a breakup that may have been somewhat acrimonious. Frank Grayson, who was a cousin of G.B. and a playing partner of Tom Ashley's, claimed that "[G.B.] and Tom didn't always get along the very best. I think that was over money maybe."[14]

Ashley went on to his own recording career, making records with several groups and as a solo artist. Because of the fame he was able to earn in these early years of the Great Depression, Tom Ashley is the banjo player most people associate with G.B. Grayson. However, Ashley was not the banjo player who most frequently performed with Grayson. Ashley would occasionally accompany Grayson on trips and at local performances, but that doesn't mean he was Grayson's primary partner. That honor goes to J.C. Smith, known locally as Calt, who performed with Grayson for years prior to his first recording session.

John Calvin Smith was almost ten years older than Grayson when the two started playing, which would have been sometime prior to 1920. Although little is known about the origins of Calt's musical ability, he was an experienced banjo player when he partnered with Grayson, utilizing a frailing style of playing. Unlike Grayson, Smith was able to support himself and his family without music, and during the day, he operated a small store on Fall Branch, a few miles from Grayson's home in Laurel Bloomery.

These two seem to have been inseparable during the years before Grayson partnered with Henry Whitter. Ray Dowell, a fiddler who learned from Grayson, remembered seeing Grayson and Smith play at molasses makings and house parties. Clarence Grayson, G.B.'s son, named Calt as his father's primary playing partner. Smith's important role as Grayson's partner has probably been ignored because Smith did not travel with Grayson like Tom Ashley nor create records with Grayson like Henry Whitter. However, his reluctance to engage in these activities is probably due to his responsibilities at home. Calt had three children to care for and a store to operate, so unlike Grayson, who depended on music for a livelihood, he would have found it difficult to leave home for extended periods. Calt's son, J.T. Smith, known affectionately as Buster, was also suffering from a deteriorating bone disease and would need constant care beginning around the time Grayson and Whitter were recording. Calt would have to stay behind in Johnson County while his lifelong playing partner built a musical career away from home.[15]

Although Calt Smith never received much acknowledgment for the important role he played in helping G.B. Grayson's career, he was able to impart his own musical influence on his children. His son Buster learned to play guitar and performed with his father until he was ultimately

From left to right: J.C. "Calt" Smith, G.B. Grayson, and J.H. Howell. This is the only known photograph of Calt Smith and G.B. Grayson who were frequent musical partners in the years before Grayson's recording career (courtesy Bessie Brown).

confined to a wheelchair. Belle, Calt Smith's daughter, also learned to play guitar and banjo, mimicking the style of her father. This familial flow of musical knowledge from one generation to the next was also manifested by G.B. Grayson's children. Edgar and Clarence, the two oldest boys, both learned to play guitar and enjoyed playing with their famous father when he was home. They had hoped to go on the road with him, but because of his untimely death, they were never able to do so. Despite his absence, the musical legacy Grayson left for his children never faded: they continued to play throughout their lives.

Perhaps in no way was Grayson more influential than with the local musicians in the areas around Johnson County. Although none of these musicians would go on to professional careers, their children and grandchildren still bear the imprint of G.B. Grayson decades after his death. Because of his dependence on music for survival, Grayson seems to have traveled constantly, a feat that is surprising when considering his near-blindness and the difficulties of transportation, difficulties like poorly-maintained roads and limited motorized vehicles. Despite these difficulties, it seems that almost every local musician who lived contemporaneously with Grayson can remember some connection with the famous fiddler.

Grayson's travels regularly took him all over the mountains of North Carolina, Virginia, and Tennessee. As opposed to other musicians who, like Henry Whitter, were traveling the professional circuit, Grayson couldn't get bookings at public venues. Instead, he would travel from one house to another, staying for one or two nights. Usually families would feed him and give him what money they could afford in exchange for the musical entertainment he provided.[16]

One of his most frequent stops was a service station in Konnarock, Virginia, owned by his distant relative, Oscar Roark, locally known as "Ock." Here he and Ock frequently played with James Robert Moore, the father of well-known musician Spencer Moore. All three men played both banjo and fiddle and would alternate instruments as they played. Local fiddlers often gathered at the store to learn songs from one another. Grayson was especially adept at drawing large crowds to listen to the performances. After one show, Corbitt Stamper, who had helped teach local fiddler Albert Hash to play, remembered seeing Grayson accurately picking coins up off the floor that had been tossed to him by the gathered crowd, leading him to conclude that Grayson's blindness must not have been total.[17]

Near West Jefferson, Grayson would sometimes stay with his childhood friend, Wylie Kemp. Although travel by car would have made this trek difficult, Grayson could easily ride the train from Damascus to West Jefferson. This helps explain why he so frequently showed up in the area around West Jefferson, where he encountered both Ola Belle Reed and Glen Neaves. Wylie Kemp didn't play, but his young son Cliff was an aspiring musician. During his stays with the Kemps, Grayson taught the young Cliff, who was learning guitar, how to play "Don't Let Your Deal Go Down" (this song must have been a favorite of Grayson's; others remember hearing Grayson play it on the street during a Mountain City fiddlers' convention).[18]

Cliff Kemp would continue playing music for the rest of his life; his son J.C. would also become a musician, one of the earliest bluegrass banjo players in Ashe County. J.C. would play regularly on a local radio station, WKSK, with other local musicians like Wayne Henderson and Albert Hash—who had also been inspired to play by G.B. Grayson. Although J.C. was locally renowned for a banjo style that mimicked the playing of Don Reno, his musical lineage can be clearly traced to G.B. Grayson.[19]

Cliff Kemp wasn't the only local musician who took direct instruction from Grayson. Ray Dowell, a local fiddler who would win first prize at the Watauga County fiddlers' convention in 1935,[20] was initially taught to play the fiddle by Grayson. Dowell had begun playing banjo but was inspired to switch instruments after seeing Grayson and Calt Smith play. He remembered Grayson giving him specific instruction on how to play tunes like "Barnyard Serenade." Before he died, Grayson had told Dowell that he would make a good fiddler someday because he was willing to listen and learn. After Grayson was killed, Dowell followed closely in his mentor's footsteps. He borrowed Grayson's fiddle and played occasionally with both Henry Whitter and Tom Ashley.

Another talented fiddler who got instruction from Grayson was Howard Miller, a resident of western Ashe County who was working toward mastering the fiddle when he met Grayson. Unlike Ray Dowell, Miller was not a beginner; in fact, although he was only a teenager, he was already a recorded artist. Miller had played fiddle with the Carolina Night Hawks on the single side they had released on the Columbia label in 1928. Sometime around 1929, Grayson, who regularly visited relatives living near the Millers, began stopping by to play with the young fiddler. These playing sessions would have a deep impact on Miller for the rest of his life. Years after Grayson's death, Miller was still playing songs like "Train 45" and "I Saw a Man at the Close of the Day" the way G.B. Grayson had taught him.

Grayson seems to have had a direct impact on dozens of musicians as he traveled around the region. Callie Clyde Trivette, the product of another musical family, recalled Grayson coming to her house to play; she lived with her parents near Horse Creek in Ashe County, North Carolina. This area, near where Grayson's mother was born, was a popular destination for Grayson, who would travel from one house to the next, staying with friends and relatives. The young Callie played the guitar. She recalled Grayson playing songs like "Roving Gambler" and "Tom Dooley." At the time, Grayson had not yet met Whitter and was trying to find a playing partner to assist him in breaking into the recording world. According to Callie's

Henry Whitter (in back with guitar) and G.B. Grayson (on right with fiddle) and the Greer Sisters. Little is known of Greer Sisters, not even their names, though they may have been from Watauga County, North Carolina. Tom Ashley would later play with this all-girl group on a radio show broadcast from Emory, Virginia (courtesy Brian and Ann Baker Forehand).

son, Grayson and Trivette had heard about the record companies' openness to unsolicited auditions, and the two had played together regularly for two weeks, hoping they could travel to one of the open call auditions occasionally held by the recording companies. Unfortunately, when Callie's mother discovered her young daughter's plan, she forbade her from leaving home. Her descendants still talk about how close they believe their mother came to being a recorded star.[21]

Grayson was always looking for people to play with. At the Mountain City fiddlers' convention, possibly in 1925, he teamed up with another young girl, Verna Dotson, who lived near his home in Johnson County. Dotson played guitar, and she and Grayson won a blue ribbon in the competition. For the rest of her life Dotson kept the ribbon she won with Grayson in her guitar case and was always eager to show it off, a testament to her brief partnership with a local legend.[22]

These influences would continue to be felt for years. G.B. Grayson died tragically when he was only forty-two years old and buried in an unmarked grave, but the impression he left behind is profound. His influence is still felt on the biggest stages in the country, and perhaps more significantly, his influence continues to resonate with new generations of musicians who can trace their musical heritage directly to the blind fiddler from Laurel Bloomery. G.B. Grayson's successes were never manifested in fame or fortune, but he did more than any other single individual to shape the music in the areas around his home of Johnson County, Tennessee, and he was no doubt one of the most important early musicians to shape the trajectory of traditional music.

I Wish I Was Single Again
Marriage and Divorce in the Grayson and Whitter Families

Country music songs, as well as their folk predecessors like ballads and Victorian-era parlor songs, have long been associated with a strong sense of tradition. Through these sometimes archaic works, listeners are able to catch a glimpse of an imagined past, one characterized by tranquil pastures, peaceful farm life, and, perhaps most pervasively, stable nuclear families. Songs of a mother's love, ramblers longing for home, and family gatherings are nearly ubiquitous in country and folk music. Generally, scholars have seen this emphasis on happy family life as a protest, a response to a rapidly changing society. In these songs, the thinking goes, artists reaffirm the disappearing values they believe once made Southern society great. This has traditionally been a core component of country music's appeal. Charles Wolfe describes country music, saying, "It spoke to the people of the rural South, helping them to come to grips with the traumatic changes of the modern age: to meet the challenges to traditional values posed by industrialization and 'progress.'"[1]

Like almost all other hillbilly artists, Grayson and Whitter were great purveyors of these traditional motifs. "I Saw a Man at the Close of the Day," "He's Coming to Us Dead," "The Red and Green Signal Lights," and "You'll Never Miss Your Mother Until She's Gone" all drip with the sentimental love of hearth and home that characterizes much of the folk canon. After listening to G.B. Grayson and Henry Whitter's recordings of these songs, it would be tempting to believe that they were themselves products of this much-celebrated system of tight-knit families and austere traditional values. However, as is so often the case, the truth is much different than might be expected. Grayson and Whitter were not, in fact, the product of generations of stable nuclear families; they were quite the opposite. They were living embodiments of the complexities of life in the Appalachian Mountains, complexities that are sometimes ignored in favor of a view more in line with the family-centered images and songs perpetuated by country music. By peering into the reality of their lives and the lives of G.B. Grayson's and Henry Whitter's preceding generations, a much different view emerges.

Frequently, early country artists were already the heads of households, earning money through farming or full-time employment and only supplementing their family incomes with the money they earned through recordings and performances. Many of these artists had no desire to become full-time professional musicians and so were content to stay close to home rather than taking up a life of traveling to live appearances. Additionally, the early record industry put a high value on age and experience, favoring older artists, like John Carson, Gid Tanner, and Ernest Stoneman, who were likely to already have established families. This would quickly change, as the Great Depression severely eroded the early record industry, providing openings for young artists willing to accept the sacrifices necessary to eke out a living as a touring musician.[2]

A formal portrait of Henry Whitter and his fourth wife Hattie Baker. Whitter met Hattie while performing at the Healing Springs High School. After marrying Baker, Whitter would spend the rest of his life in Healing Springs (courtesy Brian and Ann Baker Forehand).

G.B. Grayson was a perfect example of an older, family patriarch making a career solely through music. When he first recorded with Whitter in 1927, he was married and had seven children, and, by all accounts, Grayson was a good father and responsible family man. He married his wife, Fannie Mahaffey, on

November 26, 1908, when he was twenty-one years old. Shortly after this marriage, in June of 1909, the first of Grayson's children, Edgar, was born. His final child, a daughter, Dallas, would be born in 1925. These children remembered their father fondly, recalling his proclivity to tell jokes and ghost stories, to throw his voice, and, of course, to entertain everyone with his musicality; in fact, when recalling his father, one of Clarence Grayson's greatest regrets was that he and his brother Edgar, who both became musicians themselves, never got a chance to play publicly with their famous father.[3] Grayson was clearly a source of inspiration for the family, but he wasn't home much. During most of their childhoods, and before he ever recorded a disc or performed on the radio, Grayson was already living like a professional musician, attempting to supplement the Civil War pension inherited from his father by traveling the countryside, playing for money and food.

Despite these long absences, Grayson stayed focused on the well-being of his family. He returned home on most weekends and was able to use his meager income to support them. Even though his partial blindness was a significant handicap, he was able to create and sustain the stable nuclear family he so often depicted in song. This was not the environment he had himself known as a child.

Edgar Grayson (center with guitar), G.B. Grayson's oldest son, playing with unidentified musicians in 1966 (courtesy Charles Meadows).

When G.B. Grayson was born in 1887, his father, Benjamin, had already been married and divorced: Grayson's mother was his second wife. Benjamin had first married Catherine Johnson Daughtery on October 8, 1867, just after his departure from service in the Civil War. She was herself recently divorced and was living with three children from her previous marriage when she was married to Grayson. Benjamin and Catherine appear to have had one child together, Martha Grayson, G.B.'s Grayson's half-sister, born in 1869. However, this marriage was doomed to failure. Sometime around 1870, Benjamin Grayson divorced Catherine, a move that would have been notable at the time because it deprived her and their young daughter any right to collect Benjamin's Civil War pension after his death.

Following this divorce, Benjamin soon found himself in the company of a new woman, who was more than ten years his junior: Martha Jane Roark. Like Benjamin's first wife, Martha Roark was also divorced, having been married first to Henry Lewallen on April 3, 1869. Although unmarried, this new couple, Benjamin Grayson and Martha Roark, may have begun having children as early as 1873, quite a departure from the typical narrative about family values in nineteenth-century America. Amanda Grayson was the first child born, followed by Rebecca, born in 1875, Caroline, born in 1878, and James, born in 1883. By 1880, Benjamin was across the state line, living in Ashe County, North Carolina, in the Horse Creek Township. In 1885, Benjamin Grayson and Martha Roark were officially married, and in 1887 their last child, G.B., affectionately known as Banmon, was born. During the course of this relationship, Benjamin and Martha moved frequently, living in both Tennessee and across the state line in Ashe County, North Carolina. In the 1880 census, the oldest daughter, Amanda, was listed as having been born in Kentucky, implying that a third state was also at least briefly inhabited. These frequent moves are a primary reason it is difficult to ascertain with certainty where exactly G.B. Grayson was born.

Seven years after G.B. Grayson's birth, his father, Benjamin, died. Eight years later, in 1902, his mother, Martha, died, leaving her fifteen-year-old dependent, G.B., to rely on his late father's Civil War pension for support. Because he was the youngest of his siblings, he was legally unable to live independently. He was put in the care of a guardian, Will S. Robinson, who, it is to be assumed, cared for him for at least a year, until he was over the age of sixteen.

The fact that G.B. Grayson was able to establish such a functional and healthy family unit as an adult, despite his own difficulties in childhood, is even more surprising given that this pattern of divorce and abandonment was multi-generational. G.B.'s grandfather, William Grayson, had immigrated to America around 1800. In 1841, William was married to Rebecca Reese and had two young children: James W.M., born in 1833, and Benjamin, born in 1838. According to family history, one day William took his rifle and said he was going hunting. He never returned. His wife, Rebecca, was left to raise the children herself. Following her death in 1858, the brothers relied on each other for support until after the Civil War.

One could argue that the Grayson family curse was carried on through G.B. Grayson, whose untimely death in 1930 once again resulted in a young family being left to struggle without their father, this time without even a pension to support them. The family hadn't been rich to begin with: Clarence, G.B. Grayson's son, recalled that they routinely had to gather wild plants to supplement their diets and that his father had never had enough disposable income to even buy a record player, listening to his own recordings on neighbors' machines.[4] After the death of their primary breadwinner, the Grayson family was in dire financial straits. At the time of his untimely demise, their total property, which included Grayson's fiddle and banjo, was assessed as being worth twenty-five dollars, well insufficient to cover the $191.50[5] owed to L.H. Wright for "sickness and burial." This bill didn't even include the cost of a headstone marker, which Grayson's grave would be without for more than forty years. As a result of this financial catastrophe, the oldest boys, Clarence and Edgar, were forced to leave home and find jobs, first in sawmills and later in coal mines. This displacement resulted in several of Grayson's descendants living in Pennsylvania, far away from their ancestral home in Tennessee.

However, despite the instability that resulted from Grayson's tragic death, the strong nuclear unit he was able to cultivate during his life in Laurel Bloomery was able to persevere over the long run. Grayson's children and grandchildren, though separated across several states, maintained a strong connection and routinely saw one another. Clarence and Edgar, who lived in Pennsylvania, regularly packed their cars and made the trip to Laurel Bloomery to gather with family. In fact, it was during one of these trips that a trunk containing all of G.B. Grayson's business papers and his personal record collection fell off the roof of Clarence's car, where it had been tied, lost forever to the American interstate highway system.[6] These routine trips back to their childhood home allowed the Grayson children to share a collective memory of their father, whom they revered not only as a musician but also as a paternal figure. This ultimately stable and grounded family seems especially notable when viewed alongside the tumultuous home life of Grayson's partner, Henry Whitter.

Whitter's family background, like Grayson's, further emphasizes the fact that divorce in the rural Appalachian Mountains at this time was not the rare occurrence some would imagine. Whitter's father James Ellis Whitter had first married Mary Reeves in Alleghany County, North Carolina, in 1888. Like both of Grayson's parents, Whitter's mother, Mary Reeves, was herself previously married. She had been born Mary Ring but had married J.D. Reeves in 1880 at the age of fourteen. This marriage had produced a child. As a result, Henry Whitter grew up with a half sibling: Martha Reeves.

The Whitter family moved from the Old Town district of Grayson County to Fries to seek work in the newly-constructed Washington Mill sometime in the early 1900s. By 1910, they were living in a mill house at 109 Main Street, but this move was not easy on their relationship; the census record from that year shows cracks already appearing in the marriage. At this time, the Whitters were still living together in the same household with five children, Rosa, the eldest, twenty-one at the time, Henry, eighteen, Callie, sixteen, James Emmet, twelve, and Blanche, four (a baby, Sidney, had died when only a few months old in 1902). Oddly, Mary Reeves gave her maiden name to the census taker, rather than her married name. Further illustrating the strains in the household, Whitter's youngest sister, Blanche, was also recorded with the last name Reeves, despite the fact that the older children were listed as Whitters. James Ellis and Mary both reported themselves as divorced, and, under profession, Mary was listed as "servant"—one can only imagine the stress of the poor census taker attempting to objectively record this drama.

Soon after, the family officially broke apart. James Ellis and Mary went their separate ways, although both continued to live and work in Fries, and their son, Henry, soon found himself smitten with a local girl, Orene Jones.

At first glance, the marriage of Orene and Henry Whitter seems fairly commonplace. The two met, as was typical in a mill town like Fries, at work.[7] Orene had worked in the Washington Mill since 1906. In 1913, the couple ventured across state lines into neighboring Alleghany County, North Carolina, to get married. This elopement, aside from its romantic appeal, was interesting as a mill town phenomenon. The advancement of transportation, combined with a desire to momentarily escape the tight-knit mill town community, led many young couples in these towns to run away to neighboring areas to get married.[8]

On June 24, 1916, Orene and Whitter's only child, Paul, was born. By the time Paul was five, sometime around 1921, Henry and Orene's marriage

Henry Whitter and his first wife, Orene Jones. After marrying Jones, Whitter lived with her family in Stevens Creek, just outside of Fries, Virginia (courtesy Brian and Ann Baker Forehand).

was untenable, and the pair divorced. The specific causes are unclear. Callie Payne, Whitter's sister, placed the blame for the separation on Orene's neglect; however, in later interviews, Orene never seemed to bear any resentment to Whitter, although she did describe him as "emotional."[9] She and Whitter must have gotten along well enough, though: the two stayed in contact for several years after they were separated.

Whatever the ultimate reason for the divorce, the unusual reality of the couple's married life has never fully been understood. When Archie Green, the well-known folklorist, interviewed Orene Jones and Paul Whitter in 1961, Green wrote in his notes that he chose not to press Orene about her marital problems, noting that he could detect discomfort around the topic. The reason for the discomfort around the topic is understandable:

during that interview in Fries, Orene was accompanied by her identical twin sister, Irene: Irene had also had a child with Whitter.

According to family sources, while Whitter was married to Orene Jones, he was also carrying on a relationship with her identical twin sister, Irene Jones. Apparently, Whitter found both girls equally attractive and desirable and had difficulty choosing between them. Despite the fact that Whitter was married to Orene, Irene became pregnant, and on April 15, 1915, one year before Paul's birth, Arnold Herbert Jones was born.[10] Although this dramatic turn of events would have derailed most marriages, Whitter's marriage to Orene was able to persist for six more years. Interestingly, Whitter in no way shunned or avoided his second family; in fact, he lived with them. Moving out of downtown Fries, Whitter settled in the nearby community of Stevens Creek. There he lived in the Jones household with his father-in-law, his wife, her twin sister, their brother, and Whitter's two boys, Paul and Arnold. By this time, Orene had left her job at the mill, staying at home to take care of the household. Her twin sister Irene, however, continued to work and provide a supplementary income for the large family.

Arnold Herbert Jones, the son of Henry Whitter and Irene Jones. Jones was born April 29, 1915, and grew up in Stevens Creek with his half-brother, Paul Whitter (courtesy Benson Jones).

During the boys' adolescence, Whitter was attempting to launch his music career, and, like Grayson, was away from home much of the time. However, he still performed the paternal role for the boys. He provided for them, disciplined them, and lived with them in Stevens Creek until he finally left town permanently sometime before 1926. After that, the boys had less contact with their father. Paul recalled that one of the last times he saw Whitter was in 1934. After that, their next meeting wasn't until 1939, when he traveled to Crumpler to visit his father. When Whitter died in 1941, both sons, Paul Whitter and Arnold Jones, went to Crumpler for the funeral.

About the same time his marriage to Orene was falling apart, Whitter's musical career was taking off. He recorded almost thirty songs in 1924 and would record more than twenty in 1926. The fact that he started recording before anyone else and the fact that he could accompany himself on harmonica have been held up as explanations for his early successes. However, one often overlooked element of the Whitter mystique was his sexual appeal. Whitter's third wife recalled that he was a ladies' man and that he "fooled a lot of women."[11] In an interview, Ernest "Pop" Stoneman's wife recalled that he was an attractive figure in his early days to which Stoneman replied, "He was a fine looking man as far as that's concerned."[12]

Whitter seems to have had a strong attraction to women as well. In 1925, a young singer, fifteen-year-old Roba Stanley, from Georgia, was rising in popularity, having recorded several songs for OKeh records. After seeing a photo of her, Whitter wrote a letter to her father asking if he could perform with their family band. In June 1925, Whitter ended up playing guitar backup on recordings with the young woman. After the recording session, Whitter joined the Lawrenceville Trio, composed of young Roba, her father R.M., and William Patterson, on the radio, broadcasting a show on WSB. Roba recalls that "he was a handsome young man ... but he also explained right away that he was married at the time."[13] Given the number of artists performing for OKeh records during this period, Whitter's decision to seek out this particular group seems to have been motivated by more than just music.

When Whitter left Fries, and his unusually large family, for the last time, sometime around 1926, he was apparently not ready to give up domestic life. He soon found himself married again, this time to a girl from Wilkes County, North Carolina. This marriage was so short lived that the name of Whitter's second wife has slowly been eroded from memory. Whitter's sister thought her name was Vindie but couldn't recall her maiden name. She apparently played the guitar, something that may have been attractive to Whitter. Perhaps this desire to seek out musical women was inborn, since Whitter's mother and aunt had both been musicians.[14] Tragically, Vindie became pregnant with twins and all three died in childbirth just over a year after her marriage to Whitter.

Whitter was able to move on from this tragic relationship. On May 9, 1927, he was married again, this time to Gretchen Nellie Cook. Whitter was thirty; Gretchen was eighteen. Around this time, Whitter had moved to Mooresville to live with his sister, Callie, who was working in a local

"Single Life" by Roba Stanley featuring Henry Whitter's harmonica and guitar accompaniment. At the time this record was recorded, Whitter's solo career was thriving. Despite the fact he made few appearances on the recordings of other artists, he chose to travel to Georgia to accompany the young Roba Stanley (courtesy Marshall Wyatt).

cotton mill. Gretchen Cook recalled that when she first met Whitter, he was a successful musician. He was being represented by a talent agent, George Bridges of West Virginia, and was making a good living performing on the road. Gretchen apparently enjoyed Henry's success and aspired to a more elegant life than the cotton mill town could provide. She remembered Whitter taking her to Fries where she was taken aback by what she perceived to be the town's primitive nature.[15]

Unfortunately, Whitter's ability to provide the life Gretchen wanted had begun to fade along with his record sales. Luckily for both Whitter and Gretchen, his newly-established partnership with G.B. Grayson gave a final boost to his career, and Gretchen recalled Grayson staying with them in Mooresville while the duo was recording in Atlanta. Incidentally, this was the same session in which the duo recorded their version of "Train

Henry Whitter and his second wife, believed to have been named Vindie. This second marriage was a brief one; Vindie died in childbirth only a year after they were married (courtesy Southern Folklife Collection, Louis Round Wilson Special Collections Library, University of North Carolina at Chapel Hill).

45" for Victor, in which Whitter shouts out the name of his hometown: Mooresville. By the start of the Depression, Whitter's career was almost over. Grayson was dead, the entire recording industry was dying, and the older artists, like Whitter, were being supplanted by younger musicians performing on radio. Gretchen found her marriage to the now-struggling Whitter increasingly difficult and the couple separated.

Of course, Whitter's third marriage did not dissolve solely because of financial hardship. He was also having an affair. The divorce decree specifically stated that the couple "had lived together as man and wife until the third day of March, 1932, at which time the defendant [Whitter] without cause or excuse abandoned the plaintiff [Cook] ... and while [the marriage] was subsisting between plaintiff and defendant, the defendant has committed adultery with one Bertha Roberts at various times and places."[16] Based on the evidence of this document, one can confirm with reasonable assurance that Whitter had been engaged in at least five serious relationships over the course of three marriages.

Whitter was still able to appeal to younger women, and he was soon engaged again, and once again, his wife-to-be was eighteen years old. Whitter at the time of this fourth marriage would have been forty-one. His new wife was named Hattie Baker. According to Gretchen Cook, Whitter had also been seeing Baker while he was still married to Cook,[17] meaning he either engaged in two subsequent affairs while living with his third wife in Mooresville or was attempting to juggle three women simultaneously. Hattie Baker had first met Whitter when he played at her former school in Healing Springs, just a few hundred yards from where Whitter would eventually settle for the final time.[18] Hattie was young but already had a child, Earl Baker, who was about four years old when the couple first met. Hattie had been working at the nearby Healing Springs Hotel, a resort marketed for its healing water. After separating from Gretchen, Whitter married Hattie.

At first, no one seemed to know for sure whether Whitter and Hattie Baker were in fact legal partners. In the early 1950s, Whitter's royalties became a topic of debate among his heirs. Paul Whitter, Henry's biological son, argued that Hattie Baker (or Hattie Hader, as she was by that time remarried) was not entitled to payouts because she had never been legally married to Henry Whitter. Elliot Shapiro, of the Shapiro Bernstein music company, hired a private investigator to confirm this claim. He found instead that the couple was wed, but as with Henry's first marriage, they had traveled across state lines to make the union official. On September 12, 1933, they had been married before George Ryan, Justice of the Peace in Carter County, Tennessee.[19]

Hattie Baker, Henry Whitter's fourth wife, pictured holding Whitter's guitar (courtesy Brian and Ann Baker Forehand).

At this point, it may

seem as if divorce was ubiquitous in the southern Appalachian region. Both of G.B. Grayson's parents had been married and divorced; Grayson's grandfather had abandoned his family; Henry Whitter's parents were divorced; and Whitter himself was married four times. It may prove useful to examine census data from the era to determine the extent to which this pattern of marriage and divorce existed in the general population. In 1930, in Whitter's home county of Grayson, Virginia, a total of twenty divorced males over the age of fifteen lived in the entire county while 3,927 were married. This divorce rate was below the state average for Virginia, which had 5,801 total divorced males over the age of fifteen residing in 118 counties and cities (approximately forty-nine divorced males each). Interestingly, the number was notably higher in Tennessee. In the same census, 1930, 8,269 divorced males over fifteen were residing in ninety-five counties (about eighty-seven each). In Grayson's home county of Johnson, twenty-two divorced males were recorded. Obviously, these numbers do not take into account the exact number of divorces; for example, Whitter, who was involved in two official divorces, would only count as one divorced male. However, these numbers still seem to suggest that the prevalence of divorce and multiple marriages seen in Grayson's and Whitter's lives was an aberration; nevertheless, divorce and remarriage, even in rural mountain areas, were more frequent than an early country music fan would likely assume.

Whitter's pattern of divorce and remarriage ended with Hattie Baker, who would be his final wife, and, as was the case with his first marriage, Whitter found himself once more playing the role of a father. Earl Baker's biological father was married with a family of his own and had never claimed paternity (another instance of the Appalachian region failing to live up to its perceived image as a world of sanctified family units). As a result, Henry Whitter became the central father figure in young Earl's life. Baker learned to play the guitar and harmonica with Henry's assistance and got a chance to experience the life of a professional hillbilly musician, as Henry traveled around to local venues throughout the 1930s, playing at schools and tourist attractions like the Healing Springs and Shatley Springs resorts. These shows were a true family affair: Hattie also came along to collect money at the door (and receive a third of the ensuing profits, something that annoyed Whitter's young playing partner, Albert Hash[20]). Earl sold songbooks during intermissions. Earl always recalled with fondness the memory of a performance in West Jefferson during which Henry's performance of "Fox Chase," which involved a lot of howling and dog mimicry, called some curious hounds through the open door of the schoolhouse.[21] After Henry's death in 1941, Earl Baker continued to play guitar, sing, and play harmonica. For the rest of his life, he worked diligently to celebrate the sometimes neglected memory of his beloved stepfather. He could recall almost every song performed by Whitter. Baker eventually inherited the only guitar still owned by Whitter when he died, a 1929 Martin model 000–18, which Baker continued to play for years afterward.

Although these performances in local schools, theaters, and individual homes helped support the family, by the time of his fourth marriage, Whitter's once-lucrative performing career was over. Even though Whitter's fame was diminishing, his family was obviously aware of Whitter's former stature in the music world. During this time, someone, either Hattie or Henry himself, began creating a series of elaborate collages celebrating the scope of Whitter's achievements. Looking at these lovingly-constructed works of art creates the impression that the maker saw Whitter as the center of the musical universe: newspaper clippings, photographs, and publicity from the record companies all combined in a shrine of adoration. His neighbors, however, who were aware of his musicianship, as he often sang and played the guitar on his porch, did not seem to be aware of the vital role he had played in popularizing the hillbilly genre. They viewed Henry Whitter as little more than a neighborhood musician.

Henry Whitter (right) and his stepson Earl Baker. Baker learned to play harmonica with Whitter and always remembered him fondly. Whitter is dressed in bib overalls, which he often wore when not performing (courtesy Brian and Ann Baker Forehand).

Things did not improve with age for Whitter. Sometime after 1935, his small house in Crumpler burned down. Whitter, his wife, and stepson were forced to move into the garage. Whitter's health was also rapidly deteriorating. His diabetes, which was untreated, was resulting in

A handmade collage celebrating Henry Whitter's career. It isn't clear whether this collage was made by Whitter himself or his fourth wife Hattie Baker (courtesy Brian and Ann Baker Forehand).

bouts of severe hypoglycemia, which were in turn causing fits of delirium. Albert Hash refused to continue playing fiddle with Henry because of his tendency to drive his car off the road. Kada McNeil, a teenage neighbor of Whitter's, recalled Whitter yelling at her to feed non-existent hogs as she was walking by his house on her way to school.[22]

This instability made life with Whitter increasingly difficult. Hattie Baker took a job with the WPA to help support Whitter, who was no longer able to perform enough to support the family. By 1941, Whitter's condition was so poor that he was no longer able to stay at home. Hattie had Whitter checked into the Broughton Hospital in Morganton, North Carolina, a hospital that specialized in the treatment of mental illnesses. A little over a month later, on November 17, Whitter died from complications arising from his untreated diabetes.

As with Grayson's family, Whitter's family in Healing Springs were ill-equipped to finance a funeral. Whitter not only had no stone but no burial plot. Hattie was determined to bury Whitter in the cemetery with the rest of her family at the Healing Springs Baptist Church. Unfortunately,

Henry Whitter and Hattie Baker (courtesy Brian and Ann Baker Forehand).

the cemetery had no available space and was fenced in, surrounded by pastureland. Undeterred, she had Henry buried anyway, outside the fence. The owners of the pasture were out of town at the time and when they returned had little recourse available. Even in death, Henry Whitter had found a way to break through barriers.[23]

Hattie would soon go on to remarry, this time to a man from Baltimore, Charlie Hader. Today, she, Charlie, and Henry are all buried together in the expanded Healing Springs Church cemetery. Ironically, the financial support Whitter was unable to provide to Hattie during his lifetime began to materialize more than a decade after his death. Because of Shapiro's confirmation of Hattie and Henry's legal marriage, Hattie, and later Earl, were entitled to collect royalties from the songs bearing Whitter's name as composer, including such standards as "Lonesome Road Blues." Earl recalled receiving a check for $1,600, a cumulative amount for six months of royalty earnings.

Equally important, during the folk revival of the 1960s, music historians like Archie Green and Eugene Earle became interested in Henry Whitter, the man who helped launch the country genre, and began showing up in Crumpler and Fries to interview family members about their famous relative. Eugene Earle even agreed to purchase a fiddle supposedly owned by G.B. Grayson from Hattie Baker. Although the instrument was almost certainly never owned by Grayson, who rarely if ever owned more than one fiddle, the money was enough to finally buy Whitter the grave marker he had done without for more than twenty years.[24]

Henry Whitter's love affair with love affairs has gone largely unnoticed by folk music historians. While the off-stage exploits of rock and pop musicians are infinitely explored and exaggerated, the personal lives of early country music artists have been largely ignored, no doubt due in part to the assumption that the culture that produced them was too pure, too conservative, and too rustic to provide any interesting scandals. However, a telling clue to Whitter's difficulties with women and relationships was always in plain sight in the form of his song repertoire. While he was touring the mountain towns around his home in Ashe County with his stepson, Whitter sold songbooks between shows. These books were supposed to be filled with the songs most associated with Henry Whitter. Of course standards like "Wreck on the Southern Old 97" and "Lonesome Road Blues" were given prominent placement, as were Grayson and Whitter classics like "He's Coming to Us Dead" and "Banks of the Old Tennessee," but between those selections was more unusual fare: "The Long Tongued Woman," which decries female talkativeness; "Oh How I Hate It," a song about the miseries of married life; "Seven Years with the Wrong Woman," a song with lyrics like "It's the same in the mountain or the dale / She'll stay awake all night / To start a fight / And have you thrown in jail"; and, of course, "I'll Be Glad When You Are Dead," a song whose title conveys all one needs to know. As is so often the case, art for Henry Whitter seems to have imitated life.

Grayson, Whitter and the Hill Billies
Manufacturers of Music

When Henry Whitter first walked into the OKeh offices in New York sometime in 1923, commercial country music did not exist in any form. When he and G.B. Grayson began recording together in 1927, the legendary "Bristol sessions" had just taken place, introducing the world to both the Carter Family and Jimmie Rodgers, who would carry country music across the United States and turn a regional phenomenon into a national one. When Grayson died in 1930, essentially ending Whitter's recording career, the entire country record industry was about to die as well, killed by the weight of the Great Depression. Record sales, which had topped 100 million in 1927, would slow to a mere six million by 1932.[1] When Whitter himself passed away in 1941, the start of World War II was about to reinvigorate the U.S. economy, including the music industry. Sailors and soldiers with money to spend would soon fuel yet another explosion of popularity in country music.

Through these tumultuous formative years, country music underwent rapid growing pains. Bill Malone notes that "the early hillbilly musicians, for the most part, were folk performers who stood in transition between the traditional milieu that had nourished them and the larger popular arena which beckoned. They performed in the only way they knew, according to the dictates of the culture that had shaped their values and musical tastes."[2] What had begun as traditional folk material recorded by unpolished, rustic amateurs would soon be a sleek and industrial product, churned out commercially and with great attention to audience preferences. Grayson and Whitter, like their peers, did not know that they were playing the role of experimental test subjects. Record companies, radio stations, theater owners, music publishers, and others were silently wrestling behind the scenes to transform American folk music into a marketable commodity.

Luckily for record producers, a few musicians, like Henry Whitter, were already eager to find a way to turn their traditional music into a profitable enterprise. It has already been established that Henry Whitter was as much an entrepreneur as a musician, and, as a result, he was himself constantly in a state of transformation, trying to find ways to appeal to broader audiences. This drive was what led him to New York, seeking an unsolicited recording session. In July 1924, just a few months after his first formal recording session for OKeh, Whitter's desire to expand his sound and his appeal again led him to travel to New York, this time with a newly minted band: the Virginia Breakdowners. This band's name was eerily similar to Fiddlin' John Carson's band the Virginia Reelers, who had just recorded their first record in March 1924. Like Whitter, Carson was an early star for the OKeh label, having recorded his first record a year earlier,

Whitter's Virginia Breakdowners. This group, featuring (from left to right) James Sutphin, Henry Whitter, and John Rector, recorded several sides in 1924. Whitter formed the band to expand his sound, but the group quickly dissolved. John Rector would use his experience recording with Whitter to help secure recording sessions for the Hill Billies (courtesy Southern Folklife Collection, Louis Round Wilson Special Collections Library, University of North Carolina at Chapel Hill).

and, like Whitter, by early 1924 Carson seems to have been looking for a band to fill out the sound of his records. Carson's decision to record with a band was possibly motivated by OKeh records, who wanted to experiment with a new sound, but they still continued to record Carson solo, waiting to see which approach would sell more records.[3]

Whether the decision to show up in New York in the summer of 1924 with a band of his own was Whitter's idea or the idea of the OKeh recording company is unclear. However, the results of the session were fortuitous both for Whitter and his new banjo player John Rector. Rector had owned the store in which Whitter had first gotten the idea to make a record, but Rector had refused to journey with Whitter to New York initially. Rector did not refuse Whitter's second request to join him, and, along with James Sutphin, another Fries store owner, a new band was quickly formed. The group traveled to New York and recorded six traditional fiddle tunes, some featuring Whitter's pinched vocal refrains. Unfortunately for Whitter, but luckily for the country music industry, John Rector must have been ultimately dissatisfied with the records he created with Whitter. Although the records themselves did not live up to his expectations, the trip had provided Rector with contacts at OKeh records. Armed with this newly-discovered knowledge of the New York recording world, Rector committed to set out on his own, hoping to form a new band, one that would rival, if not surpass, Whitter in popularity.

In the summer of 1925, it seems every hillbilly artist was in Mountain City, Tennessee, for the town's first-ever fiddlers' convention. Fortunately, someone had the foresight to snap a photograph of the contestants, perhaps the most famous photo of hillbilly performers ever taken. In the upper left hand corner, G.B. Grayson stands next to his frequent playing partner, Tom Ashley. In the center of the back row one can make out Smokey Davis, who played locally with Grayson; Fiddlin' Powers and family stand in the center, and sitting in the front row is famous fiddler Charlie Bowman. Standing at the right end of center row is Fiddlin' John Carson himself, no doubt the biggest celebrity in the crowd at the time the photo was taken, and standing on the far right of the front row is a group of four men: brothers Joe and John Hopkins, Uncle Am Stuart, and John Rector, Henry Whitter's former partner; standing just behind them are Al Hopkins and Tony Alderman. Together, this group of men would form one of the most commercially savvy country bands of the 1920s: the Hill Billies.

After parting ways with John Rector, Henry Whitter had no formal contact with Rector's new group, the Hill Billies. He never recorded with them, and there is no evidence he ever appeared with them. However, there is no doubt he would have known of them and their successes. Both groups had roots in Grayson County, Virginia, and both recorded on the OKeh label. Charlie Bowman, who would eventually become one of the fiddlers for the Hill Billies, told Mike Seeger in an interview in 1961 that, though he had never met Henry Whitter, he knew him to be a great friend to the Hill Billies. Although the Hill Billies' existence is indeed indebted to Henry Whitter, the two acts were, from the outset, quite different. Echoing a sentiment expressed by other early country artists who found impetus to record after hearing Whitter's records, Tony Alderman recalled that one of the group's early ambitions was to best Whitter. Alderman said the group believed "we could outclass him a country mile."[4] However, the contrast between the two groups is more profound than just competing musicians from a similar area. To view the Hill Billies' rise to stardom alongside the rise of Henry Whitter and G.B. Grayson is to see two separate movements in country music occurring simultaneously: the conscientious attempt to appeal to the wider, more urban and less distinctly Southern audience that brought the Hill Billies success versus Whitter's attempt to carve out a working class, rural following in and around the areas that originally gave birth to the music.

One characteristic that Whitter and the Hill Billies had in common that separated them from many of their musical peers in the early 1920s was a legitimate desire to become professional musicians. Although there were many musicians recording by the time the Hill Billies made their first record for OKeh in January 1925, these individuals and groups were often amateurs, performers who made money on weekends or in their free time playing for social gatherings, but who relied on more steady full-time employment in order to survive. Whitter, looking for escape from the cotton mill life, had thrown himself fully into a professional musician's life, one that required regular radio and record performances along with constant personal appearances.

While Whitter was using music as an escape from a working class life, the Hill Billies ended up a successful group of professional musicians, despite (or because of) the fact that several core members of the group, the Hopkins brothers, Al and Joe, and, later, John, were products of a relatively upper class environment. Whereas Whitter needed a musical career to escape the drudgery of manual labor in the Washington Mill, setting his mind toward the seemingly unattainable goal of professional musicianship and working diligently to make the dream a reality, the Hopkins

brothers stumbled into musical fame by being in the right place at the right time.

The Hopkins brothers were born and raised in Gap Creek, North Carolina, a small community on the line separating Watauga County from Ashe County, the latter the supposed county of G.B. Grayson's birth and Henry Whitter's death. Interestingly, just as G.B. Grayson's uncle, James W.M. Grayson, had named a western Ashe County postal district after himself when the post office was located on his property, the Hopkins family took over management of the Gap Creek post office, renaming it Hopkins. As a result, for several years around the turn of the century, Ashe County had two postal districts named after the families of famous hillbilly musicians: Grayson and Hopkins.

John Benjamin Hopkins, the family patriarch, along with his wife, Celia Isabelle Green, were natives of Gap Creek; however, they in no way lived up to the stereotype of rough, uneducated mountain dwellers. John built and repaired organs in his spare time and raised his children in a large, well-kept home, very different than some of the more rustic homes of the region. One need only compare a photograph of the Hopkins family home in Gap Creek to one of G.B. Grayson's small house in Laurel Bloomery to see the disparities of lifestyle that existed in the Appalachian region.

Because of John's love of organs, the Hopkins' household was a musical one. Lucy Hopkins, the sister of Al and Joe, became interested in music after watching an automated player piano. She took lessons on piano and accordion and eventually became a music teacher herself.[5] Bill Hopkins, another sibling, moved away from the world of pianos and sheet music, learning to play fiddle instead. He later learned to transpose fiddle melodies onto the piano keyboard, something that Al Hopkins also did to great effect when playing with the Hill Billies.[6]

Opposite: **A photograph of the performers taken during the 1925 Mountain City fiddlers' convention. G.B. Grayson and Tom Ashley are on the left, one row from the top. Grayson is at the end of the row, wearing a black hat and holding the fiddle against his chest. Tom Ashley is to the right, holding a banjo and wearing a buttoned-up sweater. The Hill Billies are standing at the ends of the middle two rows on the right. John Rector is on the end of the second row, standing behind a banjo case. Uncle Am Stuart is to the left, holding a fiddle case. Joe Hopkins is to the left of Stuart, standing behind a guitar. His brother, John Hopkins, is next to him, holding a Ukulele. Directly behind John Hopkins, wearing no hat and holding no instrument, is Al Hopkins. To the right of him is Tony Alderman. At the end of the row, standing to the right of Alderman, holding a fiddle case and wearing a black hat, is another early recording star: Fiddlin' John Carson (courtesy of Marshall Wyatt).**

The Hopkins family home in Gap Creek, North Carolina (courtesy Southern Folklife Collection, Louis Round Wilson Special Collections Library, University of North Carolina at Chapel Hill).

Bill Hopkins' desire to break away from his family's formal music environment in favor of more exotic folk traditions was also what drove the Hill Billies' fiddler, Tony Alderman, to play traditional music. He had been trained as a cornet player in his father's all-brass band in Galax but slipped away to play fiddle. According to Alderman, "My father wanted to make a John Philip Sousey out of me and I didn't want to."[7] Ironically, musicians like Alderman and the Hopkins siblings were rejecting their native musical environments, which in their cases were characterized by keyboards, brass instruments, and sheet music, in favor of local folk traditions; thus, even in an era prior to the recording of American folk music, "authenticity" for a performer was a difficult term to define.

G.B. Grayson's home in Laurel Bloomery years after his death, probably in the early 1960s (courtesy Southern Folklife Collection, Louis Round Wilson Special Collections Library, University of North Carolina at Chapel Hill).

Al Hopkins, like his sister Lucy, embraced his family's proclivity to play instruments with keys, but, like his brother, adapted these instruments to the folk traditions he encountered. He became an old-time pianist, if such a thing can be said to exist, learning to play the intricate fiddle melodies that he heard from his brother on the keyboard.[8]

Despite Al and Bill's interest in traditional Appalachian music, the Hopkins family, urbane, educated, and relatively wealthy, were bound for a life outside the North Carolina mountains, and soon their opportunity came. In 1903, around the same time Henry Whitter's family was trudging into Fries, Virginia, in search of a better life at the Washington Mill, the Hopkins family was moving to Washington, D.C. John Benjamin Hopkins had been offered a lucrative job at the census bureau and the family soon settled at their new home at 63 Kennedy Street NW. Although they continued to maintain ties to their southern Appalachian Mountains, the Hopkins family would never again have a permanent home in the region. In the area around Washington, D.C., the Hopkins children would be raised in a world of opportunities much different than the rural one they had known in Gap Creek.[9]

These opportunities weren't squandered. Jacob Hopkins, one of the

Hopkins' seven children, became a doctor, and, desiring to return closer to his childhood home, moved to Galax, Virginia, to establish a medical clinic and hospital, one that used music to try and raise the spirits of his ailing patients.[10] It was here that Al Hopkins found himself in the summer of 1924. Having worked briefly as a butcher during World War I, Al was looking for a new career and had taken a job helping his brother with secretarial work at the Galax hospital.[11] Joe Hopkins, another musical sibling, was also back in the mountains, working as a railway express agent near Whitetop, Virginia.

Joe Hopkins carried his guitar with him wherever he went, playing during his free time.[12] One day, he stopped by the barber shop where fiddler Elvis "Tony" Alderman was working. Seeing the guitar case that Hopkins was carrying, Alderman asked if he would like to play. What started as a brief meeting soon turned into an entire week of regular playing. At the end of the week, John Rector, from Fries, who had just returned from a disappointing trip to New York with Henry Whitter, walked into the barber shop and was immediately enthralled. After hearing Alderman and Hopkins playing, he declared that it sounded a lot better than "my boys," referring to Whitter's Virginia Breakdowners.[13] He wrote a letter to his new contacts at the OKeh recording company asking for a recording session. Soon afterward, the entire band, which at that time was composed of Al and Joe Hopkins, Tony Alderman, and John Rector, was loaded into Rector's 1923 Ford headed to Manhattan.[14]

The recording studio that these men walked into in New York was the same one used a year earlier by Henry Whitter to record his first records. It was a much more advanced setup than the portable contraption that would have been used to record Fiddlin' John Carson's first records in Atlanta over the summer of 1923. However, by any modern measure, it was a joke. Techniques like multi-track recording, overdubbing, and other standards of modern studio recording were not even conceivable. Instead, performers like Whitter and the Hill Billies found themselves facing down a large horn. This was the "microphone" used to capture the sounds of the band. Tony Alderman recalled that he was not even able to play his own fiddle in these early recording sessions because it could not be sufficiently picked up on the final record. He had to play a studio fiddle equipped with its own sound horn to amplify the instrument's volume. This horn was stuck down inside the larger recording horn. Meanwhile, louder rhythm instruments were banished to the corners of the studio in order to muffle their sound. With no monitors or headphones to allow them to listen to the recording as it was being made, the band, spread out all over the room,

Taken during the 1925 Mountain City fiddlers' convention, this photograph captures the Hill Billies in their earliest years. The core members of the group are pictured standing next to Uncle Am Stuart and Fiddlin' John Carson on the streets of Mountain City. The flyer in the window behind them advertises the Ku Klux Klan, who were sponsors of the convention. From left to right: John Hopkins, Joe Hopkins, Tony Alderman, John Rector, Uncle Am Stuart, and Fiddlin' John Carson (courtesy Southern Folklife Collection, Louis Round Wilson Special Collections Library, University of North Carolina at Chapel Hill).

was also unable to hear themselves as they played. Alderman recalled that the first time he actually heard the songs from their first sessions was when he listened to the record that was offered for retail sale.

It is interesting to consider how many great bands were never able to overcome this awful studio setup. Perhaps groups whose records have been forgotten, or were never released, were not lacking in talent, but were rather victims of the recording process of the time. Tony Alderman argued that the difficulty of recording was a roadblock that stifled many bands. Timing was almost impossible to maintain; players couldn't even be sure if they were in the right key, perhaps explaining the awful mismatch of vocals and accompaniment found in Kelly Harrell's "Wild Bill Jones," in which Henry Whitter plays backup with the guitar and harmonica in a discordant register. Fiddlers hoping to be heard on record had to butcher their poor instruments for the cause as well. Alderman recalled that to get volume out of fiddles, both in the studio and on stage, players used metal bridges, heavy wire strings, and even scraped the varnish off the instruments.[15] Maybe when considering this recording reality, a bit more sympathy can be felt for Henry Whitter, whose early records are often held up as a unflattering reminder of what passed for recordable music in 1923.

Even though OKeh records were not very advanced technologically, they were making great progress in their commercial sensibilities. The process of squeezing marketability out of folk music had begun as soon as Fiddlin' John Carson and Whitter had begun making commercially viable records. Bob Coltman notes that

> the recording industry after 1923 had created country music as if it were out of thin air. Beginning with a scattering of musicians who played and sang in an archaic stiff, remote manner mixed from traditional and stage styles, the early A&R [artist and repertoire] men encouraged country artists to listen to each other, to learn new licks, to dig up, or make up, new tunes or songs. Thus they fostered an appetite for novelty in both artists and audience: an indisputable condition for successful marketing.[16]

By 1925, record companies had begun to distinguish the markets for their folk recordings and began cataloging "hillbilly" records, targeting white, rural Southerners, separately from "race" records, primarily blues and jazz, targeting black consumers. This divisions made it easier to direct their sales toward more precise audiences.[17] Their knowledge of what made a marketable country record was also growing. As noted earlier, when Whitter first recorded, he played mostly instrumentals; it was only with Peer's encouragement, when he "discovered that the dope could sing," that vocals were added. Peer once noted an often overlooked reality of these early country records, telling an interviewer, "all these things are so simple but I had to learn, or somebody had to learn, by experiment."[18]

By the time the Hill Billies hit the studio, Peer was definitely learning. By the mid–1920s, record producers were no longer as willing to let performers randomly choose songs. The 1909 Copyright Act made it mandatory for any company selling a cover of a copyrighted song to pay royalties to the copyright holder.[19] This meant that record companies had a strong financial interest in acquiring copyrights for themselves, while avoiding paying royalties by inadvertently releasing previously copyrighted material. Song choices were often no longer up to the whims of the singer, as they had been when Henry Whitter and John Carson began recording. In cases where money could be made despite royalty payments, the story was different. Many times, artists were made to cover songs that had been great successes for other artists; this explains the rapidity with which both Ernest Thompson and Vernon Dalhart recorded Henry Whitter's "Wreck on the

Old Southern 97." Capturing the sounds of the common folk song was incidental: the record company's bottom line was paramount.

In order to maximize sales, record companies began considering concepts like image and marketability, encouraging or discouraging songs that allowed them to help craft artists into salable commodities. This would eventually lead to artists with cultivated identities: Jimmie Rodgers, the rambling yodeler, warbling his blues-influenced songs about unfaithful girlfriends and lonely wanderers, the Carter Family, an ideal American example of home and hearth harmonizing around images of homesteads on the farm. The members of the Hill Billies were a varied group and no doubt familiar with a wide variety of songs, both traditional and modern. The Hopkins brothers were raised around pianos and organs, their older brother played the fiddle, and their mother had an affinity for old ballads. However, the Hill Billies, who would be marketed as a rustic string band, would rely on rollicking fiddle numbers almost exclusively, shying away from the more sentimental parlor songs and ballads that they occasionally featured in their live performances. This makes perfect sense given the musical trends of the mid-twenties, when hillbilly string bands were propelling country record sales: for example, in 1925 Charlie Poole and the North Carolina Ramblers sold 102,000 copies of "Don't Let Your Deal Go Down" paired with "Can I Sleep in your Barn Tonight, Mister?" That same year the Skillet Lickers were just beginning a run of records that would result in ninety sides being recorded for Columbia.[20]

Although these fiddle-driven string bands were proving a goldmine, by this time, record companies had learned that vocals sold records. This has long been cited as one of the reasons that Riley Puckett was asked to sing on almost every Skillet Lickers instrumental.[21] Similarly, Tony Alderman recalled that the Hill Billies were instructed to record instrumentals with a certain number of choruses spaced on the record at even intervals. The band was at first surprised that mere fiddle songs weren't enough to insure success. "We weren't smart enough to know you had to sing with it,"[22] Alderman recalled.

Interestingly, while the Hill Billies were carefully selecting upbeat fiddle numbers to record, knowing that those had the greatest appeal to their audience, G.B. Grayson's naiveté in self-promotion and marketing led him to select songs that were probably more personally meaningful. As a result, it could be argued that the discography created by Grayson and Whitter, which was eclectic, featuring everything from old British ballads to contemporary Tin Pan Alley compositions, was a more accurate reflection of the repertoire of Appalachian musicians of the time. In essence, Grayson's patchwork canon, which could at times be very non-traditional and much more difficult to define, was actually more "authentic" than the artificially-crafted fiddle repertoire of the Hill Billies.

When comparing these first Hill Billies records to the first records of Henry Whitter, records like "The Wreck on the Southern Old 97," it is easy to see the impact that the recording industry was having on the form of traditional songs. Whitter's recording, though probably more authentic and true to his street corner performances in Fries, was plodding and uneven. Whitter begins the song with a repetitive harmonica solo, one that lasts for approximately fifty seconds, almost a third of the overall track length, before beginning the first verse. Whitter's other early songs are similarly plagued by arrangements that are difficult for modern audiences to embrace. This uneven, unarranged form is hardly confined to Whitter. Fiddlin' John Carson, the other pioneer singer of the hillbilly recording era, created early records that defy current recording practices. His 1923 recording of "When You and I Were Young, Maggie" begins with a forty-three-second fiddle solo and ends with another thirty-second solo. The melody used in the first four lines changes to an altered melody for the chorus. However, the verse melody never returns, and the melody of the chorus is repeated until the end of the song. On another Carson song from the era, "You'll Never Miss Your Mother Until She Is Gone," the chorus is repeated seemingly at random, and on "Dixie Division" the melody quickly gives way to a medley of tunes which meander from one to the next.

By comparison, the Hill Billies iconic 1926 recording of "Sally Ann" is a concisely constructed piece, one that highlights a conscientious concern for what would appeal to a record-buying public; the first vocal chorus comes quickly, fourteen seconds into the track. From that point on, the song methodically alternates between solos by different instruments and vocal choruses. Multiple instruments are featured, and each is given a chance for a solo between verses. This alternation of vocals and brief instrumental solos was a formula that quickly came to dominate traditional forms like bluegrass and is still seen in modern recordings.

Clearly, the record companies were beginning to see the hillbilly record market as just that: a market that could be manipulated to meet audiences' desires and preconceptions. Often these audiences desired a sense of authenticity: they wanted to believe that the performers they heard on record were true hillbillies, rough and unschooled, projecting an archaic musical form that somehow captured America's traditional identity.[23] In 1924, the young Lowe Stokes defeated the much older Fiddlin' John Carson at the Atlanta fiddlers' convention. Carson closely adhered to the image of an "old timey" fiddler; Stokes by contrast was only twenty-two, and like many young fiddlers of the era, was embracing new sounds and styles more often associated with violin playing.[24] Stokes' victory undercut the notion that older fiddlers were more traditional, and, therefore, better. When the *New York Times* picked up the story, they massaged reality to create an image that more accurately fit with the outlook of an urban audience. They wrote that Stokes had "come down from the blue ridge foothills primed with all the Southern tunes that he had learned from his grand-dad."[25]

A similar outlook is evoked in a piece written for *Talking Machine World* in 1925. The article, entitled "Big City Holds No Lure for Singer from Hills of Virginia," showcases the OKeh recording company's attempt to frame Henry Whitter as a traditional hillbilly figure, rather than the relatively urbane, industrial mill worker he actually was. The article describes Whitter's trip to New York:

> Mr. Whitter is a real specimen of the hill country, coming from Galax, Va., and on his first few trips to New York could not be induced to stay over night, coming in to the city in the morning, making what recordings were necessary and Henry Whitter leaving before midnight arrived. Although he has overcome this shyness to some extent, he is still averse to what might be called "seeing the town." He insists that his trips from the railway station to the hotel and thence to the recording laboratories are sights enough for him. On his present visits to this city he divides his time between the laboratories and the room of his hotel practicing. Mr. Whitter sings the old-time tunes of the hill country, many of them of his own composition.[26]

Clearly an attempt was already underway at this early stage to turn the respectable Henry Whitter into a mysterious backwoods musician who had stumbled into a world of civilization and modernity. Unfortunately for the recording company, this image never stuck. Whitter, and later his partner, G.B. Grayson, were never willing to play the part of the hayseeds, opting instead for a more respectable and sophisticated appearance. In almost all photos of the men, they are pictured in suits and ties; in fact, Whitter especially seemed to take great pride in projecting a portrait of urban elegance. When posing for photographs to be used in songbooks and on posters, he went to great efforts to appear as cultured as possible. In one promotional photo taken in Galax, Virginia, Whitter appears in a topcoat, white fedora rakishly tilted to one side, his wristwatch and leather gloves on display to an envious audience. This is ironic, since he frequently dressed in overalls and looked the part of the rural farmer when not performing.

Immediately prior to his partnership with Grayson, Whitter had demonstrated a lack of concern with the authenticity of his own sound when he partnered with Joe Samuels, otherwise known as Fiddler Joe, for some of his 1926 OKeh recordings. Samuels was a professional musician.

The exact location of his birth is uncertain but he may have been born in Tennessee. Regardless, he was classically trained at the College of Music at Cincinnati, and, later, he was assistant concert conductor to Harry W. Savage. Samuels first garnered popular music fame directing Earl Fuller's Society Dance Orchestra. A critic of the time said, "Gosh! How that fellow had studied music."[27] As such, Fiddler Joe was deemed by some too well trained to be viewed as an authentic old-time fiddler, even though the songs he often recorded were traditional. A 1927 review in *Outlook* magazine gave the following analysis of Fiddler Joe's style: "Such fiddlers, and such fiddle tunes as have been recorded, unless quite recently, are not those most typical but those that have the jazz quality, foreign from real loose-arm fiddling, most highly developed."[28]

This photograph of Whitter, taken during the latter years of his career, was included in his self-published songbook. It conveys an image of urbane sophistication, quite different from the images being cultivated by other hillbilly artists at the time (courtesy Brian and Ann Baker Forehand).

Perhaps Whitter's desire to project himself as a sophisticated professional musician was detrimental to his career in country music. The Hill Billies, by contrast, made a lucrative career outside the South by embracing the image of the backwoods bumpkins the record companies so desired to project. In fact, their name, which has been cited as the source for the general term "hillbilly" music, was a conscious decision by the band to play to the expectations of their audience. Before leaving their family home in Washington, D.C., for their first New York recording session, the Hopkins brothers were teased by their father, a prosperous government bureaucrat. He felt that the desire to make a career performing fiddle tunes made the group seem unsophisticated. He specifically joked that they were acting like a bunch of hillbillies. Rather than deny this fact, the band embraced it, and when asked by OKeh records to give a name for their group, they decided to call themselves the Hill Billies, forever associating the previously derogatory term with the new musical form.[29]

The business savvy of the Hopkins brothers was so acute that they even copyrighted their name, suspecting that it would be co-opted by other groups. The Hill Billies consulted a lawyer and became an incorporated entity. However, as imitators did emerge on the scene, the band realized the cost involved in defending their claim to the name was too great to justify the effort.

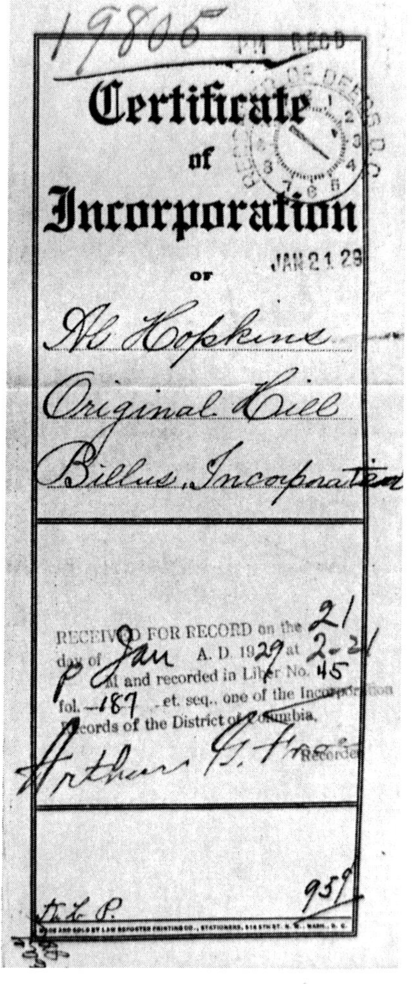

19805

Certificate of Incorporation of

JAN 21 29

Al Hopkins Original Hill Billies, Incorporated

RECEIVED FOR RECORD on the 21 day of Jan A. D. 1929 at 2-21 P M and recorded in Liber No. 45 fol. 187 et. seq., one of the Incorporation Records of the District of Columbia.

Arthur G. Froe... Recorder

959

The certificate of incorporation, dated January 21, 1929, for "Al Hopkins Original Hill Billies." Hopkins incorporated the band hoping to insure his exclusive rights to their name (courtesy Southern Folklife Collection, Louis Round Wilson Special Collections Library, University of North Carolina at Chapel Hill).

By 1926, Ralph Peer had left the OKeh label. The Hill Billies left as well, seeking out a new label for their releases. Ever conscientious of their image and with a deep desire for self-promotion, they ended up recording for Brunswick, a company originally founded to sell pianos and which is today best known as a purveyor of bowling equipment. This choice immediately magnified the group's marketability, for Brunswick was in fact two labels rolled into one. In 1924, Brunswick had acquired the Vocalion label from the Aeolian company and continued to release material under both names. In addition, Brunswick masters were licensed to Sears' Supertone label. Consequently, recordings made for Brunswick often ended up being sold on three separate labels simultaneously.[30]

To make the brands seem independent, performers were given new names on each label. As a result, the Hill Billies continued to exist as a group on the Vocalion label, while the Brunswick label featured Al Hopkins and His Buckle Busters (a name that was supposed to make reference to the band's comedic prowess, their ability to bust the audience's belt buckles with laughter). These two names referred to the same group, but that didn't stop the band from advertising themselves as two groups for live shows. Posters tempted audiences with claims like "Starting to-morrow, the original Hill Billies with Al Hopkins and his Buckle Busters, exclusive Brunswick recording orchestra,"[31] quite a dramatic introduction for five people.

This use of aliases was quite typical in the recording world of the time. For example, Grayson and Whitter recorded for Gennett, a company that was also eager to license their masters to other labels; consequently, their recordings were issued as Greyson Thomas and Will Lotty, Dillard Sanders, Norman Gayle, and David Foley, depending on the label. These names and varied label releases seem to have been conjured up by the record company with no input from the artists themselves. Gennett artists were oftentimes unaware these alias records even existed.[32] Unlike the Hill Billies, Grayson and Whitter were never able to use these aliases to market themselves to live audiences in any way.

Along with consciously grabbing names that captured their desired image, the Hill Billies were also on the forefront of groups who used costume and stage appearance to forward their constructed image. Richard A. Peterson notes that George Hay at the Grand Ole Opry was fundamentally shaping country music's identity by pushing the hillbilly image for his performers. He writes, "While radio could create an image with words and song, live appearances and movies demanded that an artist also look and act the part to be accepted as authentic."[33] As a result, Hay changed the names of Opry groups to conjure up more rustic images: Dr. Bate and his Augmented Orchestra were renamed the Possum Hunters; the Binkley Brothers Barn Dance Orchestra were renamed the Dixie Clod Hoppers. These groups were made to wear informal apparel, overalls and patchwork clothing, despite the fact that many were urban dwellers.

When this sudden embrace of the hillbilly image was taking hold on the Grand Ole Opry around 1928, the Hill Billies were already masters of the art form. An article published in the *Radio Digest* in early 1926 tries to depict the group as a conglomeration of rustic hayseeds preserving the authentic sound of a disappearing Anglo-America, a far cry from their family's upscale home in Washington, D.C. The article claims,

> They are six keen-eyed, ruddy-cheeked youths who have captured the rhythms of the hills, and who, with fiddles and other stringed instruments present the classics of the country entertainments.... There isn't a bar of jazz in the Hill Billy music. There isn't a note of weird modern harmony or anti-harmony, nor is there a skip-stop syncopation. And yet the Hill Billy music, with its "Sally Ann" rhythm and its "Cinday" swing, starts feet to tapping unrestrainedly and unashamed. It is the folk music of America, to which the backwoods youths and the farmer boys "hoe it down" on rough-plank dance floors.[34]

In the same article the group is pictured in full costume, their slouch brimmed hats and suspenders comically capturing their supposed lack of sophistication. These outfits, a revolutionary choice to purposefully look poor and uneducated, were recalled by Tony Alderman as one of the fundamental elements of the group's performance art: he notes that the group

The Hill Billies. Notice the outfits and backdrop, which were purposefully chosen to convey a rustic image. Top row, from left to right: Charlie Bowman, Tony Alderman, and Al Hopkins; bottom row, from left to right: John Hopkins, Walter Hughes and Frank Wilson (courtesy Southern Folklife Collection, Louis Round Wilson Special Collections Library, University of North Carolina at Chapel Hill).

wanted to appear to the audience as if they had just come in from hoeing corn, "like we'd come fresh from the threshing machine."[35]

No doubt the Hill Billies' early embrace of visual presentation, in contrast to the more cultured image projected by groups like Grayson and Whitter, was rooted in their performance on the vaudeville stage. Peterson notes that when creating images for Opry performers in the late 1920s, George Hay had called upon vaudeville tradition, which "had long depended on a set of stereotyped characters, including the Yankee, Irishman, Negro, Chinaman, Jew, Indian, Swede, city slicker, and country bumpkin."[36]

The Hill Billies, unlike Henry Whitter, had chosen to abandon the image of sophisticated musicians in favor of the costumes of vaudeville. Tony Alderman recalled that in their earliest years performing, the Hill Billies first attempted to break into the New York market, performing at the Hippodrome and the Broadway Theatre. Manhattan audiences were apparently not ready for "authentic" hillbilly music; consequently, these initial performances were failures, and the group returned to Washington, D.C., where they arranged a radio performance on the local station WRC. Alderman recalled their performance being so well received that they were offered a spot on the vaudeville circuit managed by the Keith-Albee company. This company controlled one of the largest vaudeville circuits in the United States and used a system of theater ownerships, theater leases, and bookings to provide entertainment from New England to New Orleans. By signing on with this circuit, the Hill Billies would have had access to theaters and markets all across the Mid-Atlantic and Southern states, something that allowed them a much greater scope of influence than performers like Whitter, who relied on a manager to arrange bookings, or G.B. Grayson, whose performances were limited to schoolhouses and social gatherings around his hometown.[37] According to Tony Alderman, the Hill Billies touring schedule was not significantly different than would be seen in a modern musical group. He recalls that the band would go to New York to record and then begin traveling from theater to theater down the Atlantic seaboard, ultimately arriving in Memphis. Along the way, they would also stop at fiddlers' conventions in the South; unlike G.B. Grayson, who attended fiddlers' conventions hoping to earn prize money, or Henry Whitter, who attended to scout for talent, the Hill Billies saw these events as marketing opportunities. Alderman recalled that "our records were selling like hot cakes. We could almost feel the sales go up whenever we went to one of those big things because they bought hundreds of them." After finishing their long tour, they would then return to New York with songs that they had worked up and tested on audiences during the previous tour, make more records, and begin the process again.

The band's rigorous touring schedule was also supplemented by mass media communication. In the 1920s, the majority of this media was in the form of radio broadcasts. The band had broken into the vaudeville circuit by performing on Washington, D.C.'s WRC and took every opportunity to perform over the airwaves. They appeared on WSB in Atlanta, the hub of radio in the South before the rise of WSM with the Grand Ole Opry in Nashville. They appeared on several other stations around Washington, notably WTOP, formerly WJSV in Arlington.[38] These northern Virginia stations, which were able to reach audiences up and down the eastern seaboard, greatly assisted the band in breaking into new markets. As a result, when they performed in places like Ohio and Maryland, they already had name recognition with potential audiences.

Nowhere was the Hill Billies' ability to reach audiences outside of the South more obvious than their appearance in a short film for Vitaphone pictures. This film, copyrighted in 1929 and titled *The North Carolina Jazz Band*, featured the group, dressed in full rustic garb, inside a log cabin, performing five songs, "Carry Me Back to Old Virginny," "Echoes of the Chimes," "The Frank Wilson Rag," "Wasn't She a Dandy?" and "Chicken Reel." The band earned an impressive $650 for this performance.[39] This short was attached to Al Jolson's feature *The Singing Fool* which played in theaters around the country, allowing the Hill Billies to present their brand of folk music to a national audience.[40]

Henry Whitter, like many professional country musicians of the era, also appreciated the importance of mass media broadcasts. He played on the radio as frequently as he could manage, and on posters advertising his live appearances, he usually billed himself as a phonograph and radio entertainer; however, when looking through the list of large stations Whitter claims to have played on—WSM in Nashville, WSB in Atlanta, and WBT in Charlotte—it is clear that, unlike the Hill Billies, he was never able to reach beyond a predominantly Southern audience. Similarly, Whitter's limited geographical range for live performances, which were primarily centered on wherever he was living at the time, did not allow him to fully take advantage of whatever name recognition he had developed through his radio performances.

Radio and records were vital to reaching audiences, but in the 1920s, live shows were the true source of a group's successes. Unlike performers like Grayson and Whitter, who attracted audiences through compelling singing and playing, the Hill Billies had to appeal to the audiences they encountered on the vaudeville circuits, and these shows frequently sandwiched their performances between wildly disparate, non-traditional acts like pop singers and shimmy dancers. The Hill Billies could not rely simply on the power of rollicking fiddle arrangements or soulful ballads to command an audience's attention. In fact, it seems that the music itself was only one component of what made their stage shows so entertaining. Charlie Bowman, who worked with the Hill Billies as a second fiddler after the group began producing records, recalled the nature of their performances. In a biography of Bowman based on his personal recollections, Bob Cox writes, "they made people roll with laughter by the clever combination of the jokes they told, the zany outfits they wore, the way they acted, the expression on their faces, their body language, their vocal inflections, the timing of their monologues, and their keen interaction with each other."[41] Lucy Hopkins (sister to Al and Joe) and Tony Alderman similarly recall the act as being largely composed of "clowning."[42]

This professional music life, characterized by constant performing, is no doubt what led the Hill Billies to craft their pioneering image as backwoods rubes. Despite being from an affluent household in Washington, D.C., appearing with movie stars like Nora Bayes on stage, entertaining President Coolidge at the White House Correspondents' dinner, appearing on film, and playing instrumental breaks on pianos, Hawaiian guitars, ukuleles and musical saws, the Hill Billies were convincingly "authentic" to the entertainment market. Perhaps because the Hopkins brothers had spent much of their adult lives living away from the rural mountains of their Ashe County home, they were able to read their urban audiences and present the kind of image that was most appealing: fanciful rustic clowns who carried with them the lost melodies of a nostalgically-imagined Anglo-America. In his biography of Charlie Bowman, Bob Cox cites an article from the *Ohio State Journal* which captures this sentiment; the author claimed that much of the Hill Billies appeal is that they play "a collection of old-time melodies, some of which have never been written down."[43]

Apparently, this approach worked. G.B. Grayson, who was no doubt as talented as any member of the Hill Billies, struggled throughout his life to make money as a musician, relying primarily on a Civil War pension for financial security; similarly, Henry Whitter, who did successfully launch a professional music career, still struggled to maintain visibility and relevance. The Hill Billies, by contrast, were incredibly successful. At the height of his popularity, Henry Whitter was performing in schoolhouses, charging fifteen to twenty-five cents for admission. Charlie Bowman remembered that the members of the Hill Billies were upset if they made less than eighteen dollars per show. Tony Alderman recalled that at their height, the five-member band was earning $750 a day, performing between three and four shows daily.[44]

Interestingly, both Grayson and Whitter's partnership and the Hill Billies' musical group were dissolved in the same way: a tragic car accident. In October 1932, two years after G.B. Grayson was killed in a collision while riding on the running board of a car, Al Hopkins was involved in an auto accident. He wrecked his car while traveling to Winchester, Virginia. He was taken to the Walter Reed Hospital where he clung to life for four weeks before finally passing away at the age of forty-three. The loss of Al and his entrepreneurial spirit, which had been instrumental in keeping the band together and on the road, immediately resulted in the dissolution of the Hill Billies. No doubt the Great Depression and the collapsing recording industry also contributed to the end of the band. Their name and image would actually go on well after their existence as a group ended: every overall-clad hillbilly musician, whose "authentic" rural image has tickled the hearts and opened the wallets of audiences all over the country, can trace their origins back to this trailblazing group.

Because of their keen marketing sensibilities and their willingness to embrace the image desired by their audiences, the Hill Billies were famous during the 1920s in a way that Grayson and Whitter could never have imagined. When Henry Whitter was living in Crumpler in the years immediately preceding his death, his own neighbors were unaware of his former recording fame. Al Hopkins, by contrast, was being recognized on the streets far away from home and well after the peak of the Hill Billies' popularity. An article from the *Abilene Reporter*, published in 1931, just a year before Al's untimely death, describes a true celebrity:

> Al Hopkins, the "Hill Billie" musician of national broadcasting fame, was in Abilene on Sunday. While he was here, he came in for a little surprise … it all began when Al and his publicity manager, Jimmie Armour, who are on a leisurely automobile trip from Washington to the Pacific coast, dropped in a local cafe for breakfast. An enterprising city officer, spotting them, ordered the two to "stay put" and left them scratching their heads over an unusual arrest. But it wasn't, for presently the policeman was back and turned his "prisoners" over to two Sunday school workers…. Al and his manager made the class meeting just in time to surprise the members with three numbers…. Al got a kick out of his "arrest." "Now I know what Texans mean by 'round up'" he said.[45]

This magical ability to find audiences for Appalachian music away from the Appalachian Mountains was the secret to the Hill Billies' success. Although Grayson and Whitter's music has no doubt found similar reach in the modern era, it has been a slow process, with their songs and melodies filtering out of the mountains through performances by other musicians,

musicians who were themselves given opportunities to find new audiences by walking the road carved out by groups like the Hill Billies. It is ironic that the largely inauthentic Hill Billies, with their stereotypical outfits and market-tested song selections, were necessary for the discovery of truly authentic Appalachian artists like G.B. Grayson and Henry Whitter.

James W.M. Grayson, Tom Dula and the Appalachian Civil War

G.B. Grayson's knowledge of obscure songs was one of the qualities that made him desirable not only to his entrepreneurial partner but also to Ralph Peer, the Victor record executive who sought out uncopyrighted songs with as much interest as he sought out talented artists. As a result of Peer's partnership with Grayson and Whitter, his publishing company acquired the copyrights to several "original" songs that had no prior copyright assigned to them. These included "What You Gonna Do with the Baby?," "On the Banks of Old Tennessee," "Never Be as Fast as I Have Been," "I Have Lost You Darling True Love," and "Going Down the Lee Highway." By acquiring the rights to these compositions, Peer's publishing company was able to reap continued royalties from the recordings, years after the original records were out of print.

But of all the songs that G.B. Grayson brought with him out of the hills around Laurel Bloomery, no song ultimately became more popular than "Tom Dooley," a well-known mountain ballad about a tragic murder and an escaped criminal eventually brought to justice. In fact, when Ralph Peer was interviewed about his career in 1958, he still held the rights to the song, acquired from G.B. Grayson, at a time when the Kingston Trio, one of the most commercially-successful folk groups of the 1950s, had only recently re-recorded the song for Capitol records. The Kingston Trio version of the song hit number one on the Billboard charts, but, unfortunately for Peer, legal difficulties involving the copyright of the song prevented him from suing for royalties; however, at the time of the interview, he still had on his desk the original contract, with which the illiterate Grayson had signed over copyright to the song, marking his signature line with an "X."[1]

The Kingston Trio version of the "Tom Dooley" ballad is the most widely known, but it is hardly the only time the song entered into the wider sphere of popular culture. It has been recorded by many traditional artists, including Doc Watson and Frank Proffitt; it was referenced by country singer Stonewall Jackson in the lyrics of his hit song "Waterloo"; it even inspired a film, *The Legend of Tom Dooley*, starring Michael Landon. However, the first-ever recording of the song was the one made by G.B. Grayson and Henry Whitter on September 30, 1929.

Like many of the songs recorded by Grayson and Whitter, and despite what Ralph Peer may have liked to believe, "Tom Dooley" was not an original composition. It, like so many other traditional songs, had been floating around North Carolina and Tennessee for years before it was ever heard by G.B. Grayson. In fact, there were at one time three different songs about the infamous murder—"The Murder of Laura Foster," "Tom Dula," and "Tom Dula's Lament"—circulating in western North Carolina, perhaps as early as 1867.[2] Unlike many other traditional songs and ballads sung by Grayson, this song appealed to him on more than an abstract level: Grayson himself had a personal connection. The story of the events surrounding the song, and the impact they had on the culture of the region, are a useful insight into G.B. Grayson's family history, his recording of the song, and the Appalachian region in general, but perhaps most notably, how the region coped with the seismic impact of the American Civil War.

The story of the Civil War in the Appalachian Mountains is the story of long-standing divisions becoming suddenly and violently exposed on a localized level. This region, which is often treated as a monolithic entity, is in fact quite fragmented. Just between the hometowns of G.B. Grayson and Henry Whitter existed huge disparities in culture and economics. The mountain region is as varied as the mountains themselves. Some areas are flatter, less rocky, and more inviting to agriculture. Beginning in the early nineteenth century, these areas, many of which were often found near the eastern edge of the Blue Ridge, attracted wealthy farmers who were able to create large, commercially-viable farms that could produce crops with great efficiency.

Traveling away from the eastern edge of the plateau to land in western Ashe County, where G.B. Grayson was possibly born, and Johnson County, Tennessee, where Grayson lived his entire adult life, land was much higher in elevation, rockier, and less arable.[3] This difference in geography contributed to a difference in attitudes and economic realities. Farms on the eastern edge of the plateau were able to support large-scale farming and began using slave labor to increase production, growing in size and influence and creating something akin to an Appalachian planter class. Western areas, by contrast, remained populated primarily by subsistence farmers who were unable to compete with the flatter, more fertile farms to the east. Soon, large-scale wealth disparities began to emerge. In 1860, in Ashe County, North Carolina, fourteen individuals, representing less than one percent of the overall population, owned fourteen percent of the improved land. Similarly, these individuals were responsible for a disproportionate amount of slaveholding, owning 14 percent of slaves living in the county at the time.[4] Naturally, given this relatively small slave population and the disparity between the small numbers of wealthy farmers and the majority of residents surviving off subsistence farming, the idea of leaving the Union in 1861 was initially an unpopular one. In fact, in the first vote to organize a state convention in preparation for secession, Ashe County voted 84 percent against the proposal.[5]

In neighboring Johnson County, Tennessee, the vote was even more lopsided, with 88 percent of residents voting against secession.[6] In May of 1861, representatives from counties in east Tennessee even gathered in Knoxville to attempt to make an argument against Tennessee's impending departure from the Union. They declared that

> the evil which afflicts our beloved country, in our opinion, is the legitimate result of the ruinous and heretical doctrine of secession; that the people of East Tennessee have ever been, and we believe are still opposed to it by a very large majority.... That the legislature of the state, without having first obtained the consent of the people, had no authority to enter into a "military league" with the confederate states against the Federal government, and by doing so put the State of Tennessee in hostile array against the government of which it then was, and still is, a member.[7]

Ultimately, war broke out despite the best efforts of mountain communities to oppose it. As soon as the attack on Fort Sumter occurred, allegiances for many in the mountains began to shift toward the reality of secession, and pro–Confederate sentiment began to grow.[8] Some, however, refused to sign on to a cause they felt favored wealthy, lowland interests and began looking for ways to undercut the Confederates: a localized civil war was looming.

In Ashe County, which was home to several large slaveholders and wealthy farmers, Confederate sentiment eventually became dominant, and hundreds of residents signed on to fight for the Confederate cause, but in neighboring Johnson County, Tennessee, Union sentiment remained strong. In fact, proportional to population, the counties of east Tennessee would ultimately send more troops to the Federal army than any part of the Union.[9] One of the men who was involved from the early days of the war in spearheading this pro–Union movement was James W.M. Grayson, G.B. Grayson's uncle.

James W.M. Grayson, G.B. Grayson's uncle, who organized the first regiment of Union soldiers from Johnson County, Tennessee. He would later assist in capturing the Wilkes County fugitive Tom Dula (courtesy June Hubbert).

Eventually, as the war dragged on, increasing numbers of Appalachian residents would turn against the cause of the Confederacy, but James Grayson and the Union loyalists who followed him began their campaign of terror against local secessionists almost immediately. In September of 1861, just two months after Tennessee was admitted to the Confederacy, a letter was published in a Raleigh newspaper telling the tragic story of Julia H. Waugh, a resident of Johnson County, Tennessee, who was being terrorized by a group of local Unionists, led in part by James W.M. Grayson. The text of the letter paints a vivid portrait of a region locked into deep internal strife:

> About the 10th of August a mob of about 150 men … led by Johnson, Grayson, Lock and others, commenced their depredations and insults in [Johnson County], near the North Carolina line, hunting down friends of the Confederate Government, and forcing the weak and defenseless to take the oath of allegiance to Lincoln. A portion of this mob … fifty or sixty in number, visited the house of Mr. McQueen and demanded of his wife to know where he was. She refused, at the peril of her life, to tell them, and after a [severe] cursing, which they received from an old negro woman, who had no respect for Lincoln's minions, they left, and soon after visited the storehouse of Wm. R. Waugh, who was absent at the time. Their Captain marched his men up and surrounded the house and demanded of Mrs. Waugh all the arms and ammunition which her husband had. She told them her husband was absent, and had left her to take care of the store and defend the family. They assured her that if she would quietly surrender the arms, she and the family would not be hurt. She refused … and gathering an axe, placed herself on the door of the building, and told them she would split the head of the first man who attempted to enter. She had with her her stepson, about 14 years of age, armed with a double-barreled gun and pistol, her daughter, about 18, armed with a repeater and a knife, and a young man who had volunteered to defend the building, was also armed. They could and would have killed a dozen or so of the mob if the attack had been made. They endeavored to intimidate Mrs. W. but she defied them and

taunted them with the sight of a Confederate flag, which they had threatened to take from her, but she told them that before they took that flag they would have to take her, and that while they were doing that, she would be certain to have her prize in the shape of a dead tory.[10]

Of course, the Unionists weren't the only ones in the mountains terrorizing and killing their neighbors. One of the most bizarre stories of the war involves the lynching of G.B. Grayson's cousins by Confederate sympathizers. G.B. Grayson's mother, Martha Jane Roark, was the daughter of Martha Pope. Pope's first cousin, Jesse Price, was a Union sympathizer living in neighboring Ashe County, a more pro–Confederate region. Like James W.M. Grayson, Jesse Price, along with his sons, had gained a reputation during the war for instigating trouble along the North Carolina and Tennessee border. On March 22, 1863, Jesse Price, his sons, Hiram and Moses, and his nephew, Solomon, were captured by home guard forces, which served during the war as a kind of vigilante army, seeking out and attacking Union sympathizers. The four men were brought to the Ashe County Courthouse in Jefferson and jailed overnight. The next day, all four men, without having faced trial, were hanged from the same limb of a locust tree in front of the courthouse. When the group was cut down for burial hours later, it was found that the youngest son, Moses, G.B. Grayson's second cousin, once removed, was still alive. The impossibility of surviving the hanging seemed so auspicious that the Confederates refused to hang him again, instead agreeing to release him, provided he would leave for Richmond and enlist in the Confederate army. Showing the tenacity of his pro–Union sympathies, Moses would quickly desert the Confederate army and join with the Federal forces. He served out the war as a Union soldier, during which time he was blinded in one eye and shot in the shoulder. He lived to be seventy years old, and died near Abingdon, Virginia, still suffering from a notably crooked neck.[11]

Unlike some in the area, James W.M. Grayson wasn't content to merely terrorize locals; he hoped to gather enough supporters to form a functional regiment of northeast Tennessee residents to fight in the Union army. Luckily for Grayson, Kentucky, which had not seceded, was tantalizingly close to his home county. He decided to try and sneak as many men as he could across Confederate territory to enlist with the Union army. He would need help for this difficult undertaking, so he sought out the assistance of Daniel Ellis, a legendary Union guide who would eventually lead many Tennessee residents into Union territories for the purpose of fighting against the Confederacy. When Grayson met with Ellis for the first time, Ellis was inexperienced, having only made the journey to Kentucky a few times. He was shocked to hear Grayson's plan to move one hundred men through enemy territory unseen. Ellis refused to go unless Grayson lessened the size of the party. On November 14, 1862, the two set out with twenty men bound for Kentucky. The party followed a track across the Holston River and Clinch Mountain, hiding along the way from Confederate troops. At one point they did run into a small scouting party but bought their silence with provisions. Eventually the small band passed through Lee County, Virginia, and met up with some Union home guard near the Cumberland River, who helped them make contact with the larger Union force.[12]

James W.M. Grayson continued to bring troops to Kentucky to enlist in the Federal army which was forming regiments of Tennessee loyalists at Camp Nelson, a depot near Lexington. One of these young enlistees was James Grayson's only brother, Benjamin, G.B. Grayson's father, who was twenty-five years old at the time. The two Grayson brothers were very close. In both the 1850 and 1860 census, the two unmarried siblings were shown living together.

The younger Grayson, Benjamin, upon joining the army, found his experience, like that of many young Civil War soldiers, to be one characterized by hospitalization and disease. He was noted as sick on his muster sheet when he was first registered with the Federal army in June of 1863. From that time to the time he was mustered out of the army in May of 1865, he spent the war in a variety of hospitals in Kentucky and Tennessee. Although he probably never faced combat, by the end of the war, Benjamin was debilitated. He filed a pension application after the war claiming he was almost entirely disabled suffering from "rheumatism and resulting partial paralysis of the lower extremities" contracted as a result of exposure. He would never recover, and would depend on his pension for survival until his death at age fifty-six.

Benjamin's brother, James W.M., also saw little, if any, combat action; however, his initial role as agitator and organizer was instrumental in giving the Union inroads into east Tennessee, from which they were able to launch attacks into neighboring states. These forces, although originally scattered and disorganized, were eventually brought together into formal regiments, placed under the command of Federal colonel Alvin C. Gillem. An article from an 1863 edition of the *Memphis Bulletin* illustrates the respect these Tennessee Union regiments had earned:

> Organized as many of them were of refugees beyond the limits of their own State, and at a time when there was no competent State authority to recognize their existence, they rushed into the fight regardless of the forms taken in such cases. The result was that six "first Tennessee" regiments appeared in the field from the East, Middle and

> West grand divisions of the State. Col. Alvin C. Gillem, of the 2st [sic] West Tennessee infantry, has lately been appointed Adjutant General under Governor Andrew Johnson.[13]

Colonel Gillem must have been well-loved by his men. Both James W.M. Grayson and his brother Benjamin would eventually name sons after him (although with slight misspelling): Gilliam Allen Grayson and Gilliam Banmon (G.B.) Grayson, respectively.

Life calmed down somewhat after the end of the war, but the reconstruction years saw a great divergence of fortunes for the two Grayson brothers. After the war, Benjamin, G.B.'s father, married his first wife, settled in Johnson County, and was forced to rely on a meager Union pension to survive, the same pension that would later support G.B. Grayson's family. Benjamin's brother James returned to his home, having served as a lieutenant colonel in the Union army, and began buying large tracts of property in Johnson and Ashe counties.[14] In fact, a small community in Ashe County near the Tennessee line is still named Grayson after the post office which was located in a store owned by James Grayson. He had soon established a large horse farm a few miles south of Laurel Bloomery, near the place where his own father, William Grayson, had settled.

During these post-war years, the entire South was in the process of putting itself back together. James Grayson found the transition back to civilian life to be a successful one, no doubt buoyed by his successes supporting the victorious Union forces. In other places, the story was much different. On June 11, 1865, a downtrodden Confederate soldier who had fought for the Southern cause for the duration of the war was released from a Federal military prison in Maryland and began the long journey back to northwestern North Carolina. His name was Thomas C. Dula.

In many ways, Dula's story parallels the story of the Grayson brothers in east Tennessee. Dula was also living in an area notorious for its divided population during the war. Wilkes County, Dula's home, was at the time an attractive spot for deserters, disloyal to the Confederate cause and attempting to hide out for the duration of the war; over the course of the war, Confederate regiments were repeatedly sent into Wilkes County to root out these deserters and force them to re-enlist in the army.[15] Unlike the Graysons, however, Dula's loyalty was firmly with the Confederacy. He enlisted at the age of seventeen in 1862, obviously eager to fight for the Southern cause, and unlike the deserters who roamed the hills near his home in Wilkes County, Dula served loyally until the very end of the war. Like Benjamin Grayson, Dula also spent a large portion of his military career in and out of hospitals, suffering from fevers and other ailments common to Civil War soldiers. Dula was eventually taken prisoner near Kinston, North Carolina, on March 10, 1865. After his capture, Dula was transported to Point Lookout, Maryland, where he would stay as a prisoner until the end of the war.[16]

Unlike James Grayson, Dula did not profit from his time in the service and returned to an area wracked by poverty. After Dula returned to his home in Wilkes County, he immediately resumed what could generously be characterized as a promiscuous and carefree lifestyle. Whereas James Grayson seems to have devoted his post-war life to responsibly building on his successes, Tom Dula seems to have thrown himself into recapturing the youthful freedom of which the war had robbed him. Within a year, he found himself in a love triangle with a married woman he had been seeing prior to his enlistment, Ann Melton, and a young girl, aged twenty-one, from nearby Caldwell County, Laura Foster. Testimony during the eventual murder trial indicated that by the spring of 1866, Dula, Melton, and Foster had all become infected with syphilis, or "the pock," as it was commonly called. In all likelihood, the source of this infection was Pauline Foster, a distant cousin of Melton's from neighboring Watauga County who was living with Anne Melton and seeking treatment for her own infection. Court testimony indicated that, along with Laura Foster and Ann Melton, Pauline had also been involved in a sexual relationship with Dula. However, Melton and Dula instead blamed Laura Foster for infecting them. During the trial, the State argued that a desire to seek revenge for this unfortunate medical condition is what led Dula to murder.

A commonly-held belief, which was never proven in court, is that Ann Melton, with whom Dula was carrying on an affair, was at least complicit, if not active, in the murder of Foster, but all circumstantial evidence presented during the trial pointed to Dula as the actual murderer. On the morning of Friday, May 25, 1866, Laura Foster met with Dula outside her house. Shortly afterward, she gathered some clothes, climbed onto her father's horse, and set off, intending to meet up with Dula, who had promised to run away with her. She arrived in a wooded area where the two had arranged to meet, referred to during the trial as the Bates' Place. Sometime either that day or that night, Laura was killed and buried in a shallow grave that had already been dug near the home of Dula's mother.

Laura's disappearance was soon noticed, and when the mare she had been riding returned to her father's home dragging a broken lead rope, foul play was suspected. Over the course of the next month, residents actively searched for Foster's body, and a rumor began to spread that Dula, who had been seen talking to Foster on the morning of her disappearance, was the chief suspect. Tom Dula felt pressure building to escape while he could. Sometime around June 25 or 26, Dula told friends that he was leaving but would return around Christmas for Ann Melton and his mother.

Dula left Wilkes County, following the old trail carved by herds of buffalo that led across the Blue Ridge, the same trail that early longhunters like Daniel Boone had used to navigate through the mountains. This was also the trail that the early settlers of Watauga County had first used to enter the mountains, leading some of these pioneer families, like the Eggerses and Reeses, to settle near the Tennessee line around Zionville. It was here also that the wandering William Grayson, G.B.'s grandfather, had first settled and married Rebecca Reese, and it was here, across the Tennessee line in Trade, that James W.M. Grayson, G.B.'s uncle had just settled after leaving the Union army.

On June 28, a warrant was issued for Dula's arrest, and sometime around July 2, after a week of walking, the fleeing Dula arrived at Grayson's property. Grayson's home, which was located on Drake Creek, was a large, two-story log house, surrounded by a large farm. Grayson had become a large-scale farmer after the war and had established a profitable enterprise raising horses, which he would take to Sumter, South Carolina, for sale each year. Claiming that he was in need of a new pair of boots, Dula asked Grayson for a job. Grayson already had several farmhands working for him but was willing to hire Dula, who was travelling under an alias: Tom Hall.

During his brief stay at the Grayson farm, Dula seems to have made a positive impression. Family sources recall that James Grayson always said he liked Dula, allowing him to sleep in the house where Dula would entertain the family by playing the fiddle.

After a week, Dula had his new boots, and one morning, before daylight, he slipped away, heading southwest toward Johnson City. Later that same day, deputies from Wilkes County, who had been tracking Dula, arrived at Grayson's farm. Once Grayson realized the Tom Hall who had been working for him was actually the accused murderer Tom Dula from North Carolina, he seems to have developed a strong sense of personal responsibility for bringing him to justice. Assuming the responsibilities of command he had last held in the Union army, Grayson took control of the posse. He led the deputies to Taylorsville, known today as Mountain City, Tennessee, to arrange for assistance from the sheriff of Johnson County, but the sheriff was away at nearby Shady Valley with no way to be reached.

Undeterred, Grayson continued to lead the search party in pursuit of Dula. They began traveling the route they believed Dula had taken and soon spotted him sitting on the banks of Doe Creek near Pandora,

Tennessee. His new boots had rubbed blisters on his feet, and he was resting them in the creek for relief. Leaving his Civil War officer's pistol in the saddle bag where he always kept it, James Grayson picked up a large rock and demanded that Dula surrender to authorities. Dula agreed and gave himself up with no resistance. The former Confederate prisoner had finally been captured, only seventy miles away from home, by a retired Union officer.

Supposedly, based on folk sources, the party seeking Dula demanded that he be immediately hanged for his supposed crimes. They suggested that rather than return Dula to Wilkes, the group lynch him, using a tree near the creek. James Grayson, motivated by a sense of duty, warm feelings toward Dula, or both, retrieved his pistol and shot once in the air. Grayson swore that he would return Dula to North Carolina and demanded that he receive a fair trial.[17]

That night, the party, along with their prisoner, were back at Grayson's farm. Dula was locked in the corn crib, where he was guarded by twelve-year-old William Franklin Grayson, James's son. The next day, Dula was placed on the back of a horse, provided by James Grayson. His feet were tied beneath the saddle, leaving his hands free to control the animal, and he was escorted back to Wilkes County for trial.

In early September, Laura Foster's body was finally found in the shallow grave where she had been hidden, and on October 21, Dula was found guilty and sentenced to be executed. However, due to an error on the part of the judge during trial, the Supreme Court of North Carolina threw out the verdict and ordered a new trial for Dula.

This second trial was delayed because some witnesses failed to appear. One of these witnesses was James W.M. Grayson, who was fined eighty dollars by the judge in the case. By this point, Grayson was serving as an elected representative in the Tennessee government which was in session at Nashville during the trial. He would not appear.

This second trial ended the same as the first, with a guilty verdict rendered. Dula was sentenced to be executed. On May 1, 1868, Dula was hanged in Statesville. The night before his death, he wrote a note declaring that he had killed Laura Foster by himself. This note was later used to exonerate Ann Melton, who was also on trial as an accomplice.

Almost immediately after the execution of Dula, songs commemorating the event began to take shape. By the early twentieth century, three distinctly different songs about the murder were circulating. Supposedly, a man named Thomas Land, who lived near the scene of the murder in Wilkes County, wrote one, "The Murder of Laura Foster." This song, an extensive ballad, which was later cataloged as song F36 by George Malcolm Laws in his *Native American Balladry*, is in a long narrative structure, retelling Laura Foster's final hours. Notably, this song never mentions the name of the murderer. The culprits are referred to only as a faceless duo: "The grave was short and narrow too / but in it they poor Laura threw / They covered her with leaves and clay / then hastened home ere break of day." Obviously, the author seems to be implying the shared guilt of Tom Dula and Ann Melton in the murder, but he never makes the charge explicit.[18]

By contrast, the two other songs about the crime, "Tom Dula's Lament" and "Tom Dula," are more interested in the murderer than the victim. "Tom Dula's Lament" has often been associated with Dula himself, who some claim wrote the song on a banjo brought by friends to the jail in Statesville the night before he was executed. As romantic as this notion is, it probably is not true, since the story of its composition runs counter to newspaper accounts of the actual execution.[19] These accounts describe Dula spending the night before his execution pacing his cell, distressed and alone.[20]

Whoever wrote "Tom Dula's Lament" was definitely attempting to recast Dula as a victim, someone who had lost his true love and whose ultimate execution was at least as much the fault of Ann Melton as his own. The song is the only one of the three songs about the crime told in first person, which gives the audience a stronger sense of personal connection to the accused murderer. In the song, Dula laments, "Poor Laura loved me well / she was both fond and true / How deep her love for me / I never really knew," and then goes on to complain, "I've lived my life of sin / I've had a bit of fun / Come, Ann, kiss me goodbye, / My race is nearly run."

The desire on the part of writers and performers to re-characterize Dula as the victim rather than the villain was apparently a strong one. "Tom Dula's Lament" was one example, but it is also interesting to note how some examples of the more well-known "Tom Dula" (or "Tom Dooley") have allowed this tendency toward exonerating Dula to creep in. Supposedly this song, which could have been written as early as 1867, was composed by a black songster named Charlie Davenport who originally set the words to the melody of the antebellum song "Run, Nigger, Run."[21] At the time of its composition, it was clearly an outlaw ballad, telling the tale of the murdering Tom Dula, who violently ends the life of the innocent Laura Foster and receives his just punishment. This is definitely the version that G.B. Grayson knew and sang. No doubt influenced by his uncle's capture of Dula, Grayson refuses to concede any hint of Dula's innocence. His version closely follows the traditional text of the song, placing blame for the murder, the hiding of the body, and the escape on Dula alone; no hint of innocence or Ann Melton's influence is mentioned. Other performances of the song, notably the well-known version recorded by Doc Watson in 1964, include an additional verse that laments Dula's unjust sentence, as Dula claims, "I never even harmed a hair on poor little Laura's head."

The Tom Dula case, and the songs that were inspired by it, are an enduring example of the effect that memorable events can have on music, and that music can have on memorable events. Although G.B. Grayson recorded many songs, and several ballads, none is as personally linked to the artist himself as "Tom Dooley." Benjamin Grayson's pension, which G.B. received every month until his death, was a constant reminder of the realities of the Civil War, a war which had left his father forever handicapped and his uncle forever famous. Singing "Tom Dooley" allowed Grayson to bridge the divide between his own life and the lives of these heroic forbearers through music. Through his recording of the song, he was also able to preserve the memory of a crime that would otherwise have been forgotten. Although Tom Dula, Laura Foster, and Anne Melton are long dead, the memory and the nuances of their lives have gained a certain level of immortality and are still being debated and argued over, thanks in large part to G.B. Grayson, his famous uncle, and all the unknown singers who've kept the tale alive.

The Courthouse Massacre

When Henry Whitter came to New York in 1923 to make his first records, he was viewed by record executives like Ralph Peer as a nobody. When asked years later, after Whitter's recording career had come and gone, Peer was still unable to recall exactly where Henry Whitter was from.[1] When a trade magazine referred to his early recording sessions, they consistently referred to Whitter as a product of "the hill country,"[2] a dark, nebulous region somewhere south of the Mason-Dixon line. In actuality, Henry Whitter had clearer origins; he had been born in Carroll County, Virginia, and although the urbane individuals associated with the New York recording industry probably weren't aware of it, Carroll County was famous. It just wasn't famous for something a native like Henry Whitter would necessarily be proud of. When an edition of the *Radio Digest* ran a story about the Hill Billies, whose members, like John Rector and Tony Alderman, were also natives of southwest Virginia, the author didn't miss the opportunity to point out this notorious locale. He wrote, "Carroll [County] if you must know, is the county in which the famous Allen gang, feudists extraordinary, lives and has its being, and takes occasional pot shots at unsociable neighbors."[3] This comic vision of an "Allen gang," a bunch of cartoon hillbillies engaged in a stereotypical family feud, would have been popular in New York City in the 1920s, but this image belies a much more sinister story, for on March 14, 1912, members of the Allen family had, in fact, contributed to one of the most violent criminal events in early twentieth-century America, and it had happened within a few miles of Henry Whitter's birthplace. The Allens' story, which was eventually reworked by mass media sources into a caricature of Appalachian culture, was initially commemorated in a song, a ballad that was first brought to New York in 1924 by Henry Whitter. The story of this song and the tragic events that gave rise to it provide fascinating insight into the realities of life near Henry Whitter's native home.

Henry Whitter was born in Sulphur Springs, Virginia, a small community just outside the Carroll County seat of Hillsville. In 1902, when Henry was only ten years old and just before his family moved to Fries, Virginia, looking for work in the new cotton mill, his youngest brother was born. Whitter's parents, probably hoping to foster a life of luxury for their new baby, decided to name Henry's brother Sidney Allen after the wealthiest man in the area.

An early photograph of Henry Whitter, taken before his recording career began (courtesy Southern Folklife Collection, Louis Round Wilson Special Collections Library, University of North Carolina at Chapel Hill).

Sidna (pronounced with a long "e") Allen would have been in the newspaper headlines with regularity during the year leading up to the birth of Henry Whitter's brother. Allen had just returned from a long prospecting trip to the Alaska wilderness where he had made almost no money in gold but had grown his personal wealth nonetheless by selling merchandise to other miners. He had briefly traveled to Hawaii to take advantage of a growing real estate market, and by 1901, he was back in Carroll County, richer and ready to settle down. In early 1901, Sidna Allen was married and had begun construction on what would ultimately be one of the most elaborate houses in southwest Virginia, a large, eight-room dwelling with its own windmill and acetylene generator, which provided the house with both running water and gas lights.[4]

The fact that Whitter's parents chose to name their new son Sidney Allen, a name shared by no one else in the whole county at the time, demonstrates that, at the time of his birth, they saw the wealthy Allen as admirable, a symbol of possibilities. Tragically, neither Sidney Whitter nor Sidna Allen would end up experiencing very happy lives. On November 10, 1902, the three-month-old Sidney Allen Whitter died, and just over ten years later, on November 27, 1912, Sidna Allen himself would be standing trial for murder.

The events that led to Allen's trial and eventual conviction arguably began in the Civil War. The rift between Democrats, who had historically controlled Southern politics, and the Republicans, who gained power in the reconstruction years, was especially pronounced in the late nineteenth century. The Allens were a prominent band of Democrats, whereas the sheriff of Carroll County and most of the other elected officials during the period were Republicans.[5] This divide seems to have led to significant antagonism between the extended Allen family and county officials. The Allen family seems to have been under the impression that they were being unjustly persecuted by local authorities, and whether this impression was founded in reality or not, it would soon lead to a series of explosive confrontations. In the autumn of 1911, nephews of the Allen family, Sidna Edwards and Wesley Edwards, were hauled before a grand jury on charges of disturbing public worship, charges which the Allen family felt were unfounded. They argued the boys had been forced into a confrontation outside of a local church by four other individuals who were the ones actually responsible for starting the altercation.

Despite the objections of the Allen and Edwards families, the grand jury handed down an indictment. Fearing the consequences of a trial, the Edwards boys fled the jurisdiction, taking up residence in nearby Mt. Airy, North Carolina. When the location of the Edwards boys was eventually discovered by Carroll County officials, orders to arrest them were issued. Two officers traveled to Mt. Airy, captured the boys, handcuffed them, tied their feet together, placed them in a buggy and began the return to Hillsville. On the returning trip, the officers were just passing Sidna Allen's impressive new home at the top of the mountain when they were spotted by Floyd Allen, Sidna's brother. Floyd became so enraged after seeing his nephews tied up by officers, who he felt were motivated by a desire to unfairly punish the Allen family, that he committed to free them. He confronted the officers and demanded they release the Edwards boys, arguing that the arrest, made across state lines, was legally invalid. In response, the officers drew their guns but were disarmed by Floyd. After the officers fled the scene, Floyd himself brought the boys the rest of the way to the courthouse, where they were released on bond. Many more indictments were soon handed down from the grand jury of Carroll County, this time for Floyd and Sidna Allen, who were accused of interfering with officers performing their duties.

The Edwards boys were ultimately tried and given sixty-day sentences for disrupting public worship. Three months later, on March 13, 1912, it was Floyd's turn to face justice. Walking into the courtroom, Floyd found himself facing off against numerous local rivals. In addition to the sheriff and deputy officers who had been responsible for the arrest of Allens, there was the clerk of court, Dexter Goad, who had previously antagonized Allen by accusing him of falsifying expenses when Allen had served as a deputy for the county. There was also the prosecuting attorney, who had switched political parties, from Democrat to Republican, in order to defeat Allen's nephew in an election for the prosecutor's job.[6] Despite the palpable tension between the defendant and the state, the trial went smoothly, but wary of potential outbursts from the audience, the presiding judge, Thornton Massie, himself a Democrat, decided to delay the reading of the verdict until early the next morning.

Early on the morning of the 14th of March, hundreds of people crowded into the courtroom to hear the verdict against Floyd Allen. The jury found him guilty, and he was sentenced to one year in the state penitentiary. Allen's lawyer rose, asking the judge to release Floyd under his present bond while awaiting a hearing to set aside the verdict. Judge Massie refused, and Sheriff Lewis Webb was asked to take Allen into custody. Famously, Allen supposedly said, "Gentlemen, I'm not going." With those brief words, chaos erupted in the Hillsville Courthouse.

The great mystery of who fired the first shot of the Courthouse Tragedy, as it would come to be known, will probably never be solved satisfactorily. Dozens of bullets were fired in the crowded courtroom, fifty-seven of which were ultimately recovered.[7] The story of the shootout is shrouded in confusion. Who shot first, who shot at all, who shot who, who shot from where are all questions lost in the smoky haze and noise of the gunfight. What soon became apparent was the resulting carnage. Judge Massie was dead, and so were Sheriff Webb, Prosecutor William Foster, and a juror, Augustus Fowler. Along with those four, Betty Ayers, an eighteen-year-old witness, was badly wounded and would die the next day. Floyd Allen had been shot, as had his brother Sidna. Dexter Goad, the Allens' rival, had been shot through the face, but he was still able to work his way outside to continue shooting at the fleeing Allen family.

Floyd Allen was badly injured and ended up at a nearby hotel, where he was quickly arrested. The rest of the Allen family was still at large. News of the shootout was spreading from Carroll County and was soon a national headline. By this time, newspapers were more than willing to alter the facts of the story to fit their preconceived notions of mountain dwellers.

Slowly the Allen gang, as they had come to be known, were rounded up. Sidna Allen was the last one caught, six months after the shootout, in Des Moines, Iowa, after being steadily pursued by detectives from the Baldwin-Felts agency. Trials for the Allen family members quickly followed. Floyd was found guilty of murdering prosecutor William Foster; Floyd's son, Claude Allen, was found guilty of conspiracy to commit Foster's murder, despite a notable lack of evidence that Claude had anything to do with Foster's death. Father and son were sentenced to death and both would be electrocuted on March 28, 1913.

Sidna Allen was luckier than his brother: he was sentenced to thirty-five years in prison. He would stay in prison for fourteen years before being pardoned by the governor in 1926.

Throughout the trial, and afterward, the Allens denied any conspiracy to murder the officials killed during the courthouse shooting. This claim of innocence paired with the political nature of the Allens' trial, which had pitted Democratic sentiments against Republican ones, clouded the waters of objective analysis and ensured that strong public sentiment would exist in favor of the Allens, despite the court's rulings. As a result, pleas for mercy quickly arose from a section of the populace.[8] This public outcry was still very vocal years after the crime, and the notoriety of the case provided fertile ground in which songs about the Hillsville incident could take root. Randal Hall notes,

> Writers, singers, and activists seized the conflicting versions of the killings, and they have told and retold the story for the last nine decades. In wrangling to dictate the historical memory of the events, they have voiced the hostile political views both those at the local level and regarding larger issues that ignited the original violence. Ballads that glorified the Allens' bravery and criticized the governor for executing Claude emerged among Virginia musicians, and with the growth of the commercial country music industry in the 1920s, songsters recorded them for a larger audience.[9]

This pro–Allen sentiment mentioned by Hall is most popularly found in "Claude Allen," a song that centered on Floyd's son, Claude, who was executed along with his father for the dubious crime of conspiracy to commit murder. "Claude Allen" is included in Malcolm Laws' *Native American Balladry*; however, by Laws' own definition, the song can only marginally be considered a ballad at all. Laws defines the ballad form as "a narrative folksong which dramatizes a memorable event."[10] "Claude Allen" fails to meet this definition because rather than tell a story with a discernable narrative arch, the song is more of a series of emotional pleas concerning the innocence of Claude Allen and how his unjust execution affected friends and family. Most of the verses are in no particular order and could be easily rearranged, something not true of most ballads. Similarly, there is no "memorable event" being dramatized, as the song was written after Claude's death sentence and does not deal with the shooting or the trial. The song's only mention of the execution is to complain that the cruel governor of Virginia failed to pardon Claude and his father.[11]

A better example of a ballad on the subject of the Allen family and their violent exploits in Hillsville is "Sydney Allen," which places the focus on Floyd's brother and which has a much more anti–Allen viewpoint. Recorded in 1924, this is the first song about the Hillsville shooting that was committed to record. Appropriately, the singer on this first record depicting the Hillsville shooting was Carroll County native Henry Whitter.

It is necessary to note that on many occasions writers have attributed the authorship of the "Sydney Allen" ballad to Carson J. Robison, a prolific songwriter of the 1920s. Robison's assumed authorship is probably rooted in the fact that his close associate, Vernon Dalhart, would record his own version of the Virginia ballad in 1926 during a session in which he was accompanied by Robison. Recording a song about a twenty-four-year-old shooting from rural Virginia may seem like an odd choice for Dalhart at first, but it speaks to the impact the Hillsville shooting had in areas outside of Virginia and the overarching trends of country music in its earliest days. Starting with Henry Whitter's "Wreck on the Southern Old 97" and his fellow mill worker Ernest Stoneman's recording of "The Titanic," both of which became available for retail sale in 1924, companies marketing country music records became increasingly obsessed with songs that recalled tragic events. By 1925, 11 percent of all songs released by country artists were event songs and all seven top selling records for the year featured an event song on at least one side. Seven of these event song records were so popular that they accounted for almost 50 percent of all record sales on the Columbia label.[12] Vernon Dalhart and Carson Robison quickly emerged as the leaders of this event song surge. Dalhart had made a huge hit from "The Death of Floyd Collins," which recounted the 1925 death of a spelunker who had become trapped in a narrow passage near Crystal Cave, Kentucky. This song was composed following the event by Andrew Jenkins, a singer and songwriter from Atlanta. The unexpected success of "The Death of

Floyd Collins" created an explosion of event songs written for studio singers like Dalhart. Carson Robison was the man responsible for creating many of these topical ballads. Robison would eventually write many songs dealing with current events and tragedies, songs like "The Scopes Trial" and "The Santa Barbara Earthquake." Robison was also more than willing to take pre-existing songs, like the popular American ballad "Ommie Wise," and rework them, sometimes giving them new titles and taking writing credit for himself.[13] The Hillsville tragedy and the ballad that recounted it were perfect material for this age obsessed with tragic occurrences. It should then come as no surprise that Robison and Dalhart would have snatched up the pre-existing Whitter recording, claiming writing credit in the process. Consequently, the authorship may belong to Robison on paper, but the song itself is much older. In fact, Henry Whitter's recording of the song, which was made on February 24, 1924, was made just around, and probably before, the time when Robison first began working in New York for the Victor Recording Company.[14] Although Whitter was not himself the author of the song, he had obtained his version close to the original source.

"Sydney Allen," which is often spelled "Sidney Allen" in folk song collections, wasn't collected by folklorists prior to Whitter's recording, so it is difficult to ascertain exactly when the song emerged. The other famous song about the shooting, "Claude Allen," was first collected in 1917 in Surry County, North Carolina, which borders Carroll County to the south. This would suggest that retelling of the event in song began shortly after the shooting itself. Another point to consider is that the melody of "Sydney Allen" was lifted from the popular train song "Casey Jones," which was a pop hit in 1911.[15] The borrowing of this melody would imply that the song is rooted in the period of the 1912 shooting.

No doubt because of the notoriety of the Hillsville shooting, the ballad about Sidna Allen spread outward from Carroll County. It has been collected throughout the Appalachian Mountains, especially in North Carolina, Virginia, and Kentucky, but has also been found in Tennessee, Mississippi, and Nevada. Consequently, multiple versions of the song now exist, each with disparate names and details. In "The Hillsville Tragedy in Court Record Mass Media, and Folk Balladry," Peter Aceves argues that the best way to try to make sense of the varied forms of the song is to create a "popularity archetype" by comparing all known versions of the song and deciding which details are most often included. He argues that this approach is most valid because "in order to analyze general social attitudes and ideas towards an event, the historian must stress common denominators regardless of what kind of documentation he utilizes."[16] This interpretation stresses the importance of social attitudes, allowing us to use the texts of the ballad, especially their inclusions and omissions, to try to understand what about the story appealed to individuals who heard it. The problem with this approach is that it ignores authenticity; it gives no weight to the accuracy of the song's content. By looking at the details of the song itself and comparing them to the historical event it is recounting, it seems apparent that the song version recorded by Henry Whitter contains many intricate details lost in other texts, suggesting that Whitter's version of the song is very close to the original composition.

For one thing, Whitter's version of the song contains precise names of people that aren't found in most texts. Judge Massie is referenced by name; other versions refer to the first victim of the shooting as "Judge Mathey," "Judge Moses, " "Judge Mansfield," or "Blake Yancey."[17] Similarly, Sheriff Webb is hardly ever mentioned by name; he is instead usually just referred to in lines like "Sidney backed the Sheriff up against the wall." Like Webb, Dexter Goad, referred to by name in Whitter's text, also vanishes from most versions, appearing in few versions other than Whitter's.

The facts of the shooting, unclear as they were in reality, become especially muddled in texts of the ballad. In the majority of texts, Judge Massie is killed by Sidna, not Floyd. Whitter correctly identifies Floyd as the defendant and accused shooter. Whitter goes on to note the exact number of causalities, "the dead and the dying were numbered four." In most text versions, the number of deaths is unclear. Referring to the escape, Whitter notes that the Allens refused to surrender to the "Baldwin gang," a reference to the Baldwin-Felts detectives who would ultimately pursue them. This fact was lost in most translations, changing from "Baldwin gang" to "ball and chain." Most versions note that Sidna was captured in a western town. Whitter is in the minority of accounts that correctly notes that it was not only Sidna who was captured but also his nephew, Wesley. Whitter's is also in the minority of accounts that correctly identifies Galax as the place to which the outlaws were returned after their capture.

Taken together, these details could support a strong argument that Whitter's version, which is surprisingly accurate and true to the subtle facts of the event, is one of only a few collected versions that can be seen as authentic, coming directly from the original source, rather than from multiple retransmissions. This would make sense, given Whitter's background in Carroll and Grayson counties, and his family's familiarity with the Allens.

Perhaps the most interesting aspect of Whitter's version comes at the very end of the song. In his analysis of the "Claude Allen" and "Sydney Allen" ballads, Peter Aceves argues that the two ballads about the Hillsville Courthouse shooting appeal to differing viewpoints: "Claude Allen" is ensconced in family-centered sentimentality supporting the Allen cause, while "Sydney Allen" presents a more society-centered view emphasizing justice, a view which paints the Allens as villains whose subversion of societal norms ended with well-deserved punishments. He writes, "since both songs have been in oral circulation simultaneously, it would seem that carriers of oral tradition possessing strong pro or con feelings toward the defendants and their political affiliations have chosen to sing one song or the other and not both."[18] This argument holds true for every version of the "Sydney Allen" ballad except for one: Henry Whitter's. Rather than end the song with Allen's sentence to prison, as every other version of the ballad does, Whitter tags on an additional verse using a changed melody, possibly written himself, which celebrates the historical Sidna Allen and paints his capture and sentence as unjust: "Sydney Allen strong and valiant, / Sydney Allen on that sad sad day, / Sydney Allen strong and gallant, / He rode to Galax on that sad sad day."

Whitter's motivation for including this unique addition can never be known. It could have been grounded in his complex political and family loyalties rooted in Carroll County; it could have been that he felt record sales would be increased by a more upbeat ending. But perhaps he was just trying to salvage the tarnished name of his youngest brother who had died twenty-two years before.

On the Trail of Nancy Blevins

After the death of G.B. Grayson, Henry Whitter's recording career was essentially over. This has frequently been seen as a correlation: Whitter's loss of Grayson was insurmountable and, lost and grieving, he chose to abandon music rather than carry on without his friend and partner. Although this is a moving and romantic idea, it isn't actually true. Whitter was no doubt upset by Grayson's death, but his recording career wasn't over the moment Grayson was thrown from the running board of Curtis Milhorn's car. Just a few months later Whitter would record with Fisher Hendley, a banjo player from Albemarle who Whitter had assisted in getting a recording deal. Ultimately, what ended Whitter's career was the Great Depression, which ended the careers of many of the country artists recording in the middle to late 1920s.

Although he would never again make a record or be broadcast over the radio, Whitter wasn't finished working as a musician; he would continue to make what money he could through personal appearances around his home in Crumpler, North Carolina. To achieve this, he sought out young talent who could mimic the sound Whitter had perfected with G.B. Grayson; he was especially drawn to young local fiddlers, like Muncey Gaultney and Worth Taylor, who were happy to get a chance to play with a well-known musician. Eventually, Whitter found a young musician who could fill the role of fiddler in his duo: Albert Hash. Hash would later remember how he began playing with Whitter. He said, "Grayson got killed. After that his buddy Henry Whitter was alone, and I went to see Henry, who lived over at Crumpler, North Carolina. And he was a very likable fellow, a nice man, and he liked the way I played. I played so much like Grayson that he asked me if I would stay with him and play show dates with him."[1]

The grave of Nancy "Nannie" Baker, who was born Nancy Blevins (author's collection).

Whitter provided Hash with a fiddle and transportation, and the two began traveling to local schools and house parties, where Whitter attempted to impress the local crowds with tales of his former stardom. Whitter's showmanship had never left him; he often introduced Albert to the crowds as the greatest fiddle player since the death of G.B. Grayson. When Albert voiced concern that Whitter was building him up to a level his actual skill didn't merit, Whitter reassured Hash that 80 percent of the crowd at any given show would believe anything about show business that Whitter told them.[2]

Hash's short time playing with Whitter gave him his first taste of professional musical life, but, because of the Depression, it was difficult to launch a solo career as a fiddle player. Hash would continue to play sporadically, even making some home recordings with neighbors during the 1940s, but he left the professional musical world for several decades. When he started playing again in the 1960s, he performed on a local radio station, WKSK, with a band, the Virginia-Carolina Boys, that was a mixture of bluegrass, old-time, and contemporary country featuring well-known local musicians like Wayne Henderson and J.C. Kemp (whose father had been taught to play by G.B. Grayson). Hash definitely fell on the old-time end

Henry Whitter (left) and Albert Hash. Hash got his first experience playing professionally with Henry Whitter at small venues around Whitter's home in Healing Springs, North Carolina (courtesy Brian and Ann Baker Forehand).

Fleetwood Schoolhouse

Monday, October 12th

at 7:30 P. M.

HENRY WHITTER

(COMPOSER OF "WRECK OF OLD 97," "SHE'LL BE COMING ROUND THE MOUNTAIN" AND "FOXCHASE BLUES")

Will Play and Sing These Same Songs as When Recorded for Phonograph

Even late in his career, Whitter continued to rely on his early recording success to attract audiences. This flyer is for a show in 1936 at the Fleetwood Schoolhouse, just a few miles from Whitter's home in Healing Springs (courtesy Brian and Ann Baker Forehand).

of the spectrum, interspersing fiddle songs popular from the 1930s, like "Little Brown Hand," into set lists that included country songs like "Heartaches by the Number."

Albert Hash was almost sixty years old before he ever recorded his first album. Soon these commercial recordings began to introduce Albert Hash and the Whitetop Mountain Band to a larger audience. Hash was revered as a fiddle player and luthier, one of the last living embodiments of a local, orally-transmitted fiddle tradition. In addition to G.B. Grayson and Henry Whitter, Hash had inherited his playing and much of his repertoire from the fiddle players who lived around the Whitetop Mountain area, a region of western Grayson County, Virginia, that shares a border with Ashe County in northwest North Carolina. When *Whitetop*, Albert's first commercial album, became available, its track listing was a sampling of a repertoire that had been cultivated over a lifetime of playing in the region.

Most of the songs Albert recorded on his first album were not unique either to himself or to the area but rather signified a cross pollination of various traditional songs that had filtered into the Whitetop region over the years through a variety of sources. "Rabbit up a Gum Stump" had been recorded in 1929 by Hiter Colvin; "Storms Are on the Ocean" can easily be traced back to both the Carter Family and the Delmore Brothers. Other songs on the album, like "Lost John," "Sourwood Mountain," "Whistling Rufus" and "Hangman's Reel," are relatively common fiddle songs found all over America.

Despite this seemingly innocuous track listing, at least one of Hash's songs should have stood out as a truly unique piece to any avid old-time music fan, having never been heard on a record before. "Nancy Blevins" was a peppy dance number recorded in an open D tuning. The song features an A part reminiscent of the tune "Hawks and Eagles" flowing into a unique, driving B part. At the time of *Whitetop*'s release, the song had only existed as a regional anomaly, a relic of a bygone era preserved in the minds of regional fiddlers, but the overall quality of the song itself is evidenced by the fact that it has been repeatedly re-recorded. In the years since its release on the *Whitetop* LP, several other bands, including the Konnarock Critters and the Stairwell Sisters, have recorded versions of the song.

Obviously, discovering songs on records that up until their release had only existed in regional oral culture would have been nothing extraordinary in the folk music boom of the sixties and seventies, but "Nancy Blevins" had something that few orally-transmitted fiddle songs had: a very specific origin story. Albert discussed the song on the album of field recordings *Old Originals Volume Two.* His story, printed in the album's liner notes, claims that the song was "from Crumpler. Some of those people down there. When my granddad, when he was two years old he danced to that…. Anyhow, it was during the Civil War, and he had a cousin—a woman fiddler—she played that and her name was Nancy Blevins, and she just made herself a tune there. And that's the origin of that."[3] Other versions of the story, which Albert often told to interviewers, added details, specifically mentioning that Nancy Blevins was a "young lady, getting up towards grown."

An obvious question presents itself: was Albert's story true? Ashe County, the supposed location of the song's composition, has never been the hotbed for fiddle players that neighboring regions have been. The few well-known fiddler players with strong connections to the county, specifically G.B. Grayson and Frank Blevins (who recorded six songs with the Tar Heel Rattlers), have been noted at least as much for their singing as for their playing abilities. Was it possible that a native of Ashe County, an adolescent girl, for that matter, could create a song that would be carried for more than one hundred years in the oral tradition, or was Albert misremembering? The answer to this question paints a vivid portrait of life in the southern Appalachians.

To discover any possible link between Albert and the mysterious origins of his unique fiddle song requires a bit of knowledge about Albert himself. After all, Albert claims that the real Nancy Blevins was his grandfather's cousin. Unfortunately, discovering Nancy Blevins in Albert's family tree isn't as easy as it might seem.

Albert actually had three grandfathers, or, at least, three men whom he might have referred to as his grandfather in interviews. Little is known to genealogists about his maternal grandfather, Arias Long. He, along with the rest of the Long family, seems to be native to an area of Grayson County removed from the Whitetop area. As a result, the likelihood that they share a connection with a girl from Ashe County, located a considerable distance to the south of Whitetop, seems slim.

The elimination of Albert's maternal grandfather as the source of the story still leaves two possible suspects because Albert had two paternal influences in his life. His father died when Albert was fourteen, and his mother remarried a man who would become Albert's stepfather: Thomas Franklin Reedy. In fact, it is through the Reedy family that Albert first learned the song.[4] His stepfather's brother, James Wiley Reedy, was a fiddle player, and James and Thomas's father, Robert Reedy, a man Albert arguably might have referred to as his grandfather, also knew the tune.

The fact that the song originates with the Reedys seems to suggest that Nancy Blevins, if she was even real, was in fact a relative of Albert's stepfather. Unfortunately, this theory also falls apart on close examination. For one thing, the Reedy family tree, which is well documented, features no mention of a Nancy Blevins, at least not one that would credibly fit with Albert's story. The closest relationship shared to a Nancy Blevins by the Reedys is the mother-in-law of Albert's stepfather's second cousin twice removed. If that distance isn't enough, this Nancy Blevins is much too old to fit with Albert's story, which places the origin of the song around the time of the Civil War. Another point that seems to suggest the Reedy family may not be the branch of Albert's family that first began to orally transmit the song is that they never lived in the region of the song's supposed origin. According to Albert, the song was composed by a young girl living in the Crumpler area of eastern Ashe County, but an evaluation of the 1870 census of Ashe County reveals only four Reedy families living in the entire county, none of whom were closely related to Albert's stepfather, and none of whom lived in the Crumpler area.

Therefore, for Albert's story to be true, Nancy Blevins had to be related to his father, Abraham Hash, but this again seems impossible. The Hash family tree also has no connection at any point to a Nancy Blevins, let alone a young girl living in Ashe County at the time of the Civil War. It would seem, based on purely genealogical evidence, that Albert's story, like so much orally-transmitted folklore before it, was not so much a product of fact as a mutation of information, but there is more truth to Albert's story than genealogical evidence may suggest.

As it turns out, Albert's father, Abraham Hash, was not the first by that name. Albert's great grandfather was also named Abraham. He was born in 1826 and, like most of the Hash family before him dating all the way back to the time of the Revolutionary War, he grew up in Grayson County, Virginia. But Abraham wasn't content to stay where his family had historically resided; he needed a move. Consequently, sometime around 1846 he packed up and moved south to neighboring Ashe County, North Carolina. It was there he married. Whether his wife was the lure that drew him south or just an unexpected result of his relocation is unclear, but Abraham Hash had found a new home. He settled with his new wife, Catherine Stamper, had eight children (Albert's grandfather Benjamin being the sixth) and began a new life. By the time of the 1860 census, Abraham was doing well in his new home. He was listed as a farmer, and he must have been a successful one. His property was valued at six hundred dollars, considerably more than that of many of his neighbors.

Abraham had chosen to settle in the vibrant community of Chestnut Hill in eastern Ashe County, the precise community that is a possible birthplace of G.B. Grayson. The farmland of this area, near the New River, was much more arable than the rugged terrain near the Tennessee border, and it attracted many families looking for a new life.

One of the clans living near the newly-transplanted household of Abraham Hash was the Blevins family. Like the Hashes, Martha and Alvis Blevins were also looking to establish a prosperous life in the farmland around the New River. They were just one of several Blevins households living in the area and were not significantly different from the other families living around them. According to the 1870 census, they were respectively listed as homemaker and farmer and had four children: William, Frankey, Tobias, and Nancy.

Nancy Blevins was born on November 5, 1852, in the Chestnut Hill community of Ashe (an area later referred to as Crumpler). Despite the fact that she was assuredly no relation to the Hash family, she would have been the right age to be the young girl fiddler Albert recalls in his story. This is notable because at the time of the Civil War, the time Albert claims his grandfather was first exposed to the song, there were only seven residents in all of Ashe County named Nancy Blevins. Of these potential candidates, most were too old to be the Nancy Blevins of Albert's story, and only one lived in the Crumpler area. An adolescent Nancy Blevins living in the Crumpler community near the farm on which Albert's grandfather grew up suddenly provides strong evidence that there was a kernel of truth in the tale Albert remembered. But could Nancy play the fiddle?

That seems a more difficult question to answer. Marriage licenses and census records report names and dates from people of the past, but personalities and pastimes are more difficult to discover. To find out whether Nancy Blevins was indeed the same Nancy associated with Albert's fiddle tune, proof of her fiddle playing would have to emerge.

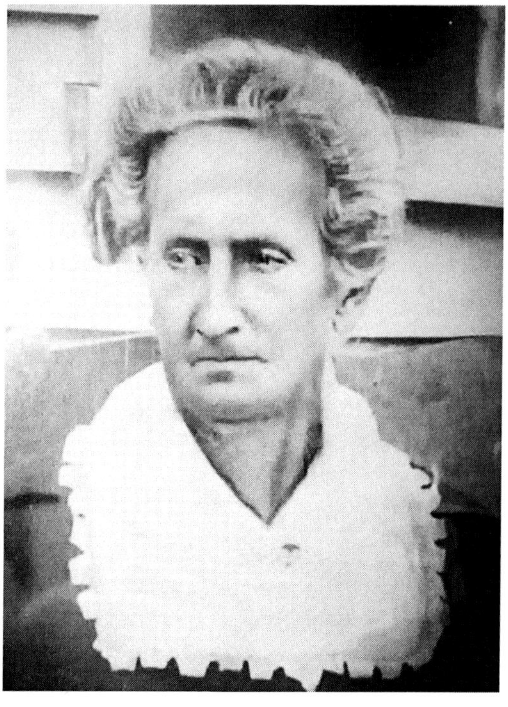

A portrait of Nancy Baker, born Nancy Blevins. Nancy Baker lived next door to Henry Whitter and was the grandmother of Whitter's wife, Hattie Baker. She was also the fiddler who composed the tune "Nancy Blevins" (courtesy Haynes Baker family).

At the end of the Civil War, the adolescent Nancy Blevins was a neighbor of Albert's grandfather, but she wouldn't stay Nancy Blevins for long. A marriage to James Franklin Baker sometime after 1870 would change her name to Nancy Baker, and she was known affectionately to friends and family as "Nan" or "Nannie." Mrs. Baker settled in an area near her family home with her new husband and would go on to start a family. Some of her children grew up and moved on, but several stayed nearby, and it is from their descendants that a fuller picture of the mysterious Nancy Blevins Baker becomes clear.

She did play the fiddle. She played it well, and she played it in public performances. One of her descendants recalls her playing at the Healing Springs Hotel, a retreat built near Nancy's home to attract visitors to the medicinal waters that supposedly sprang from a nearby hillside, waters which one medical journal of the era described as possessing "valuable qualities as a mild antacid, tonic and alternative. It is useful in many of the afflictions benefited by this class of waters."[5] The building of the hotel dates to 1888, so Mrs. Baker, then a wife and mother of seven, would have then been entertaining guests as a middle-aged woman.

But being a female fiddle player entertaining guests seeking curative mineral water wasn't all that made Nancy Baker unique. She was a witch. Or at least that's the claim of many descendants who recall dabbling in witchcraft to be one of her defining traits. She was also a lover of tobacco and made an impression on several grandchildren with the archaic clay pipe she smoked in her later years.

But discovering a fiddle-playing, pipe-smoking practitioner of witchcraft is actually not the most surprising thing about this bizarre story. In one of the most coincidental turns possible, this mysterious Nancy Blevins Baker, the composer of the mysterious fiddle song that Albert would proudly record multiple times in his later years, was the grandmother of Hattie Baker, Henry Whitter's fourth wife. In fact, when Whitter married Hattie, they moved next door to Nannie, who was still living in Healing Springs at the time. That means that during the period when Albert was first playing with Henry Whitter, possibly even playing "Nancy Blevins," he was literally next door to the song's composer. Neither Whitter nor Hash ever suspected the strange connection they shared through this Civil War–era fiddle tune.

The circumstantial evidence that Nancy Blevins Baker was in fact the Nancy Blevins of Albert's story seems strong. Not only was she a fiddle player, but she was also the right age and living in the right community to be the young musician Albert's grandfather remembered. But one key question remains. How did the song migrate? According to Albert, he didn't learn the song from the Hash side of the family; he instead claims to have learned it from the Reedy family, a clan that never lived in Ashe County. If the Hashes were the first branch of Albert's tree to hear the song, why didn't they teach it to the young Albert? Why didn't his father teach him the song?

The answer, to that last question, at least, is an easy one. Albert's father, Abraham Hash, couldn't play the fiddle. It wasn't because he had no interest or no talent. What he was lacking was an arm. His had been lost as a result of a hunting accident, making it impossible for him to play. If the young Albert was to find instruction about fiddle playing, it would have had to come from other sources, like his uncle Emmet Long, his neighbor Corbitt Stamper, or the family of his stepfather.

But how did a song written and popularized by a girl in eastern Ashe County, North Carolina, make it to Grayson County, Virginia? The answer to that question might be closely tied to the Civil War.

As in G.B. Grayson's Johnson County, Tennessee, the mood in the Appalachian mountain communities where the Hash and Blevins families would have lived during the Civil War was tense. Although they were far removed from the famous battles and generals of Tennessee and northern Virginia, Ashe County residents suffered greatly as a result of the conflict. One historian notes that "what existed in the western counties [of North Carolina], from about mid–1862 until the war's end … was a sullen, smoldering atmosphere of deprivation and anxiety, of the constant possibility of violence."[6]

As was seen in experiences of G.B. Grayson's ancestors in Tennessee, the Appalachian region suffered particularly from political divisions during the Civil War, with some regions and families favoring the Confederate cause, others favoring the Union. In Grayson's home of Johnson County, local sympathies were overwhelmingly in favor of the Union. In neighboring Ashe County, where the Hash and Blevins family were living, allegiances were more divided. In fact, a clear line of demarcation, in the form of the New River's north fork, roughly divided the county between the pro–Confederate landholders of eastern Ashe, an area of large prosperous farms nestled near the relatively flat, fertile soil of the New River, and the generally poorer Union sympathizers living on more rugged tracts in the western half of the county near the Tennessee border. Among residents, even those not directly engaged in military conflict, these allegiances were taken very seriously. In fact, young Nancy Blevins' future father-in-law, Bolen Bill Baker, is remembered as being so staunchly pro–Confederate that he assisted in the lynching of deserters whom he felt were disloyal to the Southern cause.

It was sometime around the Civil War that the Hash family chose to leave their farm in Chestnut Hill in order to return to western Grayson County, Abraham Hash's family home. It could be argued that the timing of this move away from the pro–Confederate environment of eastern Ashe County was a coincidence. However, the fact that, as late as 1860, Abraham

Hash and his family seemed so rooted in Ashe County seems to suggest that their sudden move was unplanned, his wife and children all having been born in Chestnut Hill and his property exceeding the value of many of his neighbors. The fact that the Hash family may have suddenly found hostility among their pro–Confederate neighbors can never be known for sure, but the full name of Albert Hash's father, Abraham Lincoln Hash, born after the family left Ashe County, only one generation removed from the Civil War, may provide a clue about the family's allegiances.

The family's move back to Grayson County is recorded in the census records, which show Abraham and his family disappearing from North Carolina and reappearing on the Virginia rolls in 1870. It would seem that along with their belongings, families like the Hashes brought something back with them from Crumpler: a fiddle song that would take root in the Whitetop region and continue to flourish, both through oral transmission and modern recorded media. When Albert later began playing with Henry Whitter at his home in Healing Springs, he could have never guessed that the roots of his fiddle tune could literally have been found next door.

The Music

Overview

Despite the fact that G.B. Grayson and Henry Whitter exemplify many of the influences and societal trends of the Appalachian region occurring at the beginning of the twentieth century, the duo would have been long forgotten had it not been for the recorded legacy they left behind. This legacy was created over the course of seven recording sessions between October of 1927 and October 1929. Although that may seem like a substantial career, the sessions were quite spread out: their final recording date, in late September 1929, took place a year after their previous recording date, August of 1928. Consequently, this two-year career as a duo produced only forty-one sides. Deducting unissued releases and songs that were recorded more than once for different labels, the duo left behind only thirty-two songs.[1] However, this canon of recordings has had an impressive influence over later artists. For example, compare the output of Grayson and Whitter with that of Dick Parman, who recorded thirty sides under his own name from November of 1928 to October of 1930, or John McGee and Frank Welling, who recorded more than one hundred and twenty sides from 1927 to 1929, artists whose songs have largely faded into history, rarely referenced or re-released. By contrast, Grayson and Whitter's entire catalog has been re-released, either on vinyl record or CD. Their songs have found their way into various genres, and many of the songs they were the first to record have become so ubiquitous in folk and bluegrass music that it's hard to find an artist in these genres who doesn't play at least a few. Their influence in traditional music circles is so profound that in 1996, Ralph Stanley released *Short Life of Trouble*, an entire album of Grayson and Whitter covers.

Most of the credit for this longevity and influence can be attributed to G.B. Grayson. Although it was Whitter's business acumen that brought the duo to the recording studio initially, and although Whitter's guitar backup and vocal asides were an important component of the duo's charm, it was Grayson's strong voice, straightforward playing style, and song selec-

G.B. Grayson with fiddle and Henry Whitter with guitar (courtesy Southern Folklife Collection, Louis Round Wilson Special Collections Library, University of North Carolina at Chapel Hill).

tions that would elevate the pair into the towering influence they would become. The singing and playing of Grayson is itself rewarding to hear, but an exploration of the roots of Grayson's repertoire adds an additional layer of meaning to these influential recordings.

Unlike many artists who came before and after, G.B. Grayson was hard to categorize. Some artists, like Doc Roberts and Gid Tanner, focused almost exclusively on fiddle tunes, largely ignoring ballads and Victorian parlor songs. Others, like Vernon Dalhart, gravitated almost entirely to heartfelt songs of love and loss. Still others, like Chris Bouchillon, recorded a disproportionate number of comedic and novelty songs. Grayson did all of this and more. The songs he recorded with Whitter cover a wide expanse: instrumental and vocal, tragic and comedic, ancient and modern. Consequently, Grayson and Whitter's recordings provide a glance of something that can't be seen in the catalog of the Skillet Lickers, or the Hill Billies, or Vernon Dalhart: a comprehensive view of the authentic musical influences of the southern Appalachian region. This region, which has historically been characterized as an isolated world of archaic ballads and rustic dance tunes, gains new life in the catalog of Grayson and Whitter. Clearly, the rural mountains were experiencing a bombardment of just as many, if not more, musical influences as would be found on the streets of Manhattan.

Like with any folk music canon, an attempt to codify and categorize Grayson and Whitter's output is difficult because so many of their songs can be seen as existing in multiple categories simultaneously—is "Train 45" a railroad song or a dance tune, for example?—but some clear groupings are possible. First, it is worth noting that there are some common hillbilly subgenres that are not found in their repertoire. For example, the duo recorded no gospel songs or blues songs.[2] They did, however, record examples of many other categories of hillbilly songs, including several traditional dance tunes, songs that were generally recorded dozens of times by other artists, and several well-documented native ballads. They also had a strong affinity for railroad songs and, more unusually, for temperance songs. They have a couple of comedic songs recorded solely for novelty, a few more contemporary Tin Pan Alley songs, and the remainder of their catalog can be viewed as folksongs as defined by George Malcolm Laws. By going through each of these groupings, exploring their history as well as how they were manifested in Grayson and Whitter's catalog, an overall sense of the music of the region emerges. In this capacity, Grayson and Whitter still have a lot to say as the Appalachian region advances into the twenty-first century.

G. B. GRAYSON
VICTOR AND GENETTE RECORD ARTIST
AND RADIO ENTERTAINER
LAUREL BLOOMERY, TENN.

G.B. Grayson was eager to become a recorded musician. This business card, which Grayson had printed, illustrated his desire to advertise himself as a professional (courtesy Brian and Ann Baker Forehand).

The Dance Tunes

G.B. Grayson was an excellent singer, and he sang much more than most lead instrumentalists, but he would probably have preferred to be remembered as a fiddler. He often competed against other well-known fiddlers in local contests and was a documented winner at least once. Many of the anecdotal stories surrounding him reference his prowess as a fiddle player; supposedly John Carson referred to him as the best fiddler he'd ever heard.[3]

Additionally, he performed primarily at social functions, like dances, molasses makings, and celebrations of the last day of school, which would have required at least as much fiddling as singing. However, when thinking of master fiddlers, Eck Robertson, Doc Roberts, and Clayton McMichen, for example, Grayson doesn't seem to exactly fit in. His style, although precise and clean, is unadorned in comparison to others. He also tends to closely orbit the melody of the song, refraining from the exotic mutations that can be heard in the work of these other fiddlers.

One song which fully encapsulates both the strengths and weaknesses of Grayson's fiddle playing is "Sally Gooden," an especially common tune played by almost every fiddler who ever picked up a bow. When Grayson recorded his version on February 21, 1928, during his and Whitter's second recording session for the Gennett label, the song had already been recorded by sixteen other artists. In fact, the first recording ever made of a fiddle player was a recording of Eck Robertson playing the song. This song, like many fiddle tunes, has a strong beat and is meant to be used as an up-tempo dance number. Consequently, it was not uncommon for fiddlers or dance callers to add random verses, many times nonsensical, to the song for the sake of variety. This is a common practice with dance tunes, which Norm and Anne Cohen refer to as songs in the "assembly tradition." This means that, unlike ballads, which tend to follow fairly rigid lyrical structure, dance tunes are open to creative changes, with new verses being added and subtracted at the whim of the performer.[4]

Because of this song's ubiquitous nature, "Sally Gooden" can be used to examine the variety of stylistic approaches that exist between one fiddler and the next. Grayson's version is not without its charms, but his simple playing style never elevates the song beyond its humble melody. Compare his version of "Sally Gooden," a steady recycling of a single melodic line, to the version recorded by Eck Robertson, which utilizes a dizzying array of approaches and technical skill to reframe and reinterpret the melody of the song. This is not meant to suggest that Grayson's recording is somehow worse than versions produced by more technical players. In fact, it is often the case that the most appealing part of Grayson's dance tunes is his singing and vocal asides, tossed off statements like "I don't know where I'm going but I'm on my way," and verses like "Look at Sally / Isn't she a daisy / The fiddler's drunk / And Sally's crazy." In fact, in Grayson's performance, the song fully captures the celebratory mood of a neighborhood party, something that can't be said for some of the more technically-advanced versions of the song. Through his lyrical additions, Grayson's "Sally Gooden" becomes almost as much a celebration of drinking as of Sally herself. Aside from the previously-mentioned verse, Grayson twice repeats a verse proclaiming, "It's so dark / The road's so muddy / I'm so drunk / I can't stand steady."

This rollicking approach, utilizing fiddle tunes as a gateway to debauchery, is also on display in another classic dance tune, "Shout Lula," the first fiddle tune Grayson and Whitter ever recorded. This recording was made during their first session in October 1927 for the Gennett label. Like "Sally Gooden," the strength of the song lies less in the fiddling and more in the hollering. Although ably played with the strong, steady beat necessary for a dance number, like in "Sally Gooden," Grayson's playing maintains a steady repetition of the melody, with only slight variation throughout. The lyrical additions by Grayson are what elevate the song into a boisterous tune of celebration. The song is a classic fiddle standard, commonly found in folklore collections, many of which date from decades before Grayson's recording, with various titles, including "Lulu" and "Hook and Line."

The "Hook and Line" title references verses not found in Grayson's version which deal with fishing and life near the river. Many of the traditional verses also revolve around slave life, featuring black characters and complaints about former masters. In fact, most verses of the song that have been collected by folklorists are not included in Grayson's version. It is a pity that Grayson didn't know some of the more exotic verses to the song since they are quite memorable. Lines like "Now [my old missus]'s dead and gone to hell / hope the devil'll chunk her well" and "Went to the river couldn't get across / jumped on a possum and thought he was a horse" could only have added to the overall frivolity of Grayson and Whitter's recording.[5]

The verses of "Shout Lula" that Grayson does include are traditional. He most commonly uses the "Shout Little Lula shout, shout / Tell me what you're shouting 'bout," but he also includes the much more suggestive line "How many nickels will it take / To see little Lula's body shake," a variation on a traditional verse. Further adding to the party atmosphere generated by the recording, Grayson asks Whitter, "When are you going to pass that bottle?" to which Whitter replies, "About ten minutes."

Aside from fiddle songs that celebrate women and alcohol, Grayson also seemed attracted to songs with a barnyard theme. Of the six dance tunes he recorded, two prominently feature clucking and cackling hens. The first of the two, "Cluck Old Hen," was recorded in February 1928 during Grayson and Whitter's second Gennett session. Like the previously-mentioned dance songs, this tune is in no way unique to Grayson.

Interestingly, though, every artist who did release a record of the song during the pre-war years was present at the 1925 Mountain City fiddlers' convention, Fiddlin' Powers and Family, the Hill Billies, and G.B. Grayson, so an argument could be made that the song had a stronger presence in the area around east Tennessee than it did in the piedmont region of North Carolina or the deep South.

Like "Shout Lula," this song seems to be at least partially rooted in an African American tradition. It first appeared in print five years before its first recording in *Negro Folk Rhymes*, a collection of traditionally black song lyrics.[6] Grayson's version is very similar to the versions recorded by the Hill Billies and Fiddlin' Powers and Family, which all seem to be largely pulling from a common pool of verses. For instance, all three groups begin the song with the same verse: "Cluck old hen, cluck and sing / You ain't laid an egg since way last spring." The version recorded by the Hill Billies is very similar lyrically to the version recorded by Fiddlin' Powers and Family, although the Hill Billies' version is notably more exciting and varied in its overall performance. Both versions include several references to railroads in the course of singing a song ostensibly about chickens: "My old hen's a good old hen / She lays eggs for the railroad men," for example. Grayson and Whitter's version shares two verses in common with the other recordings, but some of Grayson's verses are downright bizarre. Lines unique to Grayson's rendition include "Cluck old hen, cluck your best / You'll soon be clucking way out west" and "The old hen clucked, she clucked might loud / Because she escaped that trashy crowd." Of course, Grayson took the opportunity to make note of his own thoughts between verses, shouting, "Pass that chicken, I want a wing."

In terms of fiddling, "Cluck Old Hen" is one of Grayson's more notable performances. Unlike the Fiddlin' Powers version, which is oppressively repetitive, Grayson's fiddle work breathes vitality into the song. He maintains a strong, accented downbeat throughout, giving the song a danceable rhythm, much like the Hill Billies' version but unlike the Fiddlin' Powers version, which is a good deal slower. For variety, at several points he shifts into a new rhythm, playing a greater number of notes per measure. He also takes a different approach on the second part of the tune. Most versions of "Cluck Old Hen" are characterized by a B part in which the fiddle strings are plucked rather than bowed to mimic the sound of a clucking chicken. This technique was employed in both versions of the song recorded before Grayson and Whitter's, and most that have come afterward. Grayson does take several opportunities to show off his ability to mimic the sounds of a chicken but doesn't employ the plucked fiddle strings, instead using slurs on the fiddle, and, more unusually, his own voice, to throw in added barnyard ambience.

Grayson's interest in capturing the sounds of contented poultry is also on full display in his other farm themed tune: "Barnyard Serenade." This song is more commonly known as "Cackling Hen" and has been recorded numerous times. Like "Sally Gooden," this song dates to the very earliest country recordings; it was one of the songs recorded by Fiddlin' John Carson during his first-ever recording session, the same session that created the first commercially-marketed country record. By the time Grayson and Whitter got around to recording the song, it had already been recorded seventeen times, and by the end of the Depression, it would ultimately be recorded thirty times under various titles.

The song itself is another one with a long history. It was first documented in a folklore collection around 1905 and was defined then, as now, for its distinctive chicken mimicry.[7] The B part of the song involves imitating a cackling chicken as realistically as the fiddler can muster. Oftentimes this B part includes not only the cackle, but also various other clucks and crows, provided by the fiddler's own voice. Grayson is a bit restrained in his performance, relying on the fiddle rather than his own vocals to provide the barnyard sound effects. However, he does use two different approaches to creating the distinctive cackle: a sharp pull off and a more fluid slide.

Even though he doesn't add any vocal cackles or crows himself, Grayson can't resist the urge to talk and sing over a song that usually includes no vocal part. To find verses to include in this version of the song, Grayson raids the lyrics of "Cluck Old Hen," repeating the verse "The old hen cackled she cackled in the lot / the next time she cackled, she cackled in the pot," a line that both Fiddlin' Powers and the Hill Billies include in "Cluck Old Hen," but which Grayson only uses in "Barnyard Serenade."

The barnyard theme is also present in one of Grayson's more exotic fiddle tunes, "Old Jimmie Sutton." Before 1940, this song was only ever recorded by Grayson and Whitter. It is not quite as well known as most of his other dance tunes and is currently one of the rarest Grayson and Whitter records in existence. The song, though not as popular as many other tunes recorded by Grayson, does have a documented regional popularity. In 1959, during an interview with Alan Lomax, guitar player Spencer Moore from Chilhowie, Virginia, was recorded playing the song. When asked where he learned it he said, "Well I learned from my dad, and that Grayson." Moore added that his father, who regularly played with G.B. Grayson at Ock Roark's service station in Konnarock, had learned the song when he was young and had played it throughout his life. Alan Lomax had apparently also run into the song earlier, also in southwest Virginia. While visiting Walter Henderson at his home in Rugby, Virginia, in September of 1941, he noted that Wade Reedy performed the song on the banjo. This song was also collected from both Vester Jones and Glen Smith in southwest Virginia; these recordings were released on the Folkways album *Traditional Music from Grayson and Carroll Counties*. The liner notes to this album note that the melody to the song was still commonly played in southwest Virginia in the late 1950s, but the words were becoming harder to find.[8]

Spencer Moore's 1959 recording of the song gives a good insight into its lyrical structure, which is largely absent on the Grayson and Whitter recording. Moore's version is full of farm imagery, particularly relating to goats and sheep, lines like "Sheep and a goat sitting in a pasture / Sheep said to goat, can you go a little faster" and "Sheep fell down and bumped his chin / God almighty how the billy goat grinned." These verses are lost in the Grayson and Whitter version, but Grayson does retain some sheep imagery with the line "Picked up a rock as big as a button / and killed Jimmy Sutton just as dead as a mutton, as a sheep, sheep."

Whatever the roots of the song, its vocal component was probably neglected by Grayson because, for him, it had definitely fallen into use as a fiddle-based dance number. This is easily ascertained when listening to Grayson and Whitter's recording, which begins with a skit, something that was quite commonly found in the recordings of other artists, like the Skillet Lickers, but which Grayson and Whitter only used on this recording. Grayson says at the beginning of the record, "Each one of you get your girl, and let's fix to start the dance right away. We're going to give you an old breakdown entitled 'Old Jimmy Sutton.'" The attempt to recreate the dance atmosphere continues as Grayson shows off his ability to shout out square dance calls between verses without ever breaking the rhythm of his fiddling, scolding the fictional dancers whom he senses are falling behind. More than any other Grayson and Whitter recording, this song gives a hint to the power Grayson had as a local entertainer. For someone hosting a neighborhood dance, he would have been indispensable: a rhythmic dance fiddler who not only sang but also called intricate square dance moves—a hillbilly triple threat.

The final fiddle-based dance tune Grayson recorded moved from the barnyard to the nursery. "What You Gonna Do with the Baby" was recorded for the Victor label in 1929 during the duo's final session. Based on studio log notations, it was also possibly the last song they ever recorded together.

Grayson and Whitter weren't the first to record it; the Hodges Brothers had recorded it a year earlier, but their version was never released. The song wouldn't be recorded again until Steve Ledford, the fiddler who helped transition many of Grayson and Whitter's songs into the bluegrass realm, recorded the song in 1940 with his group, the Happy-Go-Lucky-Boys. Similarly, J.E. Mainer, another proto-bluegrass artist who carried many of Grayson and Whitter's songs into the mainstream, also recorded an upbeat version of the song in 1946.

The song is much older than Grayson, having been first noted in Cecil Sharp's second volume of *English Folk Songs from the Southern Appalachians* in 1917. Late in their careers, the Coon Creek Girls would record a version of the song that included four-line stanzas and choruses with layered harmonies. The original song is a very simple one that follows the model of a typical dance tune: a tune with strong rhythm featuring sometimes nonsensical couplets added for vocal effect. Unlike some of the more raucous dance tunes, "What You Gonna Do with the Baby" is an innocent song in which each couplet details some silly behavior directed toward a baby: "Wrap him up in calico / send him back to Georgia-O," "Wrap it up in a tablecloth / Toss it up in a stable loft," etc.

Interestingly, the song seems to have a convoluted relationship with a minstrel tune written in 1843, "Dandy Jim from Caroline." Although the two songs would at first glance seem to have absolutely nothing in common, the connection is in the line from "Dandy Jim," "I look in the glass and found twas so / Jus' what massa told me, O." Apparently this chorus, which ends the last two lines with an "O," was fertile ground for parody. By the 1920s, songs like "Sugar in my Coffee-O" and "Prettiest Little Gal in the County-O" were clearly all orbiting the same source material as "What You Gonna Do with the Baby": similar melodies, rhyming couplets, and a disproportionate number of lines ended in "O" all suggest that the songs have a common ancestor, quite possibly "Dandy Jim from Caroline."

How this version of the song came to be associated with babies is more mysterious. Well-known ballad singer Jean Ritchie has claimed that the song was developed by mothers, who used the existing tune to the song and paired it with nursery-themed couplets while rocking children.[9]

Grayson's version of the song, like "Sally Gooden," is free from much musical variety and experimentation, with vocal refrains thrown in throughout. The strong use of downbeats by Grayson drives home the song's use in his repertoire as a dance number. Despite its nursery rhyme–style imagery, Grayson clearly intends for the song to get adults on the dance floor, not to entertain children. Toward the end of the song, Grayson can't resist the urge to overtly reference this dancing beat when he shouts, "Swing that gal with the red dress on."

Grayson was clearly someone who viewed a fiddler's role as more utilitarian: his playing style and calls suggest that he saw himself as a dance orchestrator more than a virtuosic artist. However, he did record one fiddle tune whose purpose was primarily to show off the prowess of the fiddler: "Going Down the Lee Highway." This tune is not one that lends itself as easily to dancing, featuring an unusual C part, in which the fiddler slides into a sustained second position note that can be held for any number of desired measures. This structure and style of playing is something characteristic of "show off" pieces like "Orange Blossom Special."[10] Despite the fact that "Going Down the Lee Highway" isn't the typical dance number that Grayson and Whitter otherwise recorded, no other fiddle tune is so strongly associated with the duo.

This close association has led many to assume that Grayson wrote the song. The liner notes for a collection of Grayson and Whitter reissues on the Davis Unlimited label, titled *Going Down the Lee Highway*, relates a commonly retold story about the song: "Grayson's 'Going Down the Lee Highway' was composed in the back seat of Whitter's Model T Ford as the car chugged down U.S. 11 (Lee Highway) on the way to the session where the song was recorded."[11] Some elements of this story are true: the song was recorded in Memphis, which probably would have meant that the duo rode the Lee Highway for at least a short leg of the journey, but the song Grayson may have played in the backseat of Whitter's car wasn't an original composition; it had been recorded a year earlier by the Roane County Ramblers, who called the tune "Home Town Blues."

The Roane County Ramblers were led by Jimmy McCarroll, a virtuosic fiddler known for original compositions, his most famous being "Southern No. 111," in which depots are called out while the fiddle expertly mimics the sounds of a train.[12] Like "Going Down the Lee Highway," "Southern No. 111" has little use as a dance number but is designed more as a showcase for fiddling ability. Interestingly, as expert a fiddler as McCarroll was, his version of "Home Town Blues," which was quite probably his own composition, leaves room for improvement. Compared to Grayson and Whitter's version, the Roane County Ramblers' performance of the song is notably slower paced. McCarroll's fiddling on the original is skillful and features many of the complexities the Grayson version is known for—the slide into second position, the tremolo on the high note—but McCarroll's overall performance is hampered by his rhythm section, which features a constant banging of chords on the banjo and guitar.

This is one of several instances where the power of a Grayson and Whitter record comes as much from Whitter as from Grayson. Although his guitar work features none of the more elaborate bass runs that are featured in some of the duo's other songs, Whitter's ability to alternate the downbeat note on the guitar gives the song a nice bounce, which Grayson is able to build on with his precise playing.

Whitter also makes his presence known on the record through extemporaneous comments, something he usually leaves primarily to Grayson. In fact, it is Whitter who says at the end of the record, "I've got those Lee Highway Blues," a tossed-off comment that would forever change the title of the song from the wordy "Going Down the Lee Highway" to the much more commonly used "Lee Highway Blues." Whitter also takes the opportunity to insert some homespun philosophy, asking, "Why is man born to die?" during each playing of the song's C part. Why he felt this questioning of humanity's ultimate existence was an appropriate addition to a lively fiddle instrumental will have to remain a mystery, but there is no doubt that this version of the song, although not the original, is definitely the version that is most often remembered today.

The Murder Ballads

Grayson and Whitter records cover a wide expanse of material, but it is their murder ballad recordings that seem to garner much of the attention from writers. This is for good reason: every ballad they recorded has since become a standard tune for folk and bluegrass players. It could be a coincidence; it could be that Grayson just had a keen ear for which songs would attract future listeners and which would not; or it could be that Grayson's strong, clear singing, coupled with his clear, simple fiddle melodies, created a sound that would have attracted listeners to anything he chose to record. Whatever the reason, these songs are today some of the most widely known in the catalog of American murder ballads. Each of these songs—"I'll Never Be Yours," "Rose Conley," and "Ommie Wise"—tell similar stories, and when examined side by side, their commonalities become even more apparent. The other story of murder recorded by Grayson and Whitter, "Tom Dooley," which has already been examined, doesn't maintain a clear narrative arc and doesn't meet the strictest definition of a ballad.

"I'll Never Be Yours," more popularly known as "Banks of the Ohio," was one of the first songs recorded by Grayson and Whitter, during their first session for Gennett. This is oddly appropriate, since this song provides a strong link to some of the oldest ballad traditions in American music. "I'll Never Be Yours" (which George Malcolm Laws documents as "On the Banks of the Ohio") is closely linked to several other American ballads that depict couples discussing their futures before the boy violently attacks his love, killing her for a seeming rejection. Brown notes that this song bears a striking resemblance to "The Lexington Murder" and "Knoxville Girl," songs which, in turn, owe their origins to a British broadside tradition of songs like "The Oxford Girl" and "The Berkshire Tragedy," which date to at least the end of the eighteenth century. These British broadsides were lyrics to songs printed on single sheets of paper and sold to a population looking for cheap entertainment. These songs spread throughout the British Isles and were most widely disseminated during the seventeenth and eighteenth centuries. To see how effectively these ballads infiltrated the folk tradition and arrived in America, consider these lines from "The Berkshire Tragedy"[13] broadside published in England in 1796: "Told her if she'd walk with me / Aside a little way / We both together would agree / All about our wedding day." When compared to the first line of Grayson and Whitter's "I'll Never Be Yours" which begins, "I asked my love to take a walk / Just a walk a little ways / On we walked and as we talked / About our future wedding day," it seems apparent that "I'll Never Be Yours" is closely connected to a wider British tradition.

The inclusion of the chorus, which invariably features the line in which the false lover promises his ill-fated girlfriend a home "Down beside where the waters flow / On the banks of the Ohio," is what differentiates this song from some of its close cousins. Interestingly, there is evidence to suggest that this notable inclusion comes from an American pioneer song. In 1842, a song titled "Banks of the Ohio" was published in the *Forget-Me-Not Songster* to encourage pioneer settlement in the Midwest. Like the murder ballad, this song advertises domestic bliss and happiness along the banks of the Ohio River. It features the chorus, "Come all you young men who have mind for to range / Into the western country your station for to change / For seeking some new pleasure we'll all together go / And we'll settle on the banks of the pleasant Ohio,"[14] a strikingly similar phrasing and word choice which points to a cross pollination between these American songs of pioneer settlement and the larger British ballad tradition.

"I'll Never Be Yours" had been recorded once prior to Grayson and Whitter by Red Patterson's Piedmont Log Rollers. They recorded the song, which they titled "Down on the Banks of the Ohio," a few months before Grayson and Whitter, in August of 1927. The Piedmont Log Rollers version of the song contains several verses not found in the Grayson and Whitter recording, but the two are largely similar, utilizing an identical melody, a parallel narrative, and the same chorus. However, the Piedmont Log Rollers employ a very formal approach to the song's performance. The inclusion of a banjo fills out the sound and provides a lighthearted bounce to the arrangement. Similarly, lead singer Red Patterson's vocals are almost operatic, featuring a trembling delivery in a high register. The fiddle follows the melody but, like the vocals, is often played much higher, sometimes sounding almost like a musical saw. As a result, the violent ballad is robbed of some of its weightiness.

As with all their ballads, "I'll Never Be Yours" actually benefits from Grayson and Whitter's lack of instrumentation. Whereas their dance tunes can never reach the roisterous height of bands like the Skillet Lickers, which utilized a banjo, guitar, and multiple fiddles, their ballads are more intimate and haunting as a result of the simple instrumentation. Unlike the Piedmont Log Rollers, Grayson and Whitter's simpler version of the song, played at a slightly quicker pace, puts more focus on the lyrics, which are well suited to Grayson's down-to-earth delivery. Grayson's fiddle follows the melody but never overpowers the vocals, and Whitter's simple guitar backup, free from elaborate bass runs and other decorations, pushes the rhythm along subtly in the background. Unlike the dance tunes, which lent themselves to rowdy outbursts, no lighthearted asides are added by the duo during the course of the song. Instead, Whitter chimes in only on the chorus, repeating Grayson's lines, and Grayson himself ends the record with his oft repeated phrase "Girls take warning."

The verses and phrases used by Grayson are the ones that found their way into most subsequent versions of the song, released by groups like the Monroe Brothers and the Blue Sky Boys. Grayson doesn't include the typical final verse, in which the murderer is discovered by the sheriff and led to meet his fate, but this could be because of the time constraints of the record. Despite this omission, when compared to the Piedmont Log Rollers version of the song, it is clear that Grayson's recording carried the most influence on later artists. The Log Rollers include several verses which were never adopted in later versions. Similarly, notable differences in some of the phrases of the song further demonstrate the extent to which Grayson and Whitter's version became the canonical one in folk music traditions. For example, in Grayson's version, the girl is led to the river by her little hands, something common in later versions. The Piedmont Log Rollers, in contrast, sing about the girl being dragged to the river by her golden curls.

"I'll Never Be Yours" is just one of many songs that migrated into the American folk tradition from England, Scotland, and Ireland, although tracing their exact history can sometimes be challenging. One of these apparently British songs with murky backstories also found its way into Grayson and Whitter's catalogue: "Rose Conley." This song, which the duo recorded during their second session in October of 1927, traces its immediate history to the American Southeast, where it has been repeatedly collected by folklorists. John Cox noted in his collection *Folk-Songs of the South* that a version of the song collected in 1915 had been "popular in the oil fields of Wetzel County [West Virginia]" about 1895. Frank C. Brown's collection of North Carolina folk songs goes even further, theorizing that the song has a supposed Irish origin, despite the fact that it is found almost exclusively in America.

The song is clearly indebted to the same tradition that produced "I'll Never Be Yours" and "The Berkshire Tragedy." As with those songs, "Rose Conley" describes a man meeting up with a girlfriend in a remote setting and, seemingly without warning, violently attacking her and throwing her into a river, but the same can also be said of other distinctly American songs. Consequently, the belief that "Rose Conley" has a history beyond nineteenth-century America is only a theory.

However, unlike some other ballads, there is strong evidence to believe that "Rose Conley" is indeed a song rooted in the Irish tradition. In an article titled "'Rose Connoley': An Irish Ballad," D.K. Wilgus notes that the song is traditionally sung to the melody of an Irish song, "Rosin the Beau." He further notes that at least one version of the song has been collected in Ireland, and the specificity of its lyrics makes it reasonable to suspect it represents a more original version than many of the versions collected in America.

Wilgus bases his argument on the fact that "Rose Conley" exists in two distinct forms: an older, more original version, which begins with an introductory stanza, often featuring a line like "Come all young men and pretty fair ladies, and warning take from me / And never go a-courting down under the Willow Tree,"[15] and another version, more streamlined and shaped by repeated transmission, which begins with the line "Down in the willow garden."

It is the second version, which drops the introductory stanza and also a final stanza in which the murderer's name is included, that Grayson and Whitter recorded as "Rose Conley." Whether Grayson knew the fuller version and chose to record the more concise form can never be known, but his version, the first ever recorded, has become the standard for all subsequent recordings of the song.

That is not to say that all versions of the song are carbon copies of Grayson's. One of the most debated lines in the song involves the wine given to the unfortunate girlfriend just before her death. Most versions collected by folklorists, as well as Grayson's version, refer to it as the nonsensical "burglar's wine." Other performers, notably Charlie Monroe, whose 1947 recording of the song "Down in the Willow Garden" is probably the most widely known, attempted to clean up this bizarre image with the substitution of "burgundy wine." Other versions include strange concoctions like "merkley wine,"[16] adding further confusion to the death of the poor female victim, who in many versions is systematically poisoned, stabbed, and thrown in the river. An explanation that might have some historical merit contends that "burglar's wine" is actually a mutation of burgaloo, a popular early American pear variety.[17] Given that the only version of the song collected in Ireland doesn't contain anything close to "burglar wine," instead merely stating, "A bottle of poison I bought her,"[18] this potential explanation seems plausible.

Grayson and Whitter's performance of the song had a strong influence on later versions of the song, particularly the previously mentioned version recorded by Charlie Monroe. Like with all of their songs, they utilize sparse instrumentation which Grayson keeps to a minimum by adding no flourishes on the fiddle, instead rigidly adhering to the melody line. As previously mentioned, this sparse approach seems especially well suited to the ballads, which would historically have been sung with no instrumentation at all. This limited arrangement was later adopted by Charlie Monroe in his version, which features only a guitar to accompany the vocals. Given the fact that these two versions of the song have become so widely known, it seems clear that Grayson and Whitter's purposefully limited arrangement was an appealing one.

Grayson and Whitter's limited instrumentation, relying on only fiddle and guitar, didn't have much room to be stripped down any further, but Grayson manages to do so on "Ommie Wise," a song whose familiar story is given an additionally haunting sound by using only the fiddle for instrumental support.

The song itself follows a story very familiar by this point: a man lures his love away from home with promises of marriage and unexpectedly murders her. Clearly, this narrative arch is indebted to the British tradition, but Ommie Wise is most assuredly not British. In fact, it isn't even fictional. The song is generally considered to be one of the oldest native American ballads, songs written in a British style but composed and performed in America.

The song retells the events surrounding the murder of Naomi Wise, a girl who was living in the home of William Adams in Randolph County, North Carolina, during the first decade of the nineteenth century. According to recollections published in 1874, Naomi was romantically involved with Jonathan Lewis, a clerk from nearby Guilford County. Unfortunately, Lewis's mother was not happy with her son's romance and pushed him to instead marry the daughter of his boss. To accomplish this goal, Lewis threatened to ruin Naomi's reputation if she did not agree to break off their relationship; Naomi, in turn, threatened to make it known that she was pregnant. Sometime around 1808, this heated argument came to a tragic conclusion when Lewis asked Wise to meet him at the spring behind her house ("Adams' spring" in the song), promising he would accompany her to a nearby magistrate and marry her. Instead he led her to Deep River, tied her dress over her head, and pushed her under the water, attempting to drown her. Lewis was interrupted when he saw approaching travelers, but for Naomi, it was already too late. Her body was soon discovered, drowned in the river. Jonathan Lewis was a prime suspect from the beginning and was shown the body in hopes of eliciting a confession. Lewis remained unmoved but was arrested regardless. He managed to escape his confines and ran, escaping North Carolina and heading west. For years his whereabouts were unknown. Eventually, rumor spread that Lewis had started a new life in Indiana, near Falls of the Ohio. Deputies found Lewis, arrested him, and brought him back for trial, but by that point, most material witnesses were dead or gone, and no compelling case could be made. He was acquitted of the crime and lived out his life in Kentucky, supposedly confessing to the murder on his deathbed.[19]

This story so closely mirrors the fictional accounts of murdered lovers found in the British ballad tradition that it seems only natural that a song relating the events would appear. That song, which is titled both "Naomi Wise" and "Ommie Wise," has become one of the most recognizable native American ballads and has been called "North Carolina's principal single contribution to American folk song."[20] The song has been recorded by many folk musicians, including Doc Watson, Roscoe Holcomb, and Bob Dylan, and many versions of the song exist in folklore collections. Despite all this famous competition, Grayson's version still stands out. In his recording, he does something unique to all the Grayson and Whitter records: he plays solo. Without Whitter's guitar rhythm in the background to anchor the song, it becomes downright archaic, sounding very much like a traditional, unaccompanied ballad. The fiddle provides some depth to the arrangement, using a combination of single strings and double stops, but, as was his trademark, Grayson plays a simple, repeated melody line with no elaborations. Grayson also refrains from including any personal comments; even the ever popular phrase "Girls, take warning" is absent.

Grayson's lyrics to "Ommie Wise" indicate a good deal of distance between his version and the original. A version published in the *Greensboro Patriot*, April 29, 1874, which is probably much closer to the original, contains a number of details lost by Grayson. Similarly, *The Frank C. Brown Collection of North Carolina Folklore* contains the words to nine other versions of the songs. In each version, John Lewis lures Ommie to her death with a promise of marriage, something Grayson omits. Additionally, in every version collected by Brown the name of the murder site is given as Deep River; some versions are even more specific, placing the murder at a mill dam on the river. Grayson instead places the site of the murder at the much less specific "deep water." Almost all the versions collected by Brown also include a section dealing with the recovery of the body and witnesses identifying it. Grayson's version omits this as well.

The inclusions to the song found in Grayson's version are equally interesting. In Grayson's telling, John Lewis goes back to Ommie's house to ask about her whereabouts, something found in none of the Brown versions. Similarly, in Grayson's version, John Lewis breaks free from prison and enters the army, a detail absent in all other versions. Grayson's version is also full of clunky lines that don't rhyme or adhere to a very predictable meter. In fact, in the final nine lines of his version, not a single line clearly rhymes with another. Compared to most collected and recorded versions of the song, this seems to be a clear distortion from the tradition, as new lines and concepts were shoehorned into the framework of the original song.

Whatever one may think of Grayson's version, no one can doubt its authenticity as a product of the folk tradition. Although it may not be as true to the facts as other versions or as compellingly phrased, it clearly shows the end result of years of folk transference. Where Grayson acquired his version of the song can never be known, but it is clear that Ommie Wise did a lot of traveling after her death.

Folksongs of the British Isles

Although Grayson and Whitter recorded songs from a wide variety of genres and musical traditions, it is clear that the music of the British

Isles is of special importance. All three of the murder ballads previously discussed are either directly linked to or strongly influenced by the British traditions. The migration of British songs into America was not confined to stories of treacherous lovers and vicious murders, however; numerous other songs, some ballads with a clear narrative arc and some more loosely arranged, also captured universal human emotions and, as such, migrated into America along with the British settlers. Three of these songs, "I've Always Been a Rambler," "Where Are You Going Alice?" and "Handsome Molly," survived in America long enough to filter into G.B. Grayson's repertoire and were given greater popularity through his and Whitter's recordings.

The first of these, "I've Always Been a Rambler," tells a story familiar in country music: the wayfaring youth who shirks his home and responsibilities in order to pursue a life of reckless hedonism. One need only listen to Jimmie Rodgers' "My Rough and Rowdy Ways," Hank Williams' "Lost Highway," Bobby Bare's "500 Miles," and dozens of other songs like them to see the degree to which this motif has appeared in the country genre.

Grayson and Whitter's "I've Always Been a Rambler" is a song that itself has done a lot of rambling. It began its journey in England before the 1840s, and it first began appearing on British broadside sheets between the 1840s and 1850s. In these first publications, it was printed with the title "Margaret Walker." This initial broadside publication was a traditional, sentimental British ballad, telling the story of a poor youth who leaves his home in Ireland, gets a job as a courtier, falls in love with a neighboring farm girl, and subsequently loses her after he travels to Scotland. He then migrates to New York and meets a new girl (Peggy Walker) who falls in love with him. The song ends with the young protagonist conflicted over his desire to make Peggy Walker happy and his memories of his lost love.

The song seems to have been well known in America and existed in the repertoire of several traditional performers. Many versions, like the one performed by Clint Howard under the title "Maggie Walker Blues" (which he learned from Clarence Ashley) on *Original Folkways Recordings of Doc Watson and Clarence Ashley, 1960–1962*, actually adhere more closely to the wording of the original broadside sheet than Grayson and Whitter's version, but even the Clint Howard version has become somewhat muddled structurally, placing the meeting of Maggie (or Peggy) Walker before the breakup of the protagonist and the farmer's daughter.

Grayson's version of the song deviates from the nineteenth-century original in several key aspects, and, as a result, becomes less a song of conflicting love interests and more of a song documenting the life of a rakish rambler. The new title Grayson uses for the song comes from an added couplet not found in the original printing of the ballad or many other recordings. This line—"I've always been a rambler, my fortune's been quite hard / I've always loved the women, drink whiskey and play cards"—is sung by Grayson before he moves to the line that traditionally begins the song, "My parents reared me tenderly / Having no child but me." By beginning the song with this added characterization of the protagonist as wild and rebellious, Grayson sets a new focus for the song.

He continues to build on this focus by totally eliminating the character of Peggy Walker from the story. In Grayson's version, the wandering boy simply falls in love and is abandoned by a faithless woman. By following this arc, and leaving aside any mention of a new love, Grayson is able to end the song with the protagonist justifiably rejecting domestic life, declaring instead that he will "drink and gamble for the one I left behind."

As a result of this editing of the original, Grayson's version of this British romantic ballad becomes the prototypical American country song. This refinement of the source material, either by Grayson himself or the larger folk tradition, shows an awareness that the rambling aspect of the piece was more compelling than the romantic aspect. Such awareness of the commercial appeal of this rambling motif is what would soon propel the career of Jimmie Rodgers, who would sell himself as a rebellious wanderer and who would, in turn, provide a model for countless other artists who came after him. Grayson was not himself inventing this rambling image, nor is he placed in the same category as Charlie Poole, Jimmie Rodgers, and other wild young country musicians whose personas mirrored the wayfaring ramblers of their songs, but his decision to record an altered version of this otherwise traditional romantic ballad shows that he actually shared an appreciation for the allure of the rebel.

A more romantic viewpoint is taken in "Where Are You Going Alice?," a song that finds lovers reuniting rather than drifting apart. The storyline of this ballad is about as basic as can be imagined. A girl, Alice, wishes to go meet her lover, Sweet William. She is told he won't show up, she gets upset, and he shows up. The song ends with the reunited lovers living in a blissful "dreamland to never part again."

Grayson and Whitter were the only early country group to record a version of this song, but it, like "I've Always Been a Rambler," can trace its lineage to a much older ballad from the British Isles: "The Banks of Claudy."

This song is one of an interesting subgenre of traditionally British songs, each of which follow a similar storyline. Two lovers part, often spending years separated. The male lover decides to test his lover's faithfulness by sneaking home in disguise. He then attempts to court his own girlfriend; she refuses, pledging her love to her wayfaring boyfriend. At that point, the male character triumphantly reveals his identity and the two live in happiness together. Much in the same way that American murder ballads tend to utilize "Willy" as the name of the murderer, this category of British ballads often utilizes "Riley" as the name of the main character.[21] Multiple songs of this subgenre have found their way from British broadside sheets to America: "George Riley," "William Hall," and "Johnny Germany," along with "Banks of Claudy," are some commonly collected examples.[22]

Grayson and Whitter's version of "Banks of Claudy" has definitely lost something in translation. Although it is clear that the traditional "Riley Ballad" storyline is still present, Grayson and Whitter's version effectively obscures the narrative. More original versions of the ballad begin by introducing the returning male lover. They then feature lines like "I stepped up to her, I took her by surprise / I own she did not know me, I being in disguise." Without these clues, Grayson and Whitter's version fails to deliver on the song's surprising payoff.

This lack of detail is probably a result of the song's oral transmission in America where it was very popular and gained widespread distribution during the nineteenth century. By the time Grayson sang the ballad on record in November of 1929, many of the lines and details of the original had already been lost. Nowhere are the titular banks of the Claudy mentioned, for example. Also at one point, Grayson improvises a verse by repeating the same line, "Never mind young William, he will not meet you there," three times. Enough of the original still exists to clearly demonstrate the song's origin, but it is clear that time eroded many of the sharper details, turning an intriguing song about lovers' faith being literally tested into a simplistic tale of reunited romance.

"I've Always Been a Rambler" and "Where Are You Going Alice?" both follow the clear narrative arc customary in ballads, but not all the British songs that filtered into Grayson and Whitter's recorded output were as linear. In fact, one of their most successful songs was a British tune without a rigid narrative structure: "Handsome Molly."

This song, more than probably any other recorded by the duo, has become incredibly ubiquitous in the music world. Not only have traditional groups like the Stanley Brothers and Doc Watson recorded the song, but it has also found its way into the recordings of artists like Bob Dylan and Mick Jagger. Grayson and Whitter apparently were also aware of its appeal, as it is one of only a handful of songs they recorded twice, for both Gennett and Victor.

The fact that the duo seemed especially fond of the song can also be ascertained from the fact that it was recorded during their initial sessions for both labels. In fact, it seems quite possible it was the first song they ever recorded together. During their first session for Gennett in October of 1927, the duo recorded six songs that would ultimately be issued. Although it is impossible to know the exact order in which the songs were played in the studio, "Handsome Molly" is the only song in this or any other session in which Grayson begins the song by introducing the duo, saying, "'Handsome Molly' by G.B. Grayson and Henry Whitter." Later in the song, Whitter also takes an opportunity for an introduction, asking, "Where are you from Mr. Grayson?" At the end of "Train 45," which was recorded during the same session, the duo ends the song by saying, "Goodbye Grayson" and "Goodbye Henry." Taken together this could suggest that they viewed the whole session as an interconnected set, rather than a series of individual songs, in which case "Handsome Molly" would have been the first.

This song that Grayson and Whitter liked so well seems to trace its lineage to Ireland, although it has undergone much alteration in its journey across the ocean. It appears sometimes under the title "The Irish Girl" and was published in Ireland on broadside sheets as early as the 1820s. The song is a traditional lover's lament: the narrator pines for a mysterious maiden, Handsome Molly, wishing he could be with her despite her apparent rejection of him. The original Irish version of the song is strikingly different from Grayson and Whitter's, but the elements they do share illustrate the connections between the two: both songs feature parted lovers; in broadside versions of the song, the girl's name is also Molly; both songs also use a series of similes to compare the beauty of the parted lover to natural objects; and both songs feature a line about wishing to be in a far off city.[23] After the song found its new home in America, it began taking the shape that Grayson would ultimately record. In 1918, Cecil Sharp collected the song in Callaway, Virginia. That version of the song, still titled "The Irish Girl," contains remnants of the Irish original along with many of the verses that Grayson would ultimately record.[24]

It is interesting to note that, despite the song's obvious appeal to audiences, no other group from the 1920s recorded the song. It was recorded under the title "Hannah My Love" by the Canova family in 1930 and 1931, but it wasn't recorded again until the Stanley Brothers released their version of the song in 1961; since then, it has entered the repertoire of many bluegrass artists, including Flatt and Scruggs, Doc Watson, and the Country Gentlemen.

When listening to these modern versions of the song, it is clear that they are all indebted to the Grayson and Whitter version. Most closely adhere to Grayson's lyrics and melody, and since the only other source for the song would have come from an orally-transmitted version existing outside of recorded media, it seems unlikely that this level of similarity could occur unless later versions were based on the Grayson and Whitter recording. The fact that this particular song, which would likely have been lost to history, has instead become so well known demonstrates the potency of Grayson and Whitter's influence.

The Victorian Songs

The British Isles were definitely a strong contributor to American folk music, and nowhere is that more obvious than in Grayson and Whitter's recorded output, even though these songs do not constitute a majority of the duo's song catalog. In fact, many of the songs that the duo recorded did not bubble up from the distant history of the British Isles; they were composed and published in America on commercially-available sheet music. These publications formed an entire genre of early popular American music. They were created commercially by an industry of songwriters and publishers hoping to compose music that would appeal to the masses of middle-class Americans who could afford the luxuries of instruments and printed music. Although these songs were performed by professional musicians, most of the "parlor songs," as they are popularly known, were created in the home by amateur musicians.[25]

The public appetite for music was refined over the course of the nineteenth century, until these Victorian era parlor songs became fairly predictable. They can be distinguished by prominent thematic elements: "The subjects receiving the greatest attention in the parlor ballads were those of affection and love, mortality and time, lamentations over death, estrangement, religious feeling, social criticism, praise of nature and didacticism."[26] Although it is a romantic notion to believe that traditional performers like Grayson and Whitter were recipients of an age-old folk tradition, the reality is that much of their musical repertoire was no more than one generation removed from a published piece of sheet music.

A good example of one of these Victorian pieces is "Nobody's Darling" recorded by Grayson and Whitter in October of 1927. This song was written in 1870 by the prolific Victorian composer William Shakespeare Hays who wrote more than 350 songs during his lifetime and sold more than six million copies of sheet music. One of these songs, "Little Old Log Cabin in the Lane," is generally considered the first country song ever recorded.[27] Hays' music, though generally simplistic, demonstrates the sentimental style of the Victorian period.

When looking through the recordings of the 1920s and 30s, it is easy to see the expansive influence that Hays' sheet music had over early twentieth-century performers. Grayson and Whitter's recording of "Nobody's Darling" was the third version recorded by 1927, Kelly Harrell and the Pipers Gap Ramblers having both released versions of the song. By the end of the Depression, nine different groups recorded versions of the song.

The song itself is in no way unique in the world of early country music, which often pulled from maudlin Victorian sources. "Nobody's Darling" tells the tragic tale of an orphan trying to survive in a cruel world after the loss of their mother. As was commonly done in the post-industrial Victorian world, the song also served to criticize social disparities in Victorian society. The line "While others are sleeping so sound / Dreaming of silver and gold / I am out in the wide world alone / Just wondering around in the cold" tries to draw attention to the gulf between the haves and have-nots emerging in post-industrial America.

Like many songs of the Victorian era, it also veers into overt religious sentiment, something quite common in early country recordings but something not seen in any other Grayson and Whitter song. In true Victorian fashion, the poor orphan looks forward to death, when a heavenly home and the peace it represents will finally be found. Bizarrely, Grayson chooses to punctuate the end of this depressing song by adding, "Come on, little woman, be mine" after the final verse, seemingly unconcerned about the disconnect between his jovial comments and the dismal mood of the song.

The suffering child in "Nobody's Darling" is a common character in Victorian parlor songs, but just as common is the dead mother. This is the major thematic element of another Victorian song in the duo's repertoire: "You'll Never Miss Your Mother Until She's Gone" recorded in October of 1927. This song is actually a combination of two Victorian songs with similar thematic content. The title comes from an 1885 song written by Harry Birch, a pen name of prolific song writer Charles A. White. The actual text of the song is from another song, "Mother and Home," written by W.J. Laney.[28] The only major change in the text comes at the end of the chorus, when the line "I can never forget my mother and my home" is swapped out for the poached titled "You'll never miss your mother until she's gone."

This song is a quintessential example of the Victorian song style. A narrator laments the loss of his dead mother who has gone off to a better world, leaving behind the mourning family she held together while on earth. This strict adherence to the market-driven appetites of the Victorian era is probably responsible for the later popularity of the song in the early country music world. The song was first recorded by Fiddlin' John Carson, who codified the new title for the song and may very well have created its melody. Gene Wiggins notes that the tune to Carson's "You Will Never Miss Your Mother Until She Is Gone" is essentially the same as his recording of "Little Old Log Cabin in the Lane." Those songs are themselves almost identical to "Lulu Walls" and "Lily of the Valley," further complicating the origin of the melody.[29] Whether Carson cobbled together these various components himself or recorded an older song he had inherited through oral transmission, it is clear that most of the versions of the song that came later relied on Carson's version of the song for their title and melody.

The song was definitely a popular one during the 1920s and 30s. When considering songs recorded under both titles "Mother and Home" and "You'll Never Miss Your Mother Until She Is Gone," it was recorded nineteen times. Grayson and Whitter's version of the song was the seventh recording under the Carson title, which would be recorded six more times after Grayson and Whitter. This ubiquitous popularity, coupled with the unique features of the original Carson recording, suggests that records, rather than oral transmission, were the source of Grayson's knowledge of the song. This was probably an instance when Grayson and Whitter chose to record a piece with a strong track record rather than one that formed an authentic part of their usual repertoire. Even in the 1920s, weepy Victorian songs were still attracting audiences.

The Temperance Songs

The Victorian parlor song industry was propelled by sentimental songs of home and loss, but songs of dead mothers and wayfaring orphans are not the full picture of compositions from the nineteenth century. Within the broader realm of Victorian sheet music, another, more narrowly focused, genre emerged: the temperance songs. Whereas the parlor songs of the Victorian age easily migrated into the popular music of the twentieth century, these temperance songs, proselytizing lectures on the ruin caused by excessive drinking, generally fell into musical decay and were forgotten in the twentieth century. However, G.B. Grayson seems to have been well acquainted with them. Two of these songs, "Don't Go Out Tonight My Darling" and "I Saw a Man at the Close of the Day," would find their way into the modern world through the recordings of Grayson and Whitter.

Unlike fiddle tunes and ballads of love and murder, which have been consistently popular for centuries, temperance songs paralleled the movement that created them: experiencing incredible popularity in the nineteenth century before declining into total obscurity by the early twentieth century. At their peak, poems and songs of the temperance movement would have been one of the largest musical genres in America. Hundreds of thousands of individual songbooks were in print around the time of the Civil War,[30] and, at one time, temperance songs and poems would have been known to almost every American,[31] but by the time Grayson and Whitter stepped into the studio in 1927, they were already fading from the public consciousness. In fact, despite the ocean of poems and songs that flooded the nation during the temperance movement of the nineteenth century, only a handful of these songs, probably fewer than a dozen, were ever commercially recorded by traditional artists.

To a student of history, the reason for this discrepancy seems obvious: by the time these early country artists were recording, prohibition was in full effect and the realities of government mandated temperance made songs on the subject less attractive. Many temperance songs of the later nineteenth and early twentieth centuries were also written with political objectives, and as such, did not age well in the era of prohibition. The few songs that did survive showcase a less politicized side of the temperance movement. Instead, these songs were often written in an attempt to help individuals privately battle alcohol abuse by presenting them simple moralistic tales.

These moralizing temperance songs, which generally date to the middle, rather than late nineteenth century, owe their longevity to the fact that they can be enjoyed apart from their anti-alcohol rhetoric, providing listeners with the same kind of pathetic appeal that was popular in so many songs of the Victorian era. Songs of dead parents and starving children were enjoyable to nineteenth-century listeners, regardless of the heavy handed moralizing they may have been engaged in. Most listeners could enjoy the depressing imagery while discarding the temperance element. As one writer notes, "a person in those lachrymose days could weep through 'Just a Bird in a Gilded Cage,' 'After the Ball,' or 'Woodman, Spare that Tree' without being anti-wealth, anti-dance, or even anti-lumbering."[32]

Although these songs could be enjoyed merely as tales of pathos, passed around through oral transmission in the same way many maudlin songs from the nineteenth century were, Grayson may very well have come by his temperance songs in their original context, as he had an unusually direct connection to the movement that spawned them. When Laurel Bloomery, Grayson's home community, was first being established, there was only one large building in the area. This building had been built on land deeded in 1852 and was shared by the Methodist Episcopal Church, which met downstairs, and the Sons of Temperance Branch 125, who met upstairs.[33]

This group, the Sons of Temperance, was a prominent early temperance organization. They began in New York City in 1842 and soon spread through the mid–Atlantic region from Pennsylvania to Massachusetts.[34] By the end of the decade, the organization had spread up and down the eastern seaboard and into the Midwestern region, though these branches were usually located in and around large towns and urban areas. Finding one in sparsely populated regions like Laurel Bloomery, Tennessee, would have been unusual, even during the nineteenth century. In 1858, there were only forty-five branches in the entire state of Tennessee, with a total combined membership of only 1,800.[35]

Although driven by a desire to eradicate alcohol altogether, the Sons of Temperance functioned originally as less of a political group and more as a secret society; an individual was selected for membership and underwent a secret initiation ceremony in which the evils of alcohol were illustrated through a short lecture. He then would pledge to abstain from drink. From that point on, the society functioned much like a modern-day support group. Members would attend regular meetings, complete with passwords, hymns, and secret ceremonies. Members relied on one another as shields against the temptations of alcohol, and the group's success was measured by how many members stayed clear of the forbidden fruit.[36]

Whether Grayson's temperance songs came directly from the meetings of the Sons of Temperance can never be known, but the existence of a branch of the group in Laurel Bloomery indicates the surrounding community must have had a strong pro-temperance sentiment; this would have made the region around Grayson's home a fertile ground for the preservation of songs from the temperance movement.

The first of these songs by Grayson and Whitter was "Don't Go Out

Tonight My Darling," which they recorded in their first session for the Victor label in October of 1927. This song, which had not been recorded prior to Grayson and Whitter's version, was written in 1895 by George Cooper and Charles Pratt, the latter having composed popular songs like "Put My Little Shoes Away" and "Bring Back My Bonnie to Me." Although it is ostensibly a song about the dangers of alcohol, it relies strongly on the overwrought maudlin emotion found in the popular songs of the Victorian era. This probably helped propel it off of printed sheet music and into the oral tradition, where it has been collected by folklorists numerous times.[37]

The song tells the tale of a woman begging her husband to stay home, away from the lure of the tavern. When he refuses her pleas, she mourns her loss; as the song ends, he is brought home and left to die, presumably from some complication due to alcohol. The song ends in classic temperance song fashion, with Grayson singing, "I asked that God's own tender mercy may save him from a drunkard's doom."

Although the song can be read purely as a sentimental tale of loss and tragedy, Grayson and Whitter make sure that the temperance lecture is not lost on the audience. Whitter shouts out, "Take warning" during the song and Grayson notes, "There's many a good man brought to his ruin this way" between verses. When compared to the rollicking celebrations of alcohol Grayson evokes on other songs, like "Sally Gooden," it seems hypocritical to hear him here lecture the listener on the dangers of drink, but it further illustrates the difficulty of simplistically categorizing the complicated individuals behind these recordings. Unlike groups like the Hill Billies, Grayson and Whitter did not feel the need to present an artificially constructed image. They obviously gravitated toward songs they liked with little concern for appearances.

Grayson recorded another temperance song for Victor during his final recording session in October of 1929. This song, "I Saw a Man at the Close of the Day," is another heart-wrenching tale of alcohol induced tragedy. It was written in 1854 by Mrs. Mary Lantz and has often been collected by folklorists under the titles "The Drunkard's Doom" and "The Drunkard and His Family." It first began appearing in temperance song books in the 1850s and was originally sung to the tune of "Auld Lang Syne."[38] Like many temperance songs of the era, it was initially less of a song than a poem, made to be sung with existing melodies.[39] Traditionally, the song has been performed in the folk tradition with a refrain, in which the last few lines of each verse are repeated each time.

Grayson's version is much more streamlined, ignoring the refrain and adhering to a more original melody. However, the emotionally overwrought story stays the same: an anonymous narrator notices a drunken father who ignores his child's pleas of hunger at home in order to buy booze; then, returning by a year later, the same narrator sees a funeral procession passing by. When he asks who has died, he discovers that it was the drunken father from a year earlier and that the wife and children of the man had preceded him in death, no doubt as a result of his alcohol-induced neglect. As with "Don't Go Out Tonight, My Darling," Grayson takes every opportunity to drive home this moral message. He declares, "Take warning girls, and don't marry a drunkard," between verses.

It is worth noting that this song also demonstrates the high point of Henry Whitter's guitar playing. Although he is often remembered as the barely competent player who banged out chords on his early OKeh recordings in 1923 and 1924, he had clearly learned a lot in six years. This was probably inevitable, as he consistently worked as a touring musician, regularly playing with great guitarists like Riley Puckett, but it is still surprising to hear how impressive his mastery of rhythms and bass runs had become by this recording session. His guitar work on this song, which helps punctuate the end of each verse with a series of cascading bass runs, would have fit in nicely on a recording by the Skillet Lickers, quite a departure from the rudimentary playing from the early career with which he is often associated.

Despite their quality as musical pieces, these two temperance era songs were clearly viewed by Grayson as moral tales warning of the dangers of alcohol; however, their greater appeal has probably resulted from their tales of angst, separation, and loss: motifs that have always found a home in country music. Nowhere were these themes more ubiquitous than in the popular music of the Victorian Age, probably explaining why songs from this era have so easily persisted with traditional musicians.

The Railroad Songs

The music of the Victorian era was able to saturate American culture through its market driven, commercial production. Unlike ballads and fiddle tunes, which floated from one generation to the next through oral transmission, Victorian songs were churned out rapidly and were constantly changing to meet audience preferences. New songs were written; old songs were forgotten; the songwriting industry fed the demands of a growing American populace. At the dawn of the nineteenth century, eighteen sheet music publishers existed in America, and by 1860, there were ninety. These companies used hundreds of retail outlets and thousands of mail orders to supply every region of America with mass produced music.[40]

This boom of population and industry that was taking place in the nineteenth century was also serving to forever change the American character. One invention especially, the railroad, was doing more than anything to foster movement of people and ideas across the rapidly expanding nation. The nineteenth century was marked by explosive growth of the rail industry. In 1835, 1,000 miles of track were in service, and by 1881, more than 100,000 miles of track were being used.[41] The presence of the railroad quickly became a universal fact of life for almost every American. Their "life and language were permeated by trains, real and symbolic."[42] Consequently, American music began to reflect this new reality. Songs about trains and the people whose lives were affected by them became an important component of American culture.

Grayson and Whitter were no exception. The duo released four records with railroad themes: "Train 45," "The Red and Green Signal Lights," "He's Coming to Us Dead," and "Nine Pound Hammer." These songs capture the mindset of a country swept up in rapid change, into a world of steel and steam, a world that simultaneously represented modern innovation and loss of the past.

Norm Cohen, in his book *Long Steel Rail: The Railroad in American Folksong*, has already done an excellent job of compiling histories of every rail-themed song released by Grayson and Whitter, so, in order to avoid redundancy, only a brief summary of each will be provided here. However, it is worth noting how these songs fit into the duo's overall recorded canon, as well as how both Grayson and Whitter were personally influenced by the arrival of the railroad industry.

It has been previously established that the railroad was an important part of both Grayson's and Whitter's lives. The rail is what allowed Henry Whitter, who used to practice his guitar on an abandoned gas tank in the town train depot, to easily travel from his home in Fries, Virginia, to Manhattan in order to pursue his dream of breaking into the music industry. Similarly, Grayson's home on Waters Branch Road in Laurel Bloomery was within several hundred yards of the rail line connecting Damascus and Mountain City. During his childhood and adolescence, he would have heard the train clattering up and down the tracks regularly as it stripped lumber out of his native county, bound ultimately for a woodworking plant in Cazenovia, New York. Grayson depended on the rail himself, using it to travel from Damascus, Virginia, to nearby towns like West Jefferson,

North Carolina. This infrastructure allowed him to easily move from one audience to the next, greatly expanding his realm of musical influence.

The train's impact on Grayson and Whitter is evident in their recorded output. In their first session for Gennett, the duo recorded "Train 45," a song that they would soon record again for Victor. This recording would go on to be one of Grayson and Whitter's biggest hits, staying in print until 1934 and selling 50,000 copies.[43]

"Train 45" is one of Grayson's most well-known songs, but the source of the song is something of a mystery. As mentioned earlier, Steve Ledford, who would go on to record the song himself along with Wade Mainer and Zeke Morris in 1938, was said by some to be the author of the song, but when looking at the song closely, it becomes clear that ascribing authorship to anyone would be difficult.

Melodically speaking, "Train 45" is "Reuben's Train" by a different title.[44] It is also nearly identical to "900 miles," although that song has traditionally featured a slightly different melody. In his attempts to untangle these three songs, Norm Cohen argues that they are best viewed as two song families: one consisting of "Reuben's Train" and "Train 45," with the other best exemplified by "900 miles." Whatever difference exists between them resides in the floating verses which can change from one performer to the next. It has been previously noted that Steve Ledford often improvised and alternated verses, but the same can also be said of Grayson. He and Whitter recorded the song twice: once for Gennett in 1927 and a few weeks later for Victor. Although both versions are similar, each recording contains unique verses. Interestingly, the floating verses favored by Grayson are more often associated with the "900 miles" song grouping than the "Reuben's Train" song grouping. In his first recording of the song, Grayson twice repeats the verse, "If you say so, I'll railroad no more / I'll sidetrack my train and go home," verses prominently featured in Riley Puckett's version of "900 Miles From Home."[45] In his second recording of the song Grayson drops those verses but adds, "If this train runs right, see my woman Saturday night / I'm 900 miles away from home," a verse which Cohen notes as being characteristic of the "900 Miles" songs.[46] Notably, in neither version is Reuben, the titular engineer of the "Reuben's Train" family of songs, mentioned. This would suggest that lyrically at least, Grayson's "Train 45" is more closely aligned with "900 Miles" than "Reuben's Train." This is not surprising, as Cohen notes that the two songs were already being intermingled as early as 1898.[47] When performing the song, Grayson did what many artists before him had done: he cobbled together a patchwork of verses from a common pool of lyrics, creating an end product unique to himself.

Of course, to a modern listener, one of the notable things about Grayson's and Ledford's versions of "Train 45" is that they are sung at all. Since their recordings, "Train 45" has become an instrumental piece, often reserved in bluegrass bands for the banjo. These rapid instrumentals, though exciting, lack some of the personality of the older versions of the song. For both Ledford and Grayson, "Train 45" was a chance to communicate with the audience. Grayson and Whitter established this practice in their two versions, which contain numerous vocal asides breaking the barrier between the faceless performer on the record and the audience. The duo begins each version of the song they recorded with a nod to the city in which they were recording, "Train 45 leaving Pennsylvania Station, New York City," for example. Aside from their normal banter ("I'm on my way somewhere") the duo also takes this song as an opportunity to introduce their hometowns, something they do on both the Gennett and Victor recordings. On the Gennett version of the recording, they also end the song by mentioning each other by name, something that was probably confusing to many listeners, as this recording was also released under two different aliases: Norman Gayle and David Foley.

During their initial recording session for Gennett in October of 1927, Grayson and Whitter performed another song saturated with railroad imagery; however, Gennett rejected the piece, and it was never released on their label. A few weeks later the duo tried again, and this time, the song "He's Coming to Us Dead" was issued. This song, along with "The Red and Green Signal Lights," which the duo would record in subsequent sessions, illustrates a style popular in the 1890s: the commercial ballad. This style of song, a culmination of the songwriting style of the Victorian age, tells a sentimental story, coupling the narrative and emotional power of the traditional ballad with the modern imagery of the late nineteenth century.

"He's Coming to Us Dead" was written in 1899 by one of the most prolific songwriters of the era: Gussie Davis. Davis was an African American songwriter from Ohio, working in the "Tin Pan Alley" of New York, who was well known for his sentimental compositions. He wrote "We Sat Beneath the Maple on the Hill," "The Fatal Wedding," and "The Baggage Coach Ahead" as well as "The Red and Green Signal Lights."[48] Because of their sentimental nature, which was especially popular among rural performers,[49] many of Davis's songs entered into the folk repertoire and were recorded by early country artists.

Grayson's version of "He's Coming to Us Dead" is the first rendition ever recorded. His version is lyrically quite similar to the Gussie Davis original, but by 1927, significant alterations had occurred, enough to suggest that Grayson's source of the song was separated from the original sheet music by years of oral transmission. Grayson's song contains no chorus, something that was found in the original composition. The original was also written, somewhat unusually to modern listeners, to alternate between a four-four time in the verse and a three-four time in the chorus. Grayson chooses to keep the entire song in a more driving four-four time; many other versions recorded later use the slower three-four time.

Although several other versions of the song emerged after Grayson's recording with fundamentally altered lyrics and the change to three-four time, the power of Grayson and Whitter's version can be traced through the number of subsequent recordings that are clearly based on their original. These include the versions by artists like Wade Mainer, Hylo Brown, and, later, Steve Ledford, who attempted to modernize the song in the 1970s by changing it to "He's Coming from Vietnam."[50]

Unlike "Train 45," this song conveys a notably negative mood. Grayson's version depicts a man sadly coming to town to receive the casket containing his son's remains. His son, a soldier, a "boy in blue," is being shipped home via the railroad; consequently, the song is set in a train depot and is full of railroad images: telegraph offices, passengers, and whistles. As a result of this setting, the song casts its depressing pallor over the rail itself. Whereas many songs about trains depict them positively, avenues of escape, promises of positive change, or embodiments of power, this song casts them coldly. The idea of a loved one being shipped home as cargo is dehumanizing and captures the ugly side of a rapidly modernizing word.

Similarly, by omitting any details about the young soldier's death, the song seems to take on more of an anti-war sentiment. This song was written around the time of the Spanish-American War, an era characterized by pro-war hysteria. In that context, the composition of this seemingly anti-war song is surprising.[51] Norm Cohen argues that the root of this anti-war sentiment is actually an earlier song, dating from the period of the Civil War, but no evidence of such a song's existence can currently be found. Grayson definitely was aware of the anti-war facet of the song, as he peppers his recording with his own warnings about military service, asking listeners to "take warning from this song" and punctuating the song's point about the probability of death during military service with "a lot of them come back that way, too." Whether Grayson, whose blindness exempted him from military service in World War I, truly held an anti-military stance cannot be deduced with certainty, although as will be noted when discussing his song "Joking Henry," Grayson was definitely familiar with other anti-war songs. He never recorded a more patriotic piece as a counterpoint, although his partner, Henry Whitter, was responsible for the first ever recording of "The Kaiser and Uncle Sam" in 1923, a song that criticized German involvement in World War I while celebrating America's military prowess.

As previously mentioned, something about Gussie Davis's style of sentimental songwriting appealed to rural audiences, and several of his songs began to circulate through folk musicians. "The Red and Green Signal Lights" also found its way into Grayson and Whitter's recorded output and was one of the few songs they recorded for both Victor and Gennett (which released the song under the title "Red or Green"). This song, which was originally titled "Go Set a Light" was composed by Davis with words credited to Henry V. Neal. It quickly entered the folk canon and became especially popular among railroad workers.[52]

The song tells the story of a train engineer who is forced to leave the side of his dying child. He asks his wife to set out a lantern so he can determine the fate of their child as his train passes near their home: a red light if the child has died or a green light if their child has taken a turn for the better. The song climaxes with the train rushing by the home and the relieved engineer seeing the green light, signaling a hope for recovery.

The song is a clever combination of sentiments common to earlier Victorian pieces—dying children, fatal illnesses, and separated families—and the modern imagery of trains, signal lights, and engineers. It was probably this hybridization that led to its immediate popularity.

Because it was so popular, it quickly entered the folk tradition, leaving its sheet music roots behind. It first appeared on record in 1926 when it was recorded under the title "The Engineer's Dying Child" by Vernon Dalhart. Because of this recording, Carson Robison, who wrote many of the songs recorded by Dalhart, is often credited as the author. It is true that he may deserve credit as an arranger, writing a new melody for commercial audiences, but the original song predates Robison by almost thirty years.

With the help of Robison's new melody, Dalhart's version of the song drips with sentimentality, from the inclusion of violins and train whistles to the vocal delivery, in which Dalhart sometimes sounds as if he's fighting back tears. Grayson's versions, by contrast, were more upbeat affairs. He and Whitter recorded the song for Gennett in February of 1928 and again for Victor in July. Although in both versions he attempts to begin the song with a tempo only slightly faster than Dalhart's, by the end of the song, he has sped up notably. This more upbeat tempo was also used by Glen Neaves, one of Grayson's biggest admirers, when he recorded the song along with the Virginia Mountain Boys on a 1977 Folkways album.

Grayson's version of the song adheres to a simpler melodic pattern than the one Robison arranged for Dalhart. From a structural standpoint, Grayson's song is also much less refined. Grayson utilizes two melodies which don't follow a clear pattern. The first verse and second verse alternate melodies. Then the second melody reappears for the third verse. The initial melody comes back for the fourth verse, and the song ends with the second melody repeated twice. Throughout all this, there is a chorus beginning with the "Just set a light as I pass tonight," which appears after every two verses. When Glen Neaves recorded his version of the song, he attempts to untangle this bizarre pattern by following a more traditional bluegrass structure, using Grayson's second melody and his chorus, featuring vocal harmony, after every verse. The end result finishes what Grayson started: turning a slow, sentimental ballad about a worried train engineer into a peppy bluegrass song.

Although songs about trains and their engineers make up a majority of railroad songs, the life of the railroad worker was also a frequent topic of song. That is the case in the final song in Grayson and Whitter's recorded output with railroad imagery, "Nine Pound Hammer." In fact, it has been noted that "Nine Pound Hammer" is so focused on the worker, and the titular tool he relies on, that it cannot really even be considered a railroad song.[53] Whatever category it is placed in, the song seems to be a true folk product, containing a patchwork of verses and motifs cobbled together from a variety of older sources. In this way, it is quite similar to "Train 45." Versions of the song often feature verses with the phrase "this old hammer" and "Roll on, buddy," verses that can be found in other folk songs, from "Driving Steel" to "Swannanoa Tunnel."[54]

The difference between verses, specifically in their underlying structure, is the criteria that scholars like Archie Green and Norm Cohen have used to divide these songs into historical families. Songs that feature rhyming couplets are considered to be in the "roll" song family, whereas stanzas featuring unrhymed couplets, with a portion of the second line repeated, constitute "hammer" songs. The latter is the structure present in Grayson and Whitter's version.

The song traces its recorded history to Al Hopkins and His Buckle Busters, another name for the Hill Billies, who first recorded the song in 1927. This first recording has led to some assertions that Charlie Bowman, the fiddler for the Hill Billies, wrote the song himself, using a melody he heard from black railroad workers in eastern Tennessee. Although it is probable that the song could have been found in the tradition of black railroad workers, the verses used by the Hill Billies had largely been collected by folklorists prior to their recording and therefore could not have been unique compositions.[55]

Bowman may be responsible for introducing the song to white recording artists, for the next two groups to record versions of the song (Grayson and Whitter and Frank Blevins' Tar Heel Rattlers) were living within seventy miles of Charlie Bowman's east Tennessee home of Gray and could have had contacts with Bowman at local fiddler's conventions. Frank Blevins and His Tar Heel Rattlers, the second group to record the song, in 1928, were from Lansing, North Carolina, near G.B. Grayson's home.

Grayson and Whitter were the third group to record the number in 1929. Their version is less polished than the Hill Billies' version, which featured tight vocal harmonies and realistic hammer sound effects (accomplished by striking a small metal rod on a banjo hoop[56]), techniques that would have served the group well on the vaudeville stage. Despite the less sophisticated arrangement, Grayson and Whitter do employ the only example of vocal harmony found on any of their records. As is the case in almost all recorded versions of the song, Whitter adds his vocals after the final line of each couplet, singing a refrain of the last few words. Despite Whitter's long and prolific career as a singer in his own right, this song is the only recorded example of him singing alongside Grayson. When heard together, it becomes obvious why Whitter volunteered to hand over the vocalizing to his partner.

The Tin Pan Alley Songs

The inclusion of railroad songs seems like a natural fit for Grayson and Whitter: both men lived in areas being rapidly altered by railway transportation, and both would have had a firsthand knowledge of the realities of the rail. However, as is so often the case, musical taste is not solely rooted in first hand experiences; just as often, people are drawn to material from outside the world of their own experiences. In Grayson and Whitter's case, this led them to record two songs, "Sweet Rosie O' Grady," and "She's Mine, All Mine," which would have been just as likely to be heard on a stage in Manhattan as a molasses making in Laurel Bloomery, Tennessee.

"Sweet Rosie O' Grady" was written by Maude Nugent in 1896. Nugent was a twenty-two-year-old native of New York City when she wrote the song. As a vaudeville performer, she was able to popularize the piece through her own performances, and consequently, "Sweet Rosie

O'Grady," her biggest hit, became one of the most popular songs of the "gay nineties" era.[57]

Unlike some of the darker, more dismal songs of the Victorian period, "Sweet Rosie O'Grady" conjures up almost every sappy romantic image imaginable. The song is told in first person, the narrator celebrating his blossoming love with Rosie O'Grady, "the sweetest little rose the garden ever grew." Although the song, which only contains two verses and a chorus, is light on narrative structure and conflicts, it is ensconced in romantic imagery. Gardens, sweet singing birds, tiny engagement rings, and the golden summertime come together to create a vibrant portrait of young love.

"Sweet Rosie O'Grady" was created during a period in popular music shaped by professional songwriters, performers, and musical publishers. Given the concentration of many of these publishers around West Twenty-Eighth Street in New York, the commercial music publishing industry was referred to as "Tin Pan Alley." By the 1890s, this industry had become a sophisticated mechanism, creating and promoting sheet music on a huge scale. Generally, a four-step process was used: musical troupes, generally performing in vaudeville or minstrel shows, would come to New York looking for gigs and materials; publishers would then enlist troupe members to perform and promote their songs; the songs would hopefully gain popularity as a result of these performances; and the music publishers would make money off the resulting sheet music sales.[58]

As was already seen with the Hill Billies, these vaudeville shows traveled throughout the eastern and southern United States. Often troupes would play in large urban centers and, while in town, perform smaller shows called "run-outs" in smaller neighboring communities.[59] This approach allowed the newest songs to be heard by all sorts of audiences, even those living in the rural South.

The effectiveness of the Tin Pan Alley model of promoting songs through live performances was profoundly successful at spreading commercially-produced music from songwriters based in New York to the rest of the country. Phrases modern Americans take for granted, like "sweet sixteen" and "a bicycle built for two," first appeared in Tin Pan Alley song lyrics, which were rapidly becoming universally known in the United States. When Grayson and Whitter traveled to New York to record "Sweet Rosie O'Grady" for Gennett in 1928, the song had already been recorded twice by hillbilly artists: once by Walter C. Peterson (known affectionately by his WLS radio audiences as "The Kentucky Wonder Bean") and once by Hugh Cross and Luther McCartt. To find a song commercially composed in New York in the repertoire of southern folk musicians was in no way unusual: clearly the popular music of the era was just as popular south of the Mason-Dixon Line.

In fact, if one examines a list of the most popular sheet music publications of the 1890s, it is clear that they formed a core part of folk performers' repertoires. "After the Ball," one of the biggest hits of 1892, was recorded by Fiddlin' John Carson and Bradley Kincaid. "My Wild Irish Rose," a defining song of 1899, was recorded by Riley Puckett and the Leake County Revelers, among others. Puckett, the Leake County Revelers, and Uncle Dave Macon all recorded one of the biggest sheet music sellers of 1902, "In the Good Old Summertime." Many other popular Tin Pan Alley songs similarly found their way into the folk canon.

"Sweet Rosie O' Grady" was incredibly popular at the turn of the century, and it would soon become nearly ubiquitous. By 1909, the Songbook of the Harvard Club included the song, along with others meant to "promote good fellowship and college loyalty and to keep alive memories that are dear to all of us."[60] In 1916, it was referenced by James Joyce in *Portrait of the Artist as a Young Man*, and it would ultimately become the title song in the 1943's feature film *Sweet Rosie O'Grady* starring Betty Grable.

Despite its clear pedigree as a commercially produced popular song, in G.B. Grayson's hands the song sounds timeless. Grayson's lyrics follow the original sheet music very closely with only slight variation, which would not be unusual in an orally transmitted song, but Grayson deviates from the original publication when he throws in a variation on his ever popular aside, calling out "Come on little Rosie and be mine" to take the song out of the realm of popular music history, making it much more personal.

Although "Sweet Rosie O'Grady" was a popular song following its composition in 1896, by 1928, when Grayson and Whitter recorded it, it was becoming old-fashioned. However, that is not to say that only older material found its way into the recordings of early country artists. "She's Mine, All Mine," which the duo recorded in same session as "Rosie O'Grady" in February of 1928, had been written in 1921, only seven years prior.

The composers of "She's Mine, All Mine," Bert Kalmar and Harry Ruby, were, like the composer of "Sweet Rosie O'Grady," products of the vaudeville circuits: Kalmar had worked as a magician and Ruby had performed as a pianist. When the two joined forces in the 1920s, they began creating songs primarily for theater shows. They wrote the music for Broadway shows *The Five O'Clock Girl* and *Good Boy* but are perhaps most well known for their collaborations with the Marx Brothers. The duo wrote the songs and screenplays for *Horse Feathers*, *Animal Crackers*, and *Duck Soup*. In addition to this theatrical output, they recorded songs which were sold as sheet music, including popular hits like "Who's Sorry Now?" and "I Wanna Be Loved by You." The duo would become so well known that in 1950 a film, *Three Little Words*, starring Fred Astaire and Red Skelton, was created to tell the story of the duo's rise to fame.

"She's Mine, All Mine" was written by Kalmar and Ruby in 1921; how it found its way into Grayson and Whitter's repertoire is anybody's guess. Unlike other commercially-written songs the pair recorded, "She's Mine, All Mine" was so modern, it hadn't had time to be picked up by folk musicians and was probably not orally transmitted. It has never been collected by folklorists, and prior to Grayson and Whitter, it had never been recorded by an early country artist. It may be possible that the song was given to Grayson and Whitter in the studio by recording executives hoping to engineer a hit; however, the song was only recorded for Gennett, a label known for its hands-off approach to the management of artists and a lack of concern for royalty generation.[61]

The song is an odd choice for another reason: its bizarre structure. Even in Grayson's hands, with his traditional fiddling and untrained singing, the song cannot be contorted into a traditional sounding folk song. Its three-four time signature coupled with its strange chord progression (by traditional country standards) and its clear melodic shift from the verses to the choruses results in a recording that is hard to define.

Other than reversing the order of the final two choruses, Grayson follows the lyrics of the original sheet almost exactly; given the complexity of the song, this would imply he received the song either directly from the source or from someone who had direct access to the original music. Although how they came to record it will probably never be known, the content of the song may provide some hint as to why it appealed to Grayson and Whitter. Lines like "I told her I worked at a glue factory / And that's how she happened to get stuck on me" and "Her pies are delicious she baked me a mince / I ate some last week and it's been with me since" would have appealed to musicians like G.B. Grayson and Henry Whitter, who are both remembered by those who knew them for their keen senses of humor and proclivity for joking, a proclivity that manifested itself in several other songs as well.

The Comedy Songs

Grayson and Whitter's comedic natures are on full display in "Never Be as Fast as I Have Been" and "Joking Henry," two songs which try (with dubious success) to drive the audience to laughter. Although one of these songs is a product of the folk tradition, the other is, at least partially, an original composition.

"Never Be as Fast as I Have Been" tells a story common in early hillbilly recordings: the abused husband warning against the horrors of married life. Songs like "I'm Glad My Wife's in Europe," "The Bald Headed End of the Broom," and "I Wish I Was Single Again" (which Henry Whitter recorded as a solo artist in 1925) each depict miserable husbands fighting against the tyranny of despotic wives. During their recording of the song, Grayson proclaims, "Lord have mercy on a married man, anyhow," something Whitter would have known quite a bit about.

Apparently this sentiment predates recorded music, as songs in a similar vein date back much earlier. "Never Be as Fast as I Have Been" is one such song. It, like so many others, outlines the exaggerated abuses heaped upon a poor married man as he struggles to financially support a demanding, unfaithful wife. Under its original title "The Sporting Bachelors" it has been collected in several folklore collections. It was first recorded in 1927 by Buell Kazee, two years before Grayson and Whitter's recording in September of 1929.

Interestingly, Kazee did not know the song before recording it. He read the song from a folklore collection *Twenty Kentucky Mountain Songs* during the recording session.[62] The ultimate origin of the song is shrouded in mystery. It seems to be the product of a commercial composer, but no record of it appearing in sheet music form or on stage exists.[63]

G.B. Grayson seems to have acquired his version of the song from the folk tradition. The wording of several lines is different than in Kazee's version, and Grayson includes two entire verses not found in the Kazee recording: the verse that begins "Six days of the week I labor for my bread / She swears three of them shall be hers" and the one beginning with the downright morbid "Now come death and take away her breath / Give me back my freedom once more" are unique to Grayson. These inclusions would suggest that Grayson's version comes from an independent source, thereby making it the only version of the song recorded directly from the folk tradition.

The other comedic piece recorded by Grayson and Whitter is probably a hybrid of folk tradition and original composition. "Joking Henry" is a bizarre song about two men, Joke and Henry, sleeping on a railroad track. Joke is turned around in his sleep and awakes thinking he has been attacked. For the remainder of the song, Joke imagines exacting vengeance on his mysterious assailant. The title of the record is obviously a butchering of the intended title "Joke and Henry" by an inattentive recording studio employee. Given the use of the name Joke, and the overall irreverence of the song, it can be assumed that Grayson intended for the piece to be humorous, but finding anything actually funny in the song itself proves challenging.

What is interesting about this song is that Grayson very probably wrote the lyrics, something uncommon for him, and for most early traditional artists. The song appears nowhere else in the recordings of earlier artists or in written folklore collections. Additionally, it has been claimed that the story of Joke and Henry was based on a true tale of two men Grayson knew in Laurel Bloomery who experienced something similar to the events in the song.[64] That grounding in reality may help account for the odd nature of the song's story.

Although he may have written the lyrics, the melody was borrowed from the folk tradition, specifically from the song "The Battleship of Maine." This song, like "He's Coming to Us Dead," was an anti-war song, albeit a lighthearted one, specifically targeting America's involvement in the Spanish-American War. The original lyrics to the song describe a reluctant soldier running away from a war he views as unwarranted. Lines like "McKinley called for volunteers / I went and got my gun / First Spaniard I saw coming / I dropped my gun and run," would hardly be considered patriotic. This song had been recorded a year before "Joking Henry" in 1927 by Red Patterson's Piedmont Log Rollers, the same group responsible for the first recording of "Down on the Banks of the Ohio." Whether Grayson lifted the melody of "Battleship of Maine" from this recording or whether he already knew the tune cannot be known for sure, but it makes for a lively backdrop to his strange tale of nocturnal railroad assault.

The American Folk Songs

The remaining five songs recorded by Grayson and Whitter fall squarely into the category of generic American folk songs. These songs lack the instrumental focus and loose lyrics of dance and fiddle tunes but are also insufficiently narrative to be considered ballads.

All of these songs were recorded during the duo's final sessions for Victor, which were recorded between July 31, 1928, and September of 1929. The first was "Short Life of Trouble." This song is one that was traditionally well known among folk musicians. Perhaps because it was well suited for banjo renditions, the song was very popular in the Appalachian region.[65] Grayson and Whitter's recording was the third version released and, by the end of the 1930s, eleven more would follow. It was also collected in multiple folksong collections, a testament to its regional popularity. Apparently, the song had a great appeal; despite the saturation of versions on the record market, it, coupled with "Nine Pound Hammer," was Grayson and Whitter's second bestselling record, moving more than 10,000 copies.[66]

The song, like "Handsome Molly," is a classic lover's lament, with a jilted romantic pining for the loss of his young love who has broken a promise to marry him. Although numerous verses exist describing the suffering of the poor abandoned boy, which vary from version to version, all recorded versions begin with the chorus rather than a verse. This is interesting because variations of the song that don't begin with the chorus do exist in the folk tradition,[67] suggesting that perhaps many of the recorded versions were relying at least in part on the model of other records.

Grayson's version is no exception. Actually his version has no substantial lyrical deviation from the multiple other versions that exist, but it is somewhat unique in its instrumentation. It is the only released version recorded before 1930 that doesn't feature a banjo as a primary instrument. Given Grayson's musical background as a banjo player, it is quite possible that he privately played the song as a banjo piece, even though he recorded it with the fiddle. By today's standard, Grayson's decision to record the song with a fiddle seems typical; by the 1930s, banjos and fiddles were quickly making way for guitars, mandolins, and tight harmonies, and recordings without banjo accompaniment became increasingly popular.

"Short Life of Trouble," like many of Grayson and Whitter's songs, was recorded many times by different artists, and clearly was not an original composition. However, since his untimely death, G.B. Grayson has gained a notoriety not only as a singer and fiddler, but also as a songwriter. To look through copyright listings, which list composers, one would think Grayson wrote several songs, including famous pieces like "Tom Dooley," but this does not actually reflect songwriting on his part. Although he is listed as composer for many of the songs he recorded, he wasn't. By listing him as the writer of certain songs, record companies could make claims to royalty and copyright to previously uncopyrighted songs floating in the ether of the folk tradition.

Despite this fact, outside of the recording industry, Grayson has still maintained quite a songwriting reputation. Many have given him credit for the composition of "Going Down the Lee Highway," a claim which has already been debunked. Ola Belle Reed claimed that he was the author of "I've Always Been a Rambler" and "Train 45."[68] Scholars have claimed "Where Are You Going Alice?" was a song he wrote about a local adulteress from Laurel Bloomery.[69] Even his daughter, Rosa, believed he had written "Don't Go Out Tonight, My Darling."[70] In every case these claims can be easily dismissed. There is, however, one song, recorded during the same session as "Short Life of Trouble," which could have been an original composition. It was never recorded by any other artists, and aside from its release on Grayson and Whitter records, it has no traceable history.

This mysterious song was "A Dark Road Is a Hard Road to Travel," which Grayson and Whitter recorded in July of 1928. It is a song that revolves around several common motifs of gospel songs—darkness and light and traveling a metaphorical road—without ever presenting an overtly religious message; instead, it is more of a song about looking on the bright side of life.

If Grayson wrote the song, it wasn't entirely original: he did pull on some floating concepts from the folk tradition to create it. These motifs and images have in turn found their way into other early country songs. Fans of the Carter Family will probably recognize the similarities between this song and the Carters' version of "Keep on the Sunny Side," which is not only similar thematically but also contains the lines "Clouds and storm will in time pass away / The sun again will shine bright and clear," a very similar sentiment to Grayson's line "Tomorrow the sun may be shining / Although it is cloudy today."

"A Dark Road is a Hard Road to Travel" also shares connective tissue with other songs from the era, specifically songs related to the traditional folksong "Little Bunch of Roses." Ephraim Woodie, from Ashe County, near Grayson's home, recorded "Last Gold Dollar" in 1930, a variation of "Little Bunch of Roses." His version contains the verse "Don't this road look long and lonely / Don't this sea look wide and deep / Would you ever think of me darling / If you could not hear me speak," an almost exact replication of the final verse from "A Dark Road Is a Hard Road to Travel." This verse in particular is so malleable and interchangeable that it consistently shows up in traditional songs. Fans of bluegrass may recognize it as the chorus to Flatt and Scruggs' 1954 recording of "Don't This Road Look Rough and Rocky."

As previously mentioned, "A Dark Road Is a Hard Road to Travel" comes very close to qualifying as a gospel song, although it never fully evolves from a generic song of optimism into one espousing a specific doctrine. Another Grayson and Whitter song, recorded almost one year later in September of 1930, also hints around the gospel motif without ever fully embracing it.

There is good reason for the seemingly gospel nature of "On the Banks of Old Tennessee": it shares a strong kinship with several songs in the gospel tradition, specifically a song entitled "I'm Alone in This World." This song, like "On the Banks of Old Tennessee," follows an incredibly simple format. Each verse is a series of three repeated lines involving a family member, "I have no father in this world," for example. After three repetitions, a recurring phrase is added, and a new verse is begun featuring a new family member. This simple pattern would have been beneficial in church settings where no hymnals were available to guide a congregation of singers, and, as would be expected, "I'm Alone in This World" has been reported in rural churches and camp meetings from Louisiana to Kentucky and as far back as the 1880s,[71] ultimately finding its way into the folk tradition.

For whatever reason, the version of the song recorded by Grayson and Whitter drops the typical final verse line "Take me home blessed Savior, take me home," replacing it with "She [or he] is sleeping tonight where the moon shines so bright / On the banks of the old Tennessee." This substitution moves the song out of the religious realm and into the secular world.

This development of the song as a secular piece obviously predates Grayson. It was recorded three times prior to Grayson and Whitter's session; however, only one—"The Banks of the Sunny Tennessee" by Mr. and Mrs. J.W. Baker—was ever issued. The Bakers' version, recorded during the famous Bristol sessions in the summer of 1927 at which Henry Whitter was also present, is basically identical to Grayson's; whether it was the source of his version or whether Grayson learned the song from a folk source cannot be fully known. It would be recorded a final time in 1930 by Fiddlin' John Carson, who would dedicate the song to Tennessee's former governor, Bob Taylor.

With songs like "On the Banks of Old Tennessee," it is unclear whether Grayson's version of a song was learned from an orally transmitted folk tradition or whether it was acquired from a previously released record. This mystery is especially pronounced with Grayson's version of "I Have Lost You Darling, True Love." Aside from a floating verse found in the song "Let Him Go, God Bless Him," this piece does not exist in any folklore collection. It was also not popularly recorded. This would suggest the possibility that the song could have been an original composition. However, that also doesn't seem to be the case, for even though the song was never released on any other early country record, it was recorded once before Grayson and Whitter's version.

That recording was made by Dock Boggs, a banjo player and singer from Norton, Virginia. Boggs had already recorded a few sides for Brunswick in March of 1927 but felt that his musical career was being neglected by the label. In 1929, he received an appeal in the mail from a variety store owner based in Richlands, Virginia: W.E. Myers. Myers was attempting to start his own record label and had sent Boggs the lyrics to four songs which Myers had written. He asked Boggs to set his words to music and record them for his new company: Lonesome Ace records. In September of 1929, Boggs travelled to Chicago and recorded Myers' songs. These records were never widely released, and Lonesome Ace records was driven out of business by the Depression shortly thereafter. However, Boggs was able to acquire a few hundred copies of the records he had made. He sold about one hundred copies of these records in the coal towns of eastern Kentucky.[72]

One of these records features a song, written by W.E. Myers, entitled "Lost Love Blues." Although the verses are in a slightly different order, this song is "I Have Lost You Darling, True Love" as recorded by Grayson and Whitter in September of 1929. Obviously, this presents a problem. Assuming the recording dates are all correct, Grayson and Whitter were recording the same song as Dock Boggs during the same month. How could they have known the song, if W.E. Myers had only just written it? Assuming all the facts are true, only two solutions are possible. Either the song wasn't actually written by Myers and was instead a folk product that has never been collected by a folklorist, or Myers, Boggs, or someone else shared the song with Grayson and Whitter during the same period. Given that Myers wrote the song to promote his new company, it seems unlikely that he would have wanted it to be recorded on another record label, but he was known to send unsolicited letters to artists he liked, and perhaps he felt that having a song he had written released on any label was an accomplishment.

With all the people involved in the confusion no longer alive to shed light on the situation, this mystery will probably never be unraveled with assurance, but there is reason to suspect that Grayson learned the song in the same way as Boggs: from a letter that contained words with no music. When Boggs recorded the song, he used a waltz time signature and a melody closely akin to the melody for "More Pretty Girls Than One." By contrast, Grayson's version uses an entirely different melody and a more driving four-four time. Boggs' version has several verses not found in the Grayson recording, but the verses Grayson does employ are worded exactly the same way and placed in the same relative order as Boggs' version. The verses that Grayson drops were probably omitted to make room for fiddle breaks between verses. Grayson and Whitter would have had good reason to record Myers' song as well. Given the pressure to show up to the Victor studios with uncopyrighted material, the duo would have been quite tempted by an unrecorded, uncopyrighted original composition which they could pass off as their own. Whatever happened, the end result is that of the three copyrights G.B. Grayson retained through the 1950s, one of them was for "I Have Lost You Darling, True Love," a song almost certainly written by W.E. Myers.

Grayson and Whitter may not have written many songs, but many have forever come to be associated with them, forming a bridge that connects their 1920s recordings to the music still performed in campgrounds and on stages today. Perhaps no song exemplifies this connection better than a song from their next-to-last session: "Little Maggie with a Dram Glass in Her Hand."

This song, like so many American folk songs, is a loose amalgamation from older sources. Specifically, it is a close relative of the songs "Darling Corey" and "Hustling Gamblers." All these songs are patchwork compositions with little clear narrative structure. They all tend to feature similar melodies, scenes of rebellious women, and floating verses which seem to drift between versions. One need only examine this verse in Dock Boggs' "Country Blues" (his title for "Hustling Gamblers") to see the similarities to Grayson and Whitter's version: "Last time I seen my little woman good people / She had a wine glass in her hand / She was drinking down her troubles / With a low down sorry man." Clearly, Grayson, Boggs, and the hundreds of other folk musicians who performed these songs were piecing together floating verses to create songs that were in some ways very similar but also unique to the performer.

What is most interesting about this particular song is the way that "Little Maggie" has entered the canon of bluegrass. Although its parent song "Darling Corey" has also been performed by artists like Bill Monroe and Flatt and Scruggs, it has not shared the same ubiquitous presence as "Little Maggie," which was one of the first songs played on the Grand Ole Opry by Bill Monroe's first true "bluegrass" band featuring Earl Scruggs on banjo and was also the first big hit for the Stanley Brothers in 1948.[73] The song has since become one of the most widely known bluegrass standards, which is surprising, since it has only a slight presence in folklore collections. This would suggest that the song has evolved more extensively through recordings rather than through oral transmission. In this case, to understand the development of the song you must trace it back through all the early artists that recorded it, including Bill Monroe, Roy Hall and His Blue Ridge Entertainers, Wade Mainer, and Zeke Morris, eventually arriving at the original rendition: Grayson and Whitter's.

Like all of their songs, "Little Maggie with a Dram Glass in Her Hand" showcases Grayson's fine fiddling and simultaneous singing. Over the course of the song, Grayson introduces almost all of the floating verses that would find their way into later versions. Although dozens of interchangeable verses to "Hustling Gamblers," "Darling Corey," and "Little Maggie" exist, the Stanley Brothers' 1948 recording of "Little Maggie" only contains two verses not found in Grayson and Whitter's original; similarly, Bill Monroe's recorded version featured on the album *Bluegrass Ramble* has only one verse not derived from the verses recorded by Grayson.

Later versions of "Little Maggie" are not exact replicas of the version played by Grayson; some lines and verses have been added and subtracted, but Grayson's opening verse and melody have never left it. Wherever the song went, whatever famous artist performed it, Grayson and Whitter's influence was always with it, an invisible reminder of the earliest recorded origins of country and bluegrass music. This Grayson and Whitter song and the thirty-one others like it that circulated on brittle discs in the 1920s and 30s continue to memorialize the towering heights that were reached by two otherwise innocuous individuals. Their lives, like those early records, were fragile, but their influence, like their songs, will hopefully stay with us forever.

Notes

Biography and History

A Dark Road Is a Hard Road to Travel

1. Grayson, Frank, personal interview, 19 April 2009.
2. Information about William and Charles Grayson taken from genealogical manuscripts compiled by Tom Gentry.
3. Wilson, Joe, liner notes for *Grayson and Whitter* (County Records, 1968).
4. Trivette, Ted, phone interview, 28 June 2016.
5. Meadows, Jim, interview with Clarence Grayson (Broadside Television Collection, Archives of Appalachia).
6. Dowell, Ray, letter to Jim Meadows, 2 November 1974 (Broadside Television Collection, Archives of Appalachia).
7. Gentry, Thomas, "G.B. Grayson," *Johnson County Heritage Book* (Marceline: Walsworth, 1985).
8. Meadows interview with Clarence Grayson.
9. Meadows interview with Clarence Grayson.
10. Meadows interview with Clarence Grayson.
11. Donleavy, Kevin, *Songs of Life* (Blacksburg: Pocahontas, 2004) 283.
12. Sneed, Thomas, interview with Frank Grayson (Thomas Sneed Papers, Archives of Appalachia).
13. Dowell, letter to Jim Meadows, 2 November 1974.
14. Cox, Bob L., *Fiddlin' Charlie Bowman* (Knoxville: University of Tennessee Press, 2007) 48.
15. Sneed interview with Frank Grayson.
16. Cohen, Norm, "Henry Whitter: His Life and Music," *JEMF Quarterly* Summer 1975: 58.
17. Green, Archie, Callie Payne interview notes (Archie Green Collection, Southern Folklife Collection).
18. Hauslohner, A.W., "From Fries to the Big Apple," *The Gazette* [Galax, VA], 27–29 March 1998: 9B.
19. Green, Archie, "Henry Whitter Search" (Archie Green Collection, Southern Folklife Collection).
20. See "Henry Whitter and the Creation of Country Music" for a full accounting of this controversy.
21. Whitter, Henry, "Familiar Folk Songs as Sung by Henry Whitter."
22. Kennedy, Rick, and Randy McNutt, *Little Labels—Big Sound: Small Record Companies and the Rise of American Music* (Bloomington: Indiana University Press, 1999) 14.
23. Kennedy and McNutt 7.
24. Wolfe, Charles, "The Carter Family," *Encyclopedia of Country Music* (Oxford: Oxford University Press, 2012) 84.
25. Grayson, Rosa, letter to Jim Meadows, 13 November 1974 (Broadside Television Collection, Archives of Appalachia).
26. Green, Archie, Laura Green interview notes (Archie Green Collection, Southern Folklife Collection).
27. Weston, Frank, "Albert Hash: Fiddler and Fiddle Maker," *Old Time Music* 39, Winter 1982–Spring 1984: 13.

Straddling the Appalachian Divide

1. 1908 Courthouse Foundation, *Bicentennial Heritage* (Marceline: Walsworth, 1995).
2. Huber, Patrick, *Linthead Stomp* (Chapel

Hill: University of North Carolina Press, 2008) 6–19.

3. U.S. Congress, "Report on the Condition of Woman and Child Wage Earners in the United States" (Washington D.C.: Government Printing Office, 1910) 538.

4. 1908 Courthouse Foundation.

5. 1908 Courthouse Foundation.

6. Knight, Jerry, "Death of a Company Town," *Washington Post*, 19 September 1988.

7. Huber 6.

8. Green, Archie, Callie Payne interview notes (Archie Green Collection, Southern Folklife Collection).

9. Huber 284.

10. Cohen, Norm, *Long Steel Rail* (Urbana: University of Illinois Press, 1981) 210.

11. Huber 19.

12. Malone, Bill C., *Country Music U.S.A.* (Austin: University of Texas Press, 1968) 36.

13. Rorrer, Kinney, "Charlie Poole and the North Carolina Ramblers," *Encyclopedia of Country Music* (Oxford: Oxford University Press, 1998) 418.

14. Malone, Bill C., "The Dixon Brothers," *Encyclopedia of Country Music* (Oxford: Oxford University Press, 1998) 149.

15. Huber 28.

16. Porter, Rose, "The History of Fries" (Grayson County Historical Society).

17. Huber xvi.

18. "Laurel Bloomery," *History of Johnson County* (Marceline: Walsworth Press, 1985) 27–29.

19. Slap, Andrew, *Reconstructing Appalachia* (Lexington: University of Kentucky Press) 297.

20. Slap 277.

21. *Manufacturer's Record*, 15 August 1907: 131.

22. Appalachian Land Ownership Task Force, *Who Owns Appalachia?* (Lexington: University of Kentucky Press, 2015) 82.

23. Appalachian Land Ownership Task Force 75.

24. Huber 34.

25. Lewis, Ronald L., *Transforming the Appalachian Countryside* (Chapel Hill: University of North Carolina Press, 1988) 155.

26. Appalachian Land Ownership Task Force 81.

Henry Whitter and the Creation of Country Music

1. Cohen, Norm, "Henry Whitter," *Encyclopedia of Country Music* (Oxford: Oxford University Press, 2012) 585.

2. Borgeson, Lillian, Ralph Peer interview transcription (JEMF Collection, Southern Folklife Collection).

3. Walsh, Ulysses J., "By the Way," *Phonograph Monthly Review*, August 1929: 374.

4. Green, Archie, Callie Payne interview notes.

5. Green, Archie, Orene Jones interview notes (Archie Green Collection, Southern Folklife Collection).

6. Stewart, Cal, *Uncle Josh's Punkin Centre Stories* (Chicago: Thompson and Thomas) 7.

7. Green, Archie, Paul Whitter interview notes (Archie Green Collection, Southern Folklife Collection).

8. 1908 Courthouse Foundation.

9. Hauslohner, A.W., "From Fries to the Big Apple," *The Gazette* [Galax, VA], 27–29 March 1998: 9B.

10. Green, Archie, Callie Payne interview notes.

11. 1908 Courthouse Foundation 86.

12. 1908 Courthouse Foundation 86.

13. Green, Archie, "Henry Whitter Search" (Archie Green Collection, Southern Folklife Collection).

14. Hauslohner 9B.

15. Mazor, Barry, *Ralph Peer and the Making of Popular Roots Music* (Chicago: Chicago Review Press, 2016) 56.

16. Borgeson interview with Ralph Peer.

17. Seeger, Mike, and John Cohen, interview with Dock Walsh, 5 April 1961 (Mike Seeger Collection, Southern Folklife Collection).

18. Green, Callie Payne interview notes.

19. Malone, Bill C., *Country Music U.S.A.* 62.

20. Palmer, Jack, *Vernon Dalhart: First Star of Country Music* (Denver: Mainspring Press, 2005) 104.

21. Cohen, *Long Steel Rail* 209–210.

22. Johnson, Willard, interview with Ernest Stoneman (Stoneman Family Papers, Archives of Appalachia).

23. For a much more thorough exploration of the song, controversy over its authorship, and the lawsuit, see Norm Cohen's *Long Steel Rail.*

24. Spottswood, Dick, "Columbia Records," *Encyclopedia of Country Music* 105.

25. Lornell 5.

26. Malone, Bill C., *Country Music U.S.A.* 36.

27. Seeger, Mike, and John Cohen, interview with A.E. Alderman (Mike Seeger Collection, Southern Folklife Collection).

28. Malone, *Country Music U.S.A.* 43.

29. Lornell, Kip, *Virginia's Blues, Country, and Gospel Records 1902–1943: An Annotated Discography* (Lexington: University of Kentucky Press, 1989) 8.

30. Kip Lornell's *Virginia's Blues, Country and Gospel Records 1902–1943: Annotated Discography* does an excellent job of explaining how

certain areas of Virginia became hotbeds of hillbilly music while other, equally talent laden areas, were ignored. Much of the analysis in this section come from Lornell.

31. Lornell 9.

32. "Old Time Tune Artists Given Test Recordings," *Talking Machine World*, 15 October 1925: 70.

33. The story of Hendley's famous banjo, which was eventually owned by seemingly every famous player of the bluegrass Golden Era, and which now resides in the Country Music Hall of Fame, is another tale in itself, one that someone interested in early bluegrass music would be interested to learn more about.

34. Carlin, Bob, "High on the Hog," *The Old Time Herald* 10.6: 23.

35. Whitter, Henry, letter to Mary Caroline Ring, 15 November, year not noted, but my guesses are 1923 or 1924.

36. Johnson, Willard, interview with Ernest Stoneman (Stoneman Family Papers, Archives of Appalachia).

37. Hagar, Fred, letter to Paul Whitter, January 18, 1951 (Archie Green Collection, Southern Folklife Collection).

38. Donleavy 282.

39. Johnson interview with Stoneman.

40. Borgeson interview with Ralph Peer.

41. Borgeson interview with Ralph Peer.

42. Borgeson interview with Ralph Peer.

43. All information about Peer's move to Victor and his policy on copyrights was taken from an extensive interviewed conducted by Lillian Borgeson in 1958.

44. Green, Archie, Walter Jones Interview Notes (Archie Green Collection, Southern Folklife Collection).

45. Earle, Eugene, Discographical Notes (Eugene Earle Collection, Southern Folklife Collection).

46. Wolfe, Charles, "Grayson and Whitter," *Old Time Herald* 3.7: 8.

47. Wyatt, Marshall, interview with Fred Miller, 15 June 1990.

48. For a thorough accounting of how this shift would influence the country music industry, see Bob Coltman's "Across the Chasm: How the Depression Changed Country Music," *Old Time Music* 23.

49. Rosenberg, Neil, *Bluegrass: A History* (Urbana: University of Illinois Press, 1985) 26.

50. Spencer, Thornton, personal interview, 22 March 2017.

51. Typed Manuscript (Archie Green Collection, Southern Folklife Collection).

52. "Famous Composer to Appear at Dogwood Festival," *The Daily Times-News* [Burlington], 2 April 1934: 4.

53. Taylor, Ronnie. Interview with Alonzo Black. 22 July 1975.

54. Thornton Spencer interview.

55. Weston, Frank, "Albert Hash: Fiddler and Fiddle Maker," *Old Time Music* 39, Winter 1982–Spring 1984: 13.

The Long Shadow of G.B. Grayson

1. Greene, Clarence, "Fiddling Steve Ledford," *Bluegrass Unlimited* 17.11, May 1983: 63.

2. Greene 63.

3. Greene 63.

4. Spottswood, Richard, *Banjo on the Mountain* (Jackson: University Press of Mississippi, 2010) 57.

5. Mainer-Morris-Ledford Band, afternoon rehearsal (Ralph Rinzler Folklife Archives, Smithsonian Institution).

6. Johnson, David W., *Lonesome Melodies: The Lives and Music of the Stanley Brothers* (Jackson: University Press of Mississippi, 2013) 37.

7. Stanley, Ralph, and Eddie Dean, *Man of Constant Sorrow: My Life and Times* (New York: Gotham, 2009) n. pag., chapter 1.

8. Rosenberg, Neil, and Charles Wolfe, *Music of Bill Monroe* (Urbana: University of Illinois Press, 2007) 56.

9. Rosenberg and Wolfe 123.

10. Weston, Frank, "Glen Neaves of Fries, Virginia," *Old Time Herald* 8.5: 15.

11. Weston 19.

12. "A Tribute to G.B. Grayson" (Broadside Television Collection, Archives of Appalachia).

13. Meadows, Jim, interview with Clarence Grayson (Broadside Television Collection, Archives of Appalachia).

14. Sneed, Thomas, interview with Frank Grayson (Thomas Sneed Papers, Archives of Appalachia).

15. Brown, Bessie, personal interview, 4 April 2016.

16. Sneed interview with Frank Grayson.

17. Spencer, Thornton, personal interview, 22 March 2017.

18. Dowell, Ray, letter to Jim Meadows, 2 November 1974 (Broadside Television Collection, Archives of Appalachia).

19. Kemp, J.C., personal interview, 6 April 2016.

20. "Fiddlers Meet Fine Success," *Watauga Democrat* [Boone], 22 August 1935: 1.

21. Trivette, Ted, personal interview, 28 June 2016.

22. Sneed interview with Frank Grayson.

I Wish I Was Single Again

1. Wolfe, Charles, *Tennessee Strings* (Knoxville: University of Tennessee Press) vii.

2. Coltman, Bob, "Across the Chasm," *Old Time Music* 23: 9.
3. Meadows, Jim, interview with Clarence Grayson (Broadside Television Collection, Archives of Appalachia).
4. Meadows interview with Clarence Grayson.
5. Information about the overdue medical expenses comes from genealogical notes made by Tom Gentry.
6. Meadows interview with Clarence Grayson.
7. Dowd Hall, et al., *Like a Family* (New York: Norton, 1987) 140.
8. Hall 143.
9. Green, Archie interview with Orene Jones (Archie Green Collection, Southern Folklife Collection).
10. Jones, Benson, personal interview, 24 June 2016.
11. Green, Archie, Gretchen Huntsinger interview notes (Archie Green Collection, Southern Folklife Collection).
12. Johnson interview with Ernest Stoneman.
13. Wolfe, Charles, "And No Man Shall Control Me," *Women of Country Music* (Lexington: University of Kentucky Press, 2003) 26.
14. Green, Archie, Orene Jones interview notes (Archie Green Collection, Southern Folklife Collection).
15. Green interview with Gretchen Huntsinger.
16. From copy of official divorce complaint.
17. Green interview with Gretchen Huntsinger.
18. McNeil, Kada, personal interview, 4 May 2016.
19. Green, Archie, notes on Henry Whitter (Archie Green Collection, Southern Folklife Collection).
20. Spencer, Thornton, personal interview, 22 March 2017.
21. Hauslohner, A.W, "From Fries to the Big Apple," *The Gazette* [Galax, VA], 27–29 March 1998: 9B.
22. McNeil, Kada, personal interview, 4 May 2016.
23. Eller, Lee, personal interview, 26 February 2016.
24. Wilson, Joe, letter in *JEMF Quarterly*, Winter 1971.

Grayson, Whitter and the Hill Billies

1. Malone, Bill C., *Country Music U.S.A.* (Austin: University of Texas Press, 1968) 94.
2. Malone, Bill C., *Country Music U.S.A.* 43.
3. Wiggins, Gene, *Fiddlin' Georgia Crazy* (Urbana: University of Illinois Press, 1987) 79–80.
4. Seeger, Mike, and John Cohen, interview with A.E. Alderman (Mike Seeger Collection, Southern Folklife Collection).
5. Green, Archie, interview with Lucy Hopkins, 1 January 1963 (Archie Green Collection, Southern Folklife Collection).
6. Green, Archie, interview with Bill Hopkins, 9 August 1962 (Archie Green Collection, Southern Folklife Collection).
7. Seeger and Cohen interview with A.E. Alderman.
8. Green interview with Bill Hopkins.
9. Green interview with Bill Hopkins.
10. Green, Archie, "Hillbilly Music: Source and Symbol," *Torching the Fink: Books and Other Essays on Vernacular Culture* (Chapel Hill: University of North Carolina Press, 2002) 21.
11. Green interview with Bill Hopkins.
12. Green, "Hillbilly Music: Source and Symbol" 21.
13. Green, Archie, A.E. Alderman interview notes (Archie Green Collection, Southern Folklife Collection).
14. Seeger and Cohen interview with Alderman.
15. Seeger and Cohen interview with Alderman.
16. Coltman, Bob, "Across the Chasm," *Old Time Music* 23: 6.
17. Lornell, Kip, *Virginia's Blues, Country, and Gospel Records 1902–1943: An Annotated Discography* (Lexington: University of Kentucky Press, 1989) 4.
18. Borgeson interview.
19. Kenney, William Howland, *Recorded Music in American Life: The Phonograph and Popular Memory, 1890–1945* (Oxford: Oxford University Press, 2003) 118.
20. Drowne, Kathleen Morgan, *American Popular Culture Through History: The 1920s* (Westport: Greenwood Press, 2004) 212.
21. Daniel, Wayne W., *Pickin' on a Peachtree: A History of Country Music in Atlanta, Georgia* (Urbana: University of Illinois Press, 2001) 103.
22. Mike Seeger and John Cohen interview with A.E. Alderman.
23. Peterson, Richard A., *Creating Country Music: Fabricating Authenticity* (Chicago: University of Chicago Press, 1997): 3.
24. Wiggins 55.
25. Peterson 58.
26. "Henry Whitter, OKeh Artist, Real Hill Country Type," *Talking Machine World* 21, 15 May 1925: 35.
27. "One of the Bright Lights Among White Lights," *The Tatler*, May 1919: 11.
28. Bronner, Simon J., *Old Time Music Makers of New York State* (Syracuse: Syracuse University Press) 31.

29. Seeger and Cohen interview of A.E. Alderman.

30. Russell, Tony, and Bob Pinson, *Country Music Records: A Discography* (Oxford: Oxford University Press, 2008) 12.

31. Hill Billies advertisement, *Portsmouth Daily Times*, 27 June 1928: 3.

32. Kennedy, Rick, and Randy McNutt, *Little Labels—Big Sound: Small Record Companies and the Rise of American Music* (Bloomington: Indiana University Press, 1999) 14.

33. Peterson 76.

34. "Hill Billies Capture WRC, Boys from the Blue Ridge Mountains Take Washington with Guitars, Fiddle and Banjos; Open New Line of American Airs," *Radio Digest*, 6 March 1925: 5.

35. Mike Seeger and John Cohen interview with A.E. Alderman.

36. Peterson 75.

37. Cullen, Frank, Florence Hackman, Donald McNeilly, "Keith-Albee Circuit," *Vaudeville, Old and New: An Encyclopedia of Variety Performers in America* (New York: Routledge, 2007) 599–612.

38. Green and Earle interview with Lucy Hopkins.

39. Liebman, Roy, *Vitaphone Films: A Catalogue of Features and Shorts* (Jefferson: McFarland, 2003): 29.

40. Green, Archie, "Hillbilly Music: Source and Symbol," *Torching the Fink: Books and Other Essays on Vernacular Culture* (Chapel Hill: University of North Carolina Press, 2002): 24.

41. Cox, Bob, *Fiddlin' Charlie Bowman: An East Tennessee Old Time Music Pioneer and his Musical Family* (Knoxville: University of Tennessee Press, 2007) 49.

42. Green and Earle interview with Lucy Hopkins.

43. Cox 44.

44. Mike Seeger and John Cohen interview with A.E. Alderman.

45. "Artist on Tour Is 'Detained' Here, Entertains Class," *Abilene Reporter-News*, 24 February 1931: 8.

James W.M. Grayson, Tom Dula and the Appalachian Civil War

1. Borgeson, Lillian, interview with Ralph Peer Transcription (John Edwards Memorial Foundation Collection, Southern Folklife Collection).

2. *Frank C. Brown Collection of North Carolina Folklore* (Durham: Duke University Press, 1952) 2:707–713.

3. Crawford, Martin, *Ashe County's Civil War: Community and Society in the Appalachian South* (Charlottesville: University of Virginia Press, 2001) 26.

4. Crawford 35.

5. Crawford 72.

6. Nikazy, Eddie M., *Forgotten Soldiers: History of the 4th Tennessee Volunteer Infantry Regiment 1863–1865* (Bowie: Heritage Books, 1995) 2.

7. Scott, Samuel, and Samuel Angel, *History of the Thirteenth Regiment Tennessee Volunteer Cavalry* (Johnson City: Overmountain Press, 1987) 39.

8. Crawford 75.

9. Scott and Angel 53.

10. "A Brave Woman," *Standard* [Raleigh] (Civil War Sourcebook, Tennessee State Library and Archives).

11. Petty, James, "The Hanging of the Price Family on Ashe County Courthouse Lawn" 2.

12. Ellis, Daniel, *Thrilling Adventures of Daniel Ellis* (New York: Harper, 1867) 65–71.

13. "What Tennessee Loyalists Have Done," *Memphis Bulletin*, 5 August 1863 (Civil War Sourcebook, Tennessee State Library and Archives).

14. Sneed, Thomas, interview with Frank Grayson (Thomas Sneed Papers, Archives of Appalachia).

15. *North Carolina Troops 1861–1865: A Roster* (Raleigh: North Carolina Department of Archives and History) 557.

16. West, John Foster, *Lift Up Your Head Tom Dooley* (Asheboro: Down Home Press) 57.

17. Grayson, Frank, personal interview, 19 April 2009.

18. *Frank C. Brown Collection of North Carolina Folklore* (Durham: Duke University Press Durham, 1952) 2:709.

19. *Frank C. Brown Collection* 2:713.

20. "The Death Penalty: Shocking Revelations of Crime and Depravity in North Carolina-Thomas Dula Hanged for the Murder of Laura Foster," *New York Herald*, 2 May 1868: 7.

21. *Frank C. Brown Collection* 2:711–712.

The Courthouse Massacre

1. Borgeson, Lillian, interview with Ralph Peer Transcription (John Edwards Memorial Foundation Collection, Southern Folklife Collection).

2. "Henry Whitter, OKeh Artist, Real Hill Country Type," *Talking Machine World*, 15 May 1925: 35.

3. "Hill Billies Capture WRC, Boys from the Blue Ridge Mountains Take Washington with Guitars, Fiddle and Banjos; Open New

Line of American Airs," *Radio Digest*, 6 March 1925: 5.

4. Gardner, Rufus, *The Courthouse Tragedy* (Mt. Airy: Reliable Printing, 1962) 12.

5. Aceves, Peter, "The Hillsville Tragedy in Court Record Mass Media, and Folk Balladry," *Keystone Quarterly* Spring 1971: 18.

6. Berrier, Ralph, Jr., "The Courthouse Tragedy: Gunfight in Hillsville in 1912," *The Roanoke Times*, 10 March 2012.

7. Berrier.

8. Hall, Randal, "A Courtroom Massacre: Politics and Public Sentiment in Progressive-Era Virginia" *The Journal of Southern History* 70.2: 287.

9. Hall 290.

10. Laws, G. Malcolm, *Native American Balladry* (Philadelphia: The American Folklore Society, 1964) 2.

11. Aceves 10.

12. Wolfe, Charles K., "Event Songs," *Reading Country Music: Steel Guitars, Opry Stars, and Honky Tonk Bars* (Durham: Duke University Press, 1998) 194.

13. Cohen, Norm, *Long Steel Rail* (Urbana: University of Illinois Press, 1981) 268.

14. Hobson, Paul, "Radio's Hillbilly King, Carson Robison, who is with his Pioneers, a regular attraction for Oxydol every Sunday from Luxembourg, Lyons and Normandy, tells us in this interview how he writes his world-famous songs (1938)," *The Country Music Reader* (Oxford: Oxford University Press, 2014) 52.

15. Cohen, Norm, *American Folksongs* (Westport: Greenwood Press, 2008) 209.

16. Aceves 10.

17. To see all the collected versions side by side, refer to Aceves, Appendix B, pp. 27–34.

18. Aceves 18.

On the Trail of Nancy Blevins

1. Weston, Frank, "Albert Hash: Fiddler and Fiddle Maker," *Old Time Music* 39 Winter 1982–Spring 1984: 13.

2. Spencer, Thornton, personal interview, 22 March 2017.

3. Owen, Blanton, liner notes, *Old Originals: Volume Two* (Rounder, 0058).

4. Anderson-Green, Paula Hathaway, *A Hot-Bed of Musicians* (Knoxville: University of Tennessee Press, 2002) 67.

5. Walker, Emma E., "Bromine-Arsenic Springs," *A Reference Handbook of the Medical Sciences: Embracing the Entire Range of Scientific and Practical Medicine and Allied Science* (New York: William Wood, 1913) 512.

6. Trotter, William R., *Bushwhackers* (Winston Salem: John F. Blair, 1988).

The Music

1. "My Mind Is to Marry" was originally unissued. However, it has since been released using an original test pressing. For the purpose of confining analysis to the duo's original recordings, it will not be considered in this section.

2. "Going Down the Lee Highway" has since been recorded as "Lee Highway Blues," and Charles Wolfe has referred to the song as "bluesy," but the song doesn't follow a typical blues song structure and is more akin to traditional fiddle tunes.

3. Dowell, Ray, letter to Jim Meadows, 2 November 1974 (Broadside Television Collection, Archive of Appalachia).

4. Norm and Anne Cohen, "Folk and Hillbilly Music: Further Thoughts on their Relation," *JEMFQ* 13.46: 50–57.

5. See Perrow and Bascom for examples of early song versions.

6. Talley, Thomas W., *Negro Folk Rhymes* (New York: Macmillan, 1922) 50.

7. Miles, Emma B., *The Spirit of the Mountains* (New York: Pott, 1905) 165.

8. Davidson, Eric, and Paul Newman, liner notes for *Traditional Music from Grayson and Carroll Counties* (Folkways, 1962) 6.

9. Richie, Jean, *Folksongs of the Southern Appalachians as Sung by Jean Richie* (Lexington: University of Kentucky Press, 1965).

10. Wolfe, Charles, *The Devil's Box* (Nashville: Country Music Foundation Press, 1997) 61.

11. Mare, Frank, liner notes for *Going Down Lee Highway: 1927–29 Recordings by Grayson and Whitter* (Davis Unlimited, 1977).

12. Wolf, Charles, *Tennessee Strings* (Knoxville: University of Tennessee Press) 49.

13. Bod4690 in the *Bodleian Broadside Collection* (Broadside Ballads Online, Bodleian Library).

14. *Folksongs of the Catskills* (Albany: State University of New York Press, 1982) 333.

15. Cox 315.

16. Cox 314.

17. Lofgren, Lyle, "Remembering the Old Songs: Rose Conley," *Inside Bluegrass*, May 2003.

18. Wilgus, D.K., "Rose Connoley: An Irish Ballad," *The Journal of American Folklore* 92.364: 173.

19. *Frank C. Brown Collection* 2: 691–692.

20. *Frank C. Brown Collection* 2: 690.

21. Rennick, Robert M., "The Disguised Lover Theme and the Ballad" *Southern Folklore Quarterly* 23.4: 220.

22. *Folk-Songs of the South*, John Harrington Cox, ed. (New York: Dover, 1967).

23. Joyce, P.W., *Old Irish Folk Music and Songs* (Dublin: Hodges, Figgis, 1909) 190.

24. Sharp, Cecil J., *English Folk Songs from the Southern Appalachians Vol. 2* (Oxford: Oxford University Press, 1952) 254.
25. Tawa, Nicholas, *Sweet Songs for Gentle Americans* (Bowling Green: Bowling Green University Popular Press, 1980) 18.
26. Tawa 123.
27. "Hays, William Shakespeare," *Encyclopedia of Louisville* (Lexington: University Press of Kentucky) 378.
28. Sizemore, Asher, *Old Fashioned Hymns and Mountain Ballads as Sung by Asher Sizemore and Little Jimmie* (Louisville: Asher Sizemore, 1933) 20.
29. Wiggins, Gene, *Fiddlin' Georgia Crazy* (Urbana: University of Illinois Press, 1987) 261.
30. Ewing, George, *The Well Tempered Lyre* (Dallas: Southern Methodist University Press, 1977) 12.
31. Ewing 25.
32. Ewing 16.
33. "Laurel Bloomery," *History of Johnson County* (Marceline: Walsworth, 1985): 28.
34. Ellis, Samuel, *The History of the Order of the Sons of Temperance* (Boston: Stacey, Richardson, 1848) 46.
35. "Statistical Report of the Sons of Temperance of North America," *The Journal of the American Geographical and Statistical Society*, 1 December 1859.
36. White, Thomas, Jr., *An Essay on the Order of the Sons of Temperance* (Montreal: J.C. Becket, 1853) 6–12.
37. It is worth noting that few if any of these collected versions predate Grayson and Whitter's recording, so it is conceivable that the record, rather than the sheet music, is the original source for these folk version.
38. Filmore, A.D., *The Temperance Musician* (Cincinnati: Applegate, 1853) 179.
39. Ewing 14.
40. Tawa 102.
41. Cohen, Norm, *Long Steel Rail: The Railroad in American Folksong* (Urbana: University of Illinois Press, 1981) 5.
42. Cohen 18.
43. Wolfe, Charles, "Grayson and Whitter." *Old Time Herald* 3.7: 8.
44. Cohen 504.
45. Cohen 504.
46. Cohen 506.
47. Cohen 507.
48. Jasen, David A., *Tin Pan Alley: An Encyclopedia of the Golden Age of American Song* (New York: Routledge, 2003):103.
49. Cohen 298.
50. Information in the preceding two paragraphs taken from Cohen 302–303.
51. Cohen 301.
52. Cohen 327.
53. Cohen 574.
54. Cohen 574.
55. Scarborough, Dorothy, *On the Trail of Negro Folk-Songs* (Boston: Harvard University Press, 1925) 220.
56. Cox, Bob L., *Fiddlin Charlie Bowman: An East Tennessee Old Time Music Pioneer and his Musical Family* (Knoxville: University of Tennessee Press, 2007) 62.
57. Brooks, William, "Maude Nugent," *The Norton/Grove Dictionary of Women Composers* (New York: Norton, 1994) 348.
58. Crawford, Richard, *America's Musical Life: A History* (New York: Norton, 2001) 472.
59. Crawford 476.
60. *Songbook of the Harvard Club of San Francisco* (San Francisco, 1909) 75.
61. Kennedy, Rick, and Randy McNutt, *Little Labels—Big Sound: Small Record Companies and the Rise of American Music* (Bloomington: Indiana University Press, 1999) 7.
62. Wilson, Mark, liner notes for *Philip Kazee: A Family Tradition* (Rounder, 2008): 13.
63. Wilson, Mark, liner notes for *Philip Kazee: A Family Tradition* (Rounder, 2008): 33.
64. Parker, Ray, "G.B. Grayson: A Short Life of Trouble," *Old Time Music* 35 Winter 1980–Spring 1981: 12.
65. Roberts, Leonard, *Sang Branch Settlers: Folksongs and Tales of a Kentucky Mountain Family* (Austin: University of Texas Press, 1974) 341.
66. Wolfe, "Grayson and Whitter" 8.
67. *The Folksongs of Middle Tennessee: The George Boswell Collection* (Knoxville: University of Tennessee Press, 1997) 59.
68. "A Tribute to G.B. Grayson" (Broadside Television Collection, Archives of Appalachia).
69. Parker 12.
70. Grayson, Rosa, letter to Jim Meadows, 13 November 1974 (Broadside Television Collection, Archives of Appalachia).
71. Caffery, Joshua Clegg, *Traditional Music in Coastal Louisiana: The 1934 Lomax Recordings* (Baton Rouge: Louisiana State University Press, 2013) 40, and Jackson, George Pullen, *Spiritual Folk-Songs of Early America* (Locust Valley: J. J. Augustin, 1953) 219.
72. O'Connell, Barry, liner notes for *Dock Boggs: His Original Recordings* (RBF Records, 1983) 1–11.
73. Rosenberg, Neil, *Bluegrass: A History* (Chicago: University of Illinois Press, 1985) 72, 82.

Bibliography

Aceves, Peter R. "The Hillsville Tragedy in Court Record, Mass Media, and Folk Balladry: A Problem in Historical Documentation." *Keystone Quarterly*, vol. 16, no. 1, 1971, 1–39.

American Murder Ballads and Their Stories. Collected and edited by Olive Woolley Burt. New York: Oxford University Press, 1958.

Anderson-Green, Paula Hathaway. *A Hot-Bed of Musicians: Traditional Music in the Upper New River Valley–Whitetop Region*. Knoxville: University of Tennessee Press, 2002.

Appalachian Land Ownership Task Force. *Who Owns Appalachia? Land Ownership and Its Impact*. Lexington: University of Kentucky Press, 2015.

Bascom, Louise Rand. "Ballads and Songs of Western North Carolina." *The Journal of American Folklore*, vol. 22, no. 84, 1909, 238–250.

Berrier, Ralph, Jr. "The Courthouse Tragedy: Gunfight in Hillsville in 1912." *The Roanoke Times*, 10 March 2012. Accessed online.

Bordman, Gerald, and Thomas S. Hischak. *The Oxford Companion to American Theatre*. New York: Oxford University Press, 2003.

Borgeson, Lillian. Interview with Ralph Peer Transcription. From Folder 750 in the John Edwards Memorial Foundation Collection, Southern Folklife Collection, Louis Round Wilson Special Collections Library, University of North Carolina at Chapel Hill.

"A Brave Woman." *Raleigh Standard*, 20 September 1861. *Civil War Sourcebook*. Tennessee State Library and Archives. Accessed online 4 April 2016.

Broadside Ballads Online. Bodleian Libraries. Web. 29 May 2017.

Bronner, Simon J. *Old Time Music Makers of New York State*. Syracuse: Syracuse University Press, 1987.

Brooks, William. "Maude Nugent." *The Norton/Grove Dictionary of Women Composers*. Edited by Julie Anne Sadie and Rhian Samuel. New York: Norton, 1994.

Brown, Bessie. Personal interview. 8 April 2016.

Caffery, Joshua Clegg. *Traditional Music in Coastal Louisiana: The 1934 Lomax Recordings*. Baton Rouge: Louisiana State University Press, 2013.

Carlin, Bob. "High on the Hog: Fisher Hendley and the Aristocratic Pigs." *The Old Time Herald*, vol. 10, no. 6, August–September 2006, 16–25.

Cohen, Anne, and Norm Cohen. "Folk and Hillbilly Music: Further Thoughts on Their Relation." *JEMFQ*, vol. 13, no. 46, Summer 1977, 50–57.

Cohen, Norm. *American Folksongs: A Regional Encyclopedia, Volume One*. Westport: Greenwood Press, 2008.

Cohen, Norm. *Long Steel Rail: The Railroad in American Folksong*. Urbana: University of Illinois Press, 1981.

Cohen, Norm. "Henry Whitter." In Kingsbury.

Cohen, Norm. "Henry Whitter: His Life and Music." *JEMF Quarterly*, Summer 1975.

Coltman, Bob. "Across the Chasm: How the Depression Changed Country Music." *Old Time Music*, vol. 23, 6–12.

Cox, Bob L. *Fiddlin Charlie Bowman: An East Tennessee Old Time Music Pioneer and his Musical Family*. Knoxville: University of Tennessee Press, 2007.

Crawford, Martin. *Ashe County's Civil War: Community and Society in the Appalachian South*. Charlottesville: University Press of Virginia, 2001.

Crawford, Richard. *America's Musical Life: a History*. New York: Norton, 2001.

Cullen, Frank, Florence Hackman, and Donald McNeilly. "Keith-Albee Circuit." *Vaudeville, Old and New: An Encyclopedia of Variety Performers in America*. New York: Routledge, 2007. pp. 599–612.

Cushing, William. *Initials and Pseudonyms: A Dictionary of Literary Disguises*. Boston: Thomas Y. Crowell and Company, 1885.

Cusic, Don. *Gene Autry: His Life and Career*. Jefferson: McFarland, 2007.

Daniel, Wayne. W. *Pickin' on Peachtree: A History of Country Music in Atlanta, Georgia*. Urbana: University of Illinois Press, 2001.

Davidson, Eric, and Paul Newman. Liner notes. *Traditional Music from Grayson and Carroll Counties*. Folkways, 1962.

Donleavy, Kevin. *Songs of Life: Conversations with Old-Time Musicians from Virginia and North Carolina*. Blacksburg: Pocahontas Press, 2004.

Dowell, Ray. Letter to Jim Meadows, 5 October 1974. Box 11, Folder 27. Broadside Television Collection, Archives of Appalachia in the Center for Appalachian Studies and Services, East Tennessee State University Library at Johnson City, TN.

Dowell, Ray. Letter to Jim Meadows, 2 November 1974. Box 11, Folder 27. Broadside Television Collection, Archives of Appalachia in the Center for Appalachian Studies and Services, East Tennessee State University Library at Johnson City, TN.

Drowne, Kathleen Morgan, and Patrick Huber. *American Popular Culture Through History: The 1920's*. Westport: Greenwood, 2004.

Earle, Eugene. Discographical notes. From Folder 189 of the Eugene Earle Collection, Southern Folklife Collection, Louis Round Wilson Special Collections Library, University of North Carolina at Chapel Hill.

Earle, Eugene, and Archie Green. Interview with Dock Walsh (FT-20002/4155) in the Archie Green Collection, Southern Folklife Collection, Louis Round Wilson Special Collections Library, University of North Carolina at Chapel Hill.

Eller, Lee. Personal interview. 26 February 2016.

Ellis, Daniel. *Thrilling Adventures of Daniel Ellis*. New York: Harper, 1867.

Ellis, Samuel. *The History of the Order of the Sons of Temperance*. Boston: Stacey, Richardson, 1848.

Ewing, George W. *The Well Tempered Lyre: Songs and Verses of the Temperance Movement*. Dallas: Southern Methodist University Press, 1977.

"Famous Composer to Appear at Dogwood Festival." *The Daily Times-News* [Burlington], 2 April 1934, 4. Web. Accessed 6 March 2016.

"Fiddlers Meet Fine Success." *Watauga Democrat* [Boone, NC], 22 August 1935, 1. Web. Accessed 23 April 2017.

Filmore, A.D. *The Temperance Musician*. Cincinnati: Applegate, 1853. p. 179.

Folk Songs from the Southern Highlands. Collected and edited by Mellinger Edward Henry. New York: J. J. Augustin, 1938.

Folk Songs of the Catskills. Edited by Norman Cazden, Herbert Haufrecht and Norman Studer. Albany: State University of New York Press, 1982.

The Folksongs of Middle Tennessee: The George Boswell Collection. Edited by Charles Wolfe. Knoxville: University of Tennessee Press, 1997.

Folk-Songs of the South. Edited by John Harrington Cox. New York: Dover, 1967.

Frank C. Brown Collection of North Carolina Folklore, 5 vols. Durham: Duke University Press, 1952.

Gardner, Rufus J. *The Courthouse Tragedy, Hillsville, Virginia*. Mt. Airy: Reliable Printing, 1962.

Gentry, Thomas. "G.B. Grayson." *History of Johnson County*. Marceline: Walsworth Press, 1985. 135–136.

Grayson, Frank. Personal interview. 19 April 2009.

Grayson, Rosa. Letter to Jim Meadows, 13 November 1974. Box 11, Folder 27. Broadside Television Collection, Archives of Appalachia in the Center for Appalachian Studies and Services, East Tennessee State University Library at Johnson City, TN.

Green, Archie. A.E. Alderman Interview Notes. From Folder 1591 in the Archie Green Collection, Southern Folklife Collection, Louis Round Wilson Special Collections Library, University of North Carolina at Chapel Hill.

Green, Archie. Callie Payne interview Notes. From Callie Payne Folder 1295 in the Archie Green Collection, Southern Folklife Collection, Louis Round Wilson Special Collections Library, University of North Carolina at Chapel Hill.

Green, Archie. Gretchen Huntsinger Interview Notes. From Callie Payne Folder 1295 in the Archie Green Collection, Southern Folklife Collection, Louis Round Wilson Special Collections Library, University of North Carolina at Chapel Hill.

Green, Achie. Hattie Hader Interview Notes. From Hattie Hader Folder 1291 in the Achie Green Collection, Southern Folklife Collection, Louis Round Wilson Special Collections Library, University of North Carolina at Chapel Hill.

Green, Archie. Henry Whitter Notes. From Folder 6024 in the Archie Green Collection, Southern Folklife Collection, Louis Round Wilson Special Collections Library, University of North Carolina at Chapel Hill.

Green, Archie. "Henry Whitter Search." Manuscript. From Folder 6024 in the Archie Green Collection, Southern Folklife Collection, Louis Round Wilson Special Collections Library, University of North Carolina at Chapel Hill.

Green, Archie. Interview Notes from Mr. Laura Green. From G.B. Grayson Folder 518 in the Archie Green Collection, Southern Folklife Collection, Louis Round Wilson Special Collections Library, University of North Carolina at Chapel Hill.

Green, Archie. *Only a Miner: Studies in Recorded Coal-Mining Songs*. Urbana: University of Illinois Press, 1972.

Green, Archie. Walter Jones Interview Notes. From Folder 518 in the Archie Green Collection, Southern Folklife Collection, Louis Round Wilson Special Collections Library, University of North Carolina at Chapel Hill.

Green, Archie, and Eugene Earle. Interview with Bill Hopkins (FT-20002/4062). From the Archie Green Collection, Southern Folklife Collection, Louis Round Wilson Special Collections Library, University of North Carolina at Chapel Hill.

Green, Archie, and Eugene Earle. Interview with Lucy Hopkins (FT-20002/4062). From the Archie Green Collection, Southern Folklife Collection, Louis Round Wilson Special Collections Library, University of North Carolina at Chapel Hill.

Green Archie. "Hillbilly Music: Source and Symbol." *Torching the Fink Books and Other Essays on Vernacular Culture*. Chapel Hill: University of North Carolina Press, 2002.

Greene, Clarence. "Fiddling Steve Ledford." *Bluegrass Unlimited*, vol. 17, no. 11, May 1983, 63–65.

Hager, Fred. Letter to Paul Whitter, 18 January 1951. From Fred Hagar Folder 1292 in the Archie Green Collection, Southern Folklife Collection, Louis Round Wilson Special Collections Library, University of North Carolina at Chapel Hill.

Hager, Fred. Letter to Paul Whitter, 27 October 1950. From Fred Hager Folder 1292 in the Achie Green Collection, Southern Folklife Collection, Louis Round Wilson Special Collections Library, University of North Carolina at Chapel Hill.

Hall, Randal. "A Courtroom Massacre: Politics and Public Sentiment in Progressive-Era Virginia." *The Journal of Southern History*, vol. 70, no. 2, May 2004, 249–292.

Hauslohner, A.W. "From Fries to the Big Apple" *The Gazette* [Galax, VA], 27–29 March 1998, 9B.

"Hays, William Shakespeare." *The Encyclopedia of Louisville*. Edited by John Kleber. Lexington: University Press of Kentucky, 2001.

"Henry Whitter, Okeh Artist, Real Hill Country Type: Big City Holds No Lure for Singer from Hills of Virginia." *Talking Machine World*, vol. 21, 15 May 1925, 35.

Hill Billies advertisement. *Portsmouth Daily Times*, 27 June 1928: 3.

"Hill Billies Capture WRC: Boys from the Blue Ridge Mountains Take Washington with Guitars, Fiddle and Banjos; Open New Line of American Airs." *Radio Digest*, vol. 16, no. 9, 6 March 1926.

A History of the Town of Fries, VA. Edited by Avery Bond and Martha Nichols. Collinsville: Collinsville Printing Co.

Hobson, Paul. "Radio's Hillbilly King, Carson Robison, Who Is with His Pioneers a Regular

Attraction for Oxydol Every Sunday from Luxembourg, Lyons and Normandy, Tells Us in This Interview How He Writes His World-Famous Songs (1938)." *The Country Music Reader.* Edited by Travid D. Stimeling. Oxford: Oxford University Press, 2014. 51–54.

Huber, Patrick. *Linthead Stomp: The Creation of Country Music in the Piedmont South.* Chapel Hill: University of North Carolina Press, 2008.

Hudson, Arthur Palmer. *Folksongs of Mississippi and their Backgrounds.* Chapel Hill: University of North Carolina Press, 1936.

Jackson, George Pullen. *Spiritual Folk-Songs of Early America.* Locust Valley: J. J. Augustin, 1953.

Jasen, David A. *Tin Pan Alley: An Encyclopedia of the Golden Age of American Song.* New York: Routledge, 2003. 103–104.

Johnson, David W. *Lonesome Melodies: The Lives and Music of the Stanley Brothers.* Jackson: University Press of Mississippi, 2013.

Johnson, Willard. Interview with Ernest Stoneman (Cassette Item 5, 7, and 9). Stoneman Family Papers, Archives of Appalachia in the Center for Appalachian Studies and Services, East Tennessee State University Library at Johnson City, TN.

Jones, Benson. Notes on Henry Whitter. From Folder NF-2190 in the Southern Folklife Collection Artist Name File, Southern Folklife Collection, Louis Round Wilson Special Collections Library, University of North Carolina at Chapel Hill.

Jones, Benson. Phone interview. 24 June 2016.

Joyce, P.W. *Old Irish Folk Music and Songs.* Dublin: Hodges, Figgis, 1909, 190.

Kemp, J.C. Personal interview. 6 April 2016.

Kennedy, Rick, and Randy McNutt. *Little Labels-Big Sound: Small Record Companies and the Rise of American Music.* Bloomington: Indiana University Press, 1999.

Kenney, William Howland. *Recorded Music in American Life: The Phonograph and Popular Memory, 1890–1945.* Oxford: Oxford University Press, 2003.

Kingsbury, Paul, editor. *Encyclopedia of Country Music.* Oxford: Oxford University Press, 1998.

Knight, Jerry. "Death of a Company Town." *Washington Post*, 19 September 1988. Accessed online 19 August 2016.

"Laurel Bloomery." *History of Johnson County.* Marceline: Walsworth Press, 1985. 27–29.

Laws, G. Malcolm. *Native American Balladry.* Philadelphia: The American Folklore Society, 1964.

Lewis, Ronald L. *Transforming the Appalachian Countryside: Railroads, Deforestation, and Social Change in West Virginia 1880–1920.* Chapel Hill: University of North Carolina Press, 1998. Accessed online 22 April 2017.

Liebman, Roy. *Vitaphone Films: A Catalogue of the Features and Shorts.* Jefferson: McFarland, 2003.

Lofgren, Lyle. "Remembering the Old Songs: Rose Conley." *Inside Bluegrass*, May 2003.

Lomax, Alan. Interview with Spencer Moore about Jimmy Sutton, September 1959 (T857.0, Track 5). Southern United States Collection. Association for Cultural Equity. Accessed online 29 May 2017.

Lomax, John A., and Alan Lomax. *American Ballads and Folksongs.* New York: Dover, 1994.

Lornell, Kip. *Virginia's Blues, Country, and Gospel Records 1902–1943: An Annotated Discography.* Lexington: University Press of Kentucky, 1989.

Mainer-Morris-Ledford Band. Afternoon Rehearsal (FP-1969-10RR-0001). Smithsonian Folklife Festival records: 1969 Festival of American Folklife, Ralph Rinzler Folklife Archives and Collections, Smithsonian Institution.

Malone, Bill C. *Country Music U.S.A.* Austin: University of Texas Press, 1968.

Malone, Bill C. "The Dixon Brothers." In Kingsbury.

Malone, Bill C. "Stranger Passing Through Your Town: Jimmie Rodgers and the Rambler Tradition." *Sing Me Back Home.* Norman: University of Oklahoma Press, 2017.

Malone, Bill C., and David Stricklin. *Southern Music/American Music.* Lexington: University of Kentucky Press, 2015.

Manufacturer's Record. 15 August 1907, 131.

Mare, Frank. Liner notes. *Going Down Lee Highway: 1927–29 Recordings by Grayson and Whitter.* Davis Unlimited, 1977.

Mazor, Barry. *Ralph Peer and the Making of Popular Roots Music (Enhanced Edition)*. Chicago: Chicago Review Press, 2015. Ebook.

McGee, Marty. *Traditional Musicians of the Central Blue Ridge*. Jefferson: McFarland, 2000.

McGuinn, Doug. *Green Gold: The Story of the Hassinger Lumber Company of Konnarock, Virginia*. Boone: Bamboo Books, 2008.

McGuinn, Doug. *The Lopsided Three: A History of Railroading, Logging and Mining in the Holston, Doe and Watauga Valleys of Northeast Tennessee*. Boone: Bamboo Books, 2010.

McKee, John S. Letter to Archie Green, 29 January 1963. From Biographical Research Folder 1289 in the Achie Green Collection, Southern Folklife Collection, Louis Round Wilson Special Collections Library, University of North Carolina at Chapel Hill.

McNeil, Kada. Personal interview. 4 May 2016.

Meade, Guthrie T., Dick Spottswood, and Douglas S. Meade. *Country Music Sources: A Biblio-Discography of Commercially Recorded Traditional Music*. Chapel Hill: Southern Folklife Collection. University of North Carolina at Chapel Hill Libraries, 2002.

Meadows, Jim. Interview with Clarence Grayson (Video Tape 146 and 147). Broadside Television Collection, Archives of Appalachia in the Center for Appalachian Studies and Services, East Tennessee State University Library at Johnson City, TN.

Miles, Emma B. *The Spirit of the Mountains*. New York: Pott, 1905. 165–166.

Nikazy, Eddie M. *Forgotten Soldiers: History of the 4th Tennessee Volunteer Infantry Regiment 1863–1865*. Bowie: Heritage Books, 1995.

North Carolina Office of Archives and History. *North Carolina Troops, 1861–1865: A Roster*. Raleigh: North Carolina Department of Archives and History, 1966.

Oates, Joyce Carol. "Little Maggie." *The Rose and the Briar: Death, Love and Liberty in the American Ballad*. Edited by Sean Wilentz and Griel Marcus. New York: Norton, 2005.

"Old Time Tune Artists Given Test Recordings." *The Talking Machine World*, 15 October 1925, 70.

"One of the Bright Lights Among White Lights." *The Tatler*, May 1919, 11.

Owen, Blanton. Liner notes. *Old Originals: Volume Two*. Rounder, 0058.

Ozark Folksongs, Vol 1: British Ballads and Songs. Edited by Vance Randolph. Columbia: University of Missouri Press, 1980.

O'Connell, Barry. Liner notes. *Dock Boggs: His Original Recordings*. RBF Records, 1983.

Palmer, Jack. *Vernon Dalhart: First Star of Country Music*. Denver: Mainspring Press, 2005.

Parker, Ray. "G.B. Grayson: A Short Life of Trouble." *Old Time Music*, no. 35, Winter 1980–Spring 1981, 10–13.

Perrow, E. C. "Songs and Rhymes from the South." *The Journal of American Folklore*, vol. 26, no. 100, 1913, 123–173.

Peterson, Richard A. *Creating Country Music: Fabricating Authenticity*. Chicago: University of Chicago Press, 1997.

Petty, James. "The Hanging of the Price Family on Ashe County Courthouse Lawn, Jefferson, NC on 22 March 1863." Manuscript, 18 January 2013.

Porter, Rose. "The History of Fries." 1953. Manuscript. Grayson County Historical Society.

Reid, Gary. *The Music of the Stanley Brothers*. Urbana: University of Illinois Press, 2014.

Rennick, Robert M. "The Disguised Lover Theme and the Ballad." *Southern Folklore Quarterly*, vol. 23, no. 4, December 1959.

Richie, Jean. *Folksongs of the Southern Appalachians as Sung by Jean Richie*, 2d ed. Lexington: University of Kentucky Press, 1965.

Roberts, Leonard. *Sang Branch Settlers: Folksongs and Tales of a Kentucky Mountain Family*. Austin: University of Texas Press, 1974.

Rorrer, Kinney. "Charlie Poole and the North Carolina Ramblers." In Kingsbury.

Rosenberg, Neil. *Bluegrass: A History*. Urbana: University of Illinois Press, 1985.

Rosenberg, Neil, and Charles K. Wolfe. *Music of Bill Monroe*. Urbana: University of Illinois Press, 2007.

Rumble, John. "RCA Victor Records." In Kingsbury.

Russell, Tony, and Bob Pinson. *Country Music Records: A Discography, 1921–1942*. Oxford: Oxford University Press, 2004.

Scarborough, Dorothy. *On the Trail of Negro Folk-Songs*. Boston: Harvard University Press, 1925.

Schweers, Loveta Miller. *The History of the Roark Families of Northwestern North Carolina.* Salisbury, MD.

Seeger, Mike. Interview with Charlie Bowman (FT-20009/5586) in the Mike Seeger Collection, Southern Folklife Collection, Louis Round Wilson Special Collections Library, University of North Carolina at Chapel Hill.

Seeger, Mike and John Cohen. Interview with A. E. Alderman (FT-20009/5583) in the Mike Seeger Collection, Southern Folklife Collection, Louis Round Wilson Special Collections Library, University of North Carolina at Chapel Hill.

Seeger, Mike and John Cohen. Interview with Dock Walsh (FT-20009/5578) in the Mike Seeger Collection, Southern Folklife Collection, Louis Round Wilson Special Collections Library, University of North Carolina at Chapel Hill.

Sharp, Cecil J. *English Folk Songs from the Southern Appalachians, Vol 2.* Edited by Maud Karples. Oxford: Oxford University Press, 1952.

Sizemore, Asher. *Old Fashioned Hymns and Mountain Ballads as Sung by Asher Sizemore and Little Jimmie.* Louisville: Asher Sizemore, 1933.

Slap, Andrew. *Reconstructing Appalachia: The Civil War's Aftermath.* Lexington: University of Kentucky Press, 2010.

Sneed, Thomas. Interview with Frank Grayson. Thomas Sneed Papers, Box 1, Folder 17, Archives of Appalachia in the Center for Appalachian Studies and Services, East Tennessee State University Library at Johnson City, TN.

Songbook of the Harvard Club of San Francisco. San Francisco, 1909.

Spencer, Thornton. Personal interview. 22 March 2017.

Spottswood, Dick. "Columbia Records." In Kingsbury.

Spottswood, Dick. "Gennett Records." In Kingsbury.

Spottswood, Dick. "Okeh Records." In Kingsbury.

Spottswood, Richard Keith. *Banjo on the Mountain: Wade Mainer's First 100 Years.* Jackson: University Press of Mississippi, 2010.

Stanley, Ralph, and Eddie Dean. *Man of Constant Sorrow: My Life and Times.* New York: Gotham, 2009. Electronic edition.

"Statistical Report of the Sons of Temperance of North America." *The Journal of the American Geographical and Statistical Society*, 1 December 1859. Accessed online 20 December 2016.

Steve Ledford Home Recordings. Boxes 1–3. Steve Ledford Home Recordings Collection, Berea College Special Collections and Archives, Berea, KY.

Stewart, Cal. *Uncle Josh's Punkin Centre Stories.* Chicago: Thompson and Thomas, 1905.

Talley, Thomas W. *Negro Folk Rhymes: Wise and Otherwise.* New York: Macmillan, 1922.

Tawa, Nicholas. *Sweet Songs for Gentle Americans: The Parlor Song in America, 1790–1860.* Bowling Green: Bowling Green University Popular Press, 1980.

Taylor, Ronnie. Interview with Alonzo Black. 22 July 1975.

Terrill, Kathy. "Tom Ashley." *History of Johnson County.* Marceline: Walsworth Press, 1985.

"A Tribute to G.B. Grayson" (Video Tapes 141 and 142). Broadside Television Collection, Archives of Appalachia in the Center for Appalachian Studies and Services, East Tennessee State University Library at Johnson City, TN.

Trivette, Ted. Phone interview. 28 June 2016.

Trotter, William R. *Bushwhackers. The Civil War in North Carolina. Volume 3: The Mountains.* Winston-Salem: John F. Blair, 1988.

U.S. Congress. *Senate. Report on the Condition of Woman and Child Wage Earners in the United States, Vol. 1: Cotton Textile Industry.* Senate Document no. 645, 61st Congress, 2nd Session. Washington, D.C.: Government Printing Office, 1910.

Walker, Emma E. "Bromine-Arsenic Springs." *A Reference Handbook of the Medical Sciences: Embracing the Entire Range of Scientific and Practical Medicine and Allied Science, Volume 2.* Edited by Albert Henry Buck. New York: William Wood, 1913.

Walsh, Ulysses J. "By the Way." *Phonograph Monthly Review*, vol. 3, no. 11, August 1929, 372–374.

Waltz, Bob. "Remembering the Old Songs: The Banks of Claudy." *Inside Bluegrass*, March 1997.

West, John Foster. *Lift Up Your Head Tom Dooley: The True Story of the Appalachian Murder that Inspired One of America's Most Popular Ballads.* Asheboro: Down Home Press, 1993.

Weston, Frank. "Albert Hash: Fiddler and Fiddle Maker." *Old Time Music* 39, Winter 1982–Spring 1984, 12–18.
Weston, Frank. "Glen Neaves of Fries, Virginia." *Old Time Herald*, vol. 8, no. 5, 15–19.
"What Tennessee Loyalists Have Done." *Memphis Bulletin*, 5 August 1863. *Civil War Sourcebook*. Tennessee State Library and Archives. Accessed online 4 April 2016.
White, Thomas, Jr. "An Essay on the Order of the Sons of Temperance" Montreal: J. C. Becket, 1853.
Whitter, Henry. *Familiar Folk-Songs as Sung by Henry Whitter.*
Whitter, Henry. Letter to Mary Caroline Ring, 15 November, date not notes, but maybe 1923 or 1924.
Wiggins, Gene. *Fiddlin' Georgia Crazy: Fiddlin' John Carson, His Real World and the World of his Songs*. Urbana: University of Illinois Press, 1987.
Wilgus, D. K. "'Rose Connoley': An Irish Ballad." *The Journal of American Folklore*, vol. 92, no. 364, 1979, 172–195.
Wilson, Joe. Letter. *JEMF Quarterly* 6, part 4, no. 20 Winter 1971.
Wilson, Joe. Liner notes. *The Recordings of Grayson and Whitter*. County Records, 1968.
Wilson, Mark. Liner notes. *Philip Kazee: A Family Tradition*. Rounder, 2008.
Wolfe, Charles. "And No Man Shall Control Me: The Strange Case of Roba Stanley, Country's First Woman Recording Star." *The Women of Country Music: A Reader*. Edited by Charles Wolfe and James Akeson. Lexington: University Press of Kentucky, 2003.
Wolfe, Charles. "The Carter Family." In Kingsbury.
Wolfe, Charles. *The Devil's Box: Masters of Southern Fiddling*. Nashville: Country Music Foundation Press, 1997.
Wolfe, Charles K. "Event Songs." *Reading Country Music: Steel Guitars, Opry Stars, and Honky Tonk Bars*. Ed. Cecelia Tichi. Durham: Duke University Press, 1998, 188–199.
Wolfe, Charles. "Grayson and Whitter." *Old Time Herald*, vol. 3, no 7, 7–8.
Wolfe, Charles. *Tennessee Strings: The Story of Country Music in Tennessee*. Knoxville: University of Tennessee Press, 1977.
Wyatt, Marshall. Interview with Fred Miller. 15 June 1990.
Wyatt, Marshall. "Governor Al Smith for President: The Story of the Carolina Night Hawks" *The Old-Time Herald*, vol. 3, no. 6, November 1992.

Index

Numbers in ***bold italics*** indicate pages with illustrations